U-Boat Assault on America

U-Boat Assault on America

Why the US was unprepared for war in the Atlantic

KEN BROWN

Seaforth
PUBLISHING

Copyright © Ken Brown 2017

First published in Great Britain in 2017 by
Seaforth Publishing,
A division of Pen & Sword Books Ltd,
47 Church Street,
Barnsley S70 2AS

www.seaforthpublishing.com

British Library Cataloguing in Publication Data

A catalogue record for this book is available from the British Library

ISBN 978 1 4738 8728 2 (HARDBACK)
ISBN 978 1 4738 8729 9 (EPUB)
ISBN 978 1 4738 8730 5 (KINDLE)

All photographs from the author's collection unless credited otherwise.

Pen & Sword Books Limited incorporates the imprints of Atlas, Archaeology, Aviation,
Discovery, Family History, Fiction, History, Maritime, Military, Military Classics,
Politics, Select, Transport, True Crime, Air World, Frontline Publishing, Leo Cooper,
Remember When, Seaforth Publishing, The Praetorian Press, Wharncliffe Local
History, Wharncliffe Transport, Wharncliffe True Crime and White Owl.

Typeset in Ehrhardt 11 on 14 by M.A.T.S, Leigh-on-Sea, Essex
Printed and bound in Great Britain by CPI Group (UK) Ltd, Croydon, CR0 4YY

Contents

List of Illustrations

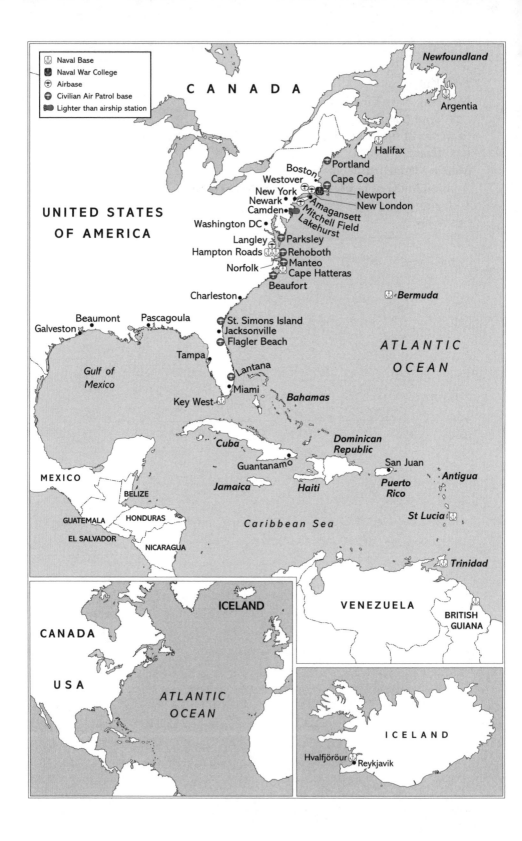

Naval Base
Naval War College
Airbase
Civilian Air Patrol base
Lighter than airship station

CANADA

Newfoundland
Argentia

UNITED STATES
OF AMERICA

Halifax

Portland
Boston
Westover   Cape Cod
New York   Newport
Newark   New London
Camden   Amagansett
           Mitchell Field
Washington DC   Lakehurst
Langley   Parksley
Hampton Roads   Rehoboth
Norfolk   Manteo
                   Cape Hatteras
                   Beaufort
Charleston   Bermuda

Beaumont   Pascagoula
Galveston   St. Simons Island
                       Jacksonville
                       Flagler Beach
Tampa   ATLANTIC
Gulf of   Lantana   OCEAN
Mexico   Miami
Key West   Bahamas

MEXICO   Dominican
                                Republic
                 Cuba
           Guantanamo   San Juan
                                          Antigua
BELIZE   Jamaica   Haiti   Puerto
                                Rico
GUATEMALA HONDURAS   St Lucia
EL SALVADOR   Caribbean Sea
        NICARAGUA
                                          Trinidad

ICELAND   VENEZUELA
                                          BRITISH
CANADA   GUIANA

USA   ATLANTIC
           OCEAN
                           ICELAND

                           Hvalfjörður Reykjavik

Acknowledgements

The production of this book has been the labour of many years. Through the course of those years I owe a great thanks to many people.

Of course, my mother Diann Brown who has been a stalwart support and great inspiration throughout my life. My brother Alex, who has always been supportive and a great friend, has been a boon all my life. My father Irvin, and his wife Nancy, have helped guide me with sober and insightful questions. My mother-in-law, Evelyn, has also been a consistent source of enthusiasm and has frequently asked probing and provocative questions. I owe a debt to my friend David Gracer, whose own writing, sense of humility and great friendship has been an irreplaceable source of solace and strength. I am deeply indebted to my professor at Bard College, Gennady Shkliarevsky, who seemed to see promise in me, regardless of whether I did.

For the production of this work in particular, I am very appreciative of Ms Laura Hayworth, librarian at the Denison, Texas, public library. She was instrumental in obtaining access to the archives related to Admiral Andrews. I would be remiss if I did not express thanks for the courage of Julian Mannering at Seaforth Press. He took the chance on an initial work by a new author. I trust that he is not dissatisfied. Through the course of writing this work, Jak Showell has helped me in obtaining resources for this work.

The City of New York: I owe a debt to the New York City Transit Authority. Countless hours spent on the subway were used (when I could get a seat) taking notes. Anyone who writes in this city owes this debt. The New York Public Library is a source of seemingly endless resources. I have had the privilege of spending many hours in the Rose Reading Room in the Schwartzman Building. This has imparted a sense of grandeur and a connection to the past that is a helpful motivator. The staff of the Brooklyn Public Library were always a pleasure to work with. They have always been knowledgeable and cheerful and the Grand Army Plaza where the library is situated is one of the great urban spaces in New York.

Finally, I would like to thank my sublime wife, Antoinette Mims. She has been an unflagging support and I owe her more than I can relay here.

Thank you all.

Introduction

The impetus for this book came about from reading Michael Gannon's excellent work, *Operation Drumbeat: The Dramatic True Story of Germany's First U-boat Attacks along the American Coast in World War II*, an enthralling tale of a desperate battle.

Between January and August 1942, German depredations along the Eastern Sea Frontier wrought the destruction of 609 ships, amounting to 3,100,000 tons. More than one thousand merchant sailors lost their lives to the U-boat assault, while only twenty-two U-boats were sunk. The German submarine assault on the US East Coast was hastily organised. The Japanese attack at Pearl Harbor was a surprise to the Kriegsmarine as much as it was to the US Navy, though with less devastating effect. Dönitz assembled all of the long-range U-boats that were available. However, Hitler diverted many to the defence of Norway, where he had an intuition the Allies were about to launch another invasion. Despite Hitler's precognition, Dönitz was able to mount 184 war patrols to North American waters. Of these patrols, all save six resulted in the sinking of at least one Allied vessel. The losses of merchant shipping created a crisis for the Allies, for the losses in American waters during this 'Second Happy Time' amounted to one-quarter of all Allied shipping sunk by U-boats throughout the entire war. Clay Blair in his magisterial work, *Hitler's U-Boat War: The Hunters, 1939–1942*, wrote: 'Thus, the campaign was the single most important of the war in terms of sinkings achieved in a relatively brief time period for effort expended – the high-water mark of the U-boat war.'

The Americans were able to avail themselves of access to copious Royal Navy intelligence during this period of the operation known as Drumbeat.

In the First World War the British had established a signals intelligence unit. They were able to locate German submarines when the latter made wireless transmissions to headquarters. The electronic emissions were intercepted, and they were able to pinpoint the location of the transmitter and the submarine. Merchant shipping was then routed around the danger. During the Second World War this capacity was revived. Once Germany had declared war on America, and Dönitz had dispatched his U-boats, the Royal Navy started to intercept the instructions to the submarines. Naval intelligence was able to surmise that an attack against the East Coast of America was in the offing, their conclusion was transmitted to the Americans and so the US Navy was thus forewarned of the coming U-boat onslaught. Admiral King, the American commander-in-chief, appraised of this information, agreed that the East Coast was in danger but he instituted no significant defensive measures.

American naval priorities both in the First World War and in the Second were for anti-submarine escorts first to protect troop ships. Escorting of merchant ships was not deemed valuable. Although there were approximately twenty destroyers along the East Coast at the time of the German attack, none of them were detailed for trade protection. The submarine assault on the East Coast was undoubtedly the nadir of the American navy after the attack on Pearl Harbor.

Unlike the constricted area of the air attack on Pearl Harbor, the German assault ranged over the length of the American coastline from Florida to Maine, a total of more than 28,000 miles (more than 46,000 kilometres). Prior to the attack on America, the Germans had dispatched submarines to Canadian waters. However, the German high command had been reluctant to send U-boats to Canadian waters on combat missions for fear of antagonising the Americans. The German naval command and Hitler were mindful that drawing the United States into the war as a belligerent could be considerably damaging to their efforts. Once there was a formal state of war between Germany and her allies, and America and her (newly overt) Allies, the naval war quickly spread from the eastern Atlantic to the west: damage mounted fast. Churchill warned Washington that the sinkings off the coast, if persistent, could jeopardise the war effort, but the commandant of the Eastern Sea Frontier, Admiral Adolphus Andrews, by nature a conservative thinker, was slow to adopt the coastal convoying that proved to be the ultimate remedy for the U-boat assault.

The initial surge of German submarines to the East Coast was code-named Operation Paukenschlag. Dönitz dispatched five submarines to American waters and they sailed from France between 23 and 27 December 1941. *U-123* was on station off the East Coast by 13 January and began the assault by torpedoing SS *Cyclops* on 12 January 1942.

The U-boats were assisted considerably not just by the lack of naval preparedness but also by absence of any co-operation between military and civilian leaders. For instance, the continuing illumination from the cities along the coast was a huge boon to the attackers. The city lights silhouetted ships as they passed along the coast making them easy targets for the raiders. Civilians wanted to maintain the illuminations, since dousing them would devastate the coastal tourist economy, but eventually sense prevailed and the military ordered the cities to turn off the lights at night. Civilian and military co-operation was to become fundamental to the American war effort, and enabled the effective mobilisation of industrial, political and scientific communities and, eventually, the marshalling of civilian scientists, industrialists and politicians, and the changing naval anti-submarine doctrine surmounted the U-boat assault on the East Coast.

A number of questions came to the fore and the issue of context became paramount through my reading Gannon's work. What were the institutional traditions in the navy that inhibited and propelled innovation? What was the political context for American naval mobilisation? The object of the attack was merchant shipping. How was industry mobilised to build the ships (and shipyards and the workforce) that made up the wartime merchant fleet? Independent of Gannon's work, I also wanted to explore New York City's unique and vital role during the war.

Another important factor was the conduct and role of the commandant of the Eastern Sea Frontier, Vice Admiral Adolphus Andrew. At the time of the attack he was sixty-two years old and approaching mandatory retirement. Hitherto he had led an unexceptional career. At the sunset of this naval career he was suddenly thrust into one of the most critical campaigns of the war. Though flawed, Andrews responded to the crisis as best he could. Eventually the German assault was turned back.

It seemed that there was a gap in the historical literature covering this campaign, addressing the traditions, doctrines and political context pertinent to the assault on the coast. Overall, there is a dearth of books that address the intuitions and traditions that provided the social, military and political context for the battle that was fought on the United States' Atlantic seaboard. It has often been recounted that America was the 'Arsenal of Democracy' for the Allies. How were the resources mobilised? These questions of context are what this work seeks to redress.

A conference held at the US Naval War College in 1993 called for a new paradigm for naval history. This call, as compiled in a volume of essays subsequent to the conference, recommended that naval history encompass issues pertaining to a context of social, economic and political importance. James Goldrick in his essay, 'The Problems of Modern Naval History', argues that in order to conduct naval history in the 'machine age ... there must be a new approach to the subject, one which integrates the elements of technology, finance, strategy, operations and personnel in achieving an understanding of the subject.' This work is written in that spirit. Navies are enmeshed into national economic, technological and political environments. The study of 'finance, manufacturing, and technology have been as peripheral if not as outside the boundaries. But they are central to navies as organisations and so must be the focus of naval historians.'

To explain the U-boat assault fully it is necessary to investigate the factors that provide the context for the battles between the assaulting German submarines and the defending Allied (American) forces. It is necessary also to elucidate the Allied anti-submarine warfare (ASW) doctrines extant at the time and the historical rationale. A part of understanding this doctrine and the small amount of attention that was spent on merchant protection during the interwar period requires understanding a number of elements, including ideas about the proper use of submarines in wartime. This was strongly influenced by the interwar treaties on permissible submarine usage in a war. Another influence on the way in which submarines were viewed relates to the historical development of the US Navy's officer corps, specifically the tensions between line and engineering officers.

For the purposes of this study, one of the most significant issues addressed by the interwar treaties were the permissible conditions for submarine warfare. The diplomatic thrusts under consideration herein address the role of the submarine. The commerce warfare that the Germans practised in both world wars was a form of 'war on communications'. Mahan writes that war on commerce affects:

the financial power of the belligerent ... These political and financial consequences bring the practice into exact line with military principle: for, being directed against the resources of the enemy, by interrupting his communications with the outer world, it becomes strictly analogous to operations against the communications of an army with its base – one of the chief objects of strategy ... upon the maintenance of commerce the vitality of a state. Money, credit, is the life of war.

Therefore, focusing upon the financial vigour of the Allies is a proper object for both historians and marauding submarines.

The U-boat assault occurred within the context of the United States' entry into the Second World War. The response to the assault was modified by the experience and assistance of the Royal Navy. Britain had been at war and engaged in anti-submarine warfare for two and a half years and had therefore accumulated techniques and experience that was pertinent to this campaign. The US and Germany (and Italy) had been officially at war as of December 1942. However, the United States had been involved in a de facto war in the Atlantic well before the formal declarations of war.

Central to an understanding of the campaign is how the country mobilised for war. This mobilisation included military and political developments. The political machinations that President Roosevelt undertook served to garner public support for the Allies and eventually participation in combat. The rationalisation of the economy on a wartime basis was central to the American contribution to Allied success.

New York City played a central role in the campaign. However, there were pro-Nazi elements that troubled the navy and the security of the waterfront was considered a vulnerability, which the navy redressed by cultivating criminals. The naval commandant at New York was Vice Admiral Adolphus Andrews. Up to the assault by the U-boats he had led an unspectacular career. When the crisis came he coped as best he could, but that entailed little innovation or initiative on his part.

By encompassing all of these factors, this book aims for a more holistic analysis of the campaign.

1

Navy Bureaucracy and the Development of Doctrine

Campaigns are fought with ships and men. Ships need to be enduring and men need to be creative in order to win the battles. The battle for the East Coast was waged with boldness on both sides but sometimes, considering the scale of the threat, with a lack of focus, even inertia, by the Americans. What bound the ships and men together and what brought them to the scene of battle was formed by the way that the contending forces were organised. Ships are deployed in formations; they train together and that training is moulded by assumptions constructed and reinforced through exercises, doctrine and tradition.

Development of the United States Navy Department

What were the anti-submarine warfare assumptions that permeated the pre-war navy? How were these assumptions reinforced through the use of doctrine and exercises? How were these assumptions eventually overturned and then replaced? These are organisational questions. The naval bureaucracy makes the environment for these traditions to flourish. How the navy was organised and how that organisation reacted to the stressors of the interwar and early war period all contributed to how tactics and assumptions were moulded to better fit the environment and needs of the forces afloat.

Since the dawn of the American republic and the birth of a national navy, the United States Navy has been divided into three parts.

The Navy Department is the headquarters of the navy. It is comprised of the Secretary of the Navy, his civilian executive assistants, the executive offices of the Secretary, the office of the Chief of Naval Operations, the several bureaus and boards, the headquarters of the Marine Corps and during World War II the headquarters of the Coast Guard.

The Shore Establishment comprises the field activities of the Department of the Navy ashore: yards and bases.

The Operating Forces are sometimes spoken of simply as the Fleet. They comprise all of the seagoing and sea frontier forces, naval aviation, the Marine Corps, the Coast Guard in time of war, and certain shore facilities assigned to the operating forces.[1]

When the Constitution was ratified in 1789, the War Department was charged with administering the army and navy, albeit there were no ships then that flew the federal flag. When the Barbary pirates began to prey upon United States–flagged merchant ships and take American sailors captive, Congress in 1794 authorised the construction of six frigates. These were the first federal warships in the new nation's history. However, it was the naval war with France nine years later that led to the creation of the Secretary of the Navy and an officer responsible to him.

The Secretary of the Navy was created due to the incompetence of the War Department: 'Economy and Efficiency are the keynotes of the principal House debates ... The Federalist speakers were specific in calling for an administrator acquainted with maritime affairs in general and shipbuilding in particular.'[2] It was at the genesis of the Navy Department that an emphasis on technical knowledge was inculcated into the navy's corporate structure. Technical proficiency and an acquaintance with the technology of shipbuilding and ship handling animated the department's development and functioning.

At the conclusion of the Spanish-American War, the Navy Department expanded its shore-side administration. The east and west coasts of the country were divided into naval districts. Each district was composed of a number of states. By 1920 the inland states were included in the naval districts and districts were also established overseas. In addition to the continental United States, naval districts were established for the Hawaiian Islands, the Philippines, the Canal Zone, Alaska and the Caribbean Sea.[3]

The 'task of the Navy Department, including the elements of military command, management control, and technical control, with provision for coordinating all elements' was mandated by law. The command of the war-making elements devolved from the Chief of Naval Operations and was exercised through the sea frontier commanders.[4] One of the strengths of this system was that through to the Second World War, career naval officers occupied nautical, technical and administrative posts within the naval hierarchy. By the time an officer reached flag rank, he would have served at least one tour at a navy yard or shore station. He therefore would have experience in civilian labour-relations, and also experience of commanding both a ship and a shore facility by the time he attained flag rank. Aboard a ship, the expectation was that any command would be followed with minimal or no questioning or deliberation. A consequence of this culture was that a captain would not be accustomed to seeking and utilising the advice of others onboard. But flag officers were adept both in commanding by dictate and by working co-operatively, as through exposure to shore billets and interactions with civilians, senior naval officers were able to attain an agility of mind that enabled them to work collaboratively, and craft effective plans with both military and civilian colleagues. This fortuitous mindset, embracing collaboration and appreciation of civilian input for decision-making, would serve the Allied war effort in good stead, and contributed to a flexibility and adaptability which ultimately contributed to the Allied victory over the U-boats.

Line versus engineering officers

The Industrial Revolution had a profound effect upon the organisation of the navy. As steam power displaced sail, a schism developed in the officer corps. The serving line officers (the officers who operated the ship, as opposed to the technical branches, like gunnery and engineering) felt threatened by the displacement of sails by steam. This was a revolutionary technology and the engineers had the potential to render obsolete the skills of officers who had grown up with sailing ships. The line officers were not content to stand passively and lose their prestige.

In 1862 the navy reorganised and the ranks of rear admiral, commodore, lieutenant commander and ensign were instated. These ranks, however, were only available to line officers, and engineers were excluded from promotion to these ranks. However, this discrimination was soon partially ameliorated. In 1864 Secretary of the Navy Gideon Welles ordered that all naval academy students should study steam engineering. Several assistant engineers were assigned as instructors to the academy. This culminated in a law passed on 4 July 1864, which authorised the Secretary

3

to appoint up to fifty cadet engineers to the academy. In 1866 fifty engineers tested for admission to Annapolis (relocated from Newport, Rhode Island, when the Civil War ended). Of these, sixteen were admitted as third assistant engineers. They underwent a two-year course, segregated from the other cadets, and the engineering classes were instituted only grudgingly. Of the sixteen cadet-engineers there were only four remaining in 1868 – only two of the four remaining engineer-cadets graduated.

Vice Admiral David D Porter, the hero of the Civil War western riverine campaigns, administered the post-bellum navy. Although Porter had used steam-driven vessels with success during the war, he was against expanding steam propulsion for warships. He saw the rise of steam power as an encroachment upon the prerogatives of the line officers, one of whom he considered himself. At the end of the Civil War there were 474 regular and 1803 volunteer engineering officers in the Union Navy. Over several years all of the volunteer engineers had been discharged.[5] This anti-engineer bias grew to such proportions that by 1876 a group of line officers established a fund to lobby Congress against the advancement of engineers.[6]

The navy's retrogressive policies had the unintended consequence of making the fleet obsolete. Eventually, the officers recognised that technical innovation was necessary if they hoped to stave off insuperable inferiority to the advanced fleets of Europe, especially those of Britain and France – the navy needed to be technologically competitive if they were to be competent to defend the nation's interests. In 1883 Congress authorised the first steel warships, *Atlanta*, *Boston*, *Chicago* and *Dolphin*.[7] The tide of technical innovation had finally dampened the navy's leadership, compelling innovation.

Despite progress building new ships, the officer corps continued to resist change. In an attempt to create more billets for officers, the Amalgamation Act of 1899 was passed. In effect, the specialist ranks in the service were subsumed into the line officer ranks, thus the distinctions between line, engineering and staff officers were obliterated. However, line officers were afforded seniority and among officers with the same time in a rank, a line officer would be considered as the superior.

One of the principal battlegrounds for this intra-officer corps conflict was at the naval academy. On 16 April 1883 Superintendent Ramsay shepherded a resolution through the board of superintendents to amalgamate the engineering and line cadets together, who would then take a combined examination for commissioning. One result of this was that the graduating class of 1883 included twenty-one engineers out of the fifty-four total graduates. The school now felt justified in concentrating on traditional naval topics, such as gunnery and navigation and there was a concomitant waning of attention to technical and engineering subjects. As a consequence, the more progressive European navies eclipsed the United States, and engineers in the American service went abroad to study.[8] This created a crisis in the naval education of officers. On the one hand, there was a demonstrable need to maintain excellence in technical education and on the other there was the conservatism and inertia of the dominating line officers. Hence a movement to have a formal course of study in engineering at the academy began.

While a course of studies at the academy was developing, there was movement outside of Annapolis for engineering classes. Officers at the Bureau of Construction and Repair were in conversation with the staff at the Massachusetts Institute of Technology (MIT) to develop a graduate course in engineering. In autumn 1901 three academy graduates entered the venerable halls of MIT and sat for class X111-A; three years later they graduated from MIT with a master's degree in science.

Not to be superseded by a private university, the academy initiated a study in February 1902 to see how an engineering course could be instituted at Annapolis. Finally, in June 1909 a two-year course in marine engineering design was instituted. By the time of America's entry into the First World War , naval engineering courses were spread among a number of institutions:

In January 1916 seventy-six officers were enrolled in technical postgraduate courses of study. Twenty naval students were enrolled at Columbia University; nine marine engineers, ten electrical engineers, and one 'metallographist.' Thirteen naval constructors were enrolled at MIT and three civil engineers at Rensselarer Polytechnic Institute. The remaining nine students were studying ordnance engineering at various steel plants, the Naval Gun Factory, and the Naval Proving Ground.[9]

There was now developing a significant corps of engineering-literate naval officers. The traditional line officers who eschewed steam technology were clearly on the defensive. Overarching these internal conflicts was the growth of the battleship as the supreme warship and as these ships developed, their technical sophistication increased. Instead of affording engineers the prestige and opportunities for advancement that should have been available to them in the new and technologically sophisticated navy, they remained subordinate to line officers. This conflict between line and engineering officers was to continue throughout the First World War.

As the twentieth century dawned, steam engineering was firmly ensconced in naval architecture. Steam frigates had been the transitional warship to bridge sail to steam propulsion; next were the heterogeneously gunned cruisers. It was these cruisers that were victorious in the Spanish-American War. Finally, once Britain's Royal Navy commissioned HMS *Dreadnought*, the era of the all big-gun battleship had arrived.

The move to resist technological progress had been faltering. In 1890 Congress authorised the building of three all-big-gun battleships, *Indiana*, *Oregon* and *Massachusetts*. These were followed between 1898 and1905 by fourteen more big-gun battleships. The US Navy had awoken from its Luddite slumber and entered the ranks of serious naval powers. This awakening was due to Benjamin Franklin Tracey, Secretary of the Navy (1889–93). In his first annual report he stated that the United States would not fight a war at sea as a *guerre de course* (the concept of an inferior fleet that would fight to damage the enemy's commerce). Instead, the United States' fleet would be strong enough to be exempt from a fight. Although hitherto the US Navy would have undertaken a *guerre de course*, once there was a strong fleet they would not be forced to follow this course of action, but could also act as a deterrent to war. He went on to say: "'The United States needed a navy that will exempt it from war, but the only navy that will accomplish this is a navy that can wage war.' That, to Tracey, was a navy of armored battleships.'[10]

When Jacky Fisher at the Royal Navy developed the all–big-gun battleship prototype, HMS *Dreadnought*, all other capital warships were rendered obsolete with that one commissioning in 1906. Fisher's innovation was to abandon the heterogeneous scheme of multiple-calibre guns on the same ship. Instead, he discarded medium–calibre guns and concentrated on designing a battleship that had the maximum number of the heaviest guns: she mounted ten 12in guns arranged in five turrets.[11]

The US Navy, and all others that hoped to be competitive, now had to labour to catch up with Britain's lead.

The Navy General Board

The new battleships would be a novel development for the US Navy – their design was a complete break from the ships that had hitherto been built. To develop the design for these new ships, the General Navy Board was created in 1900. The General Board was the 'nexus where policy was translated into force structure. Its members were senior and mid-grade officers of proven experience and promise.'[12] The board cultivated an atmosphere of free deliberation and deference to rank was not enforced. As the recognition that the navy needed to have state-of-the-art battleships permeated the hierarchy, the board was charged with developing ships that incorporated the newest notions of warship design. The development of a new battleship design also proved to be the battleground where the line and technical officers now fought.

In July 1902 Congress authorised six new *Connecticut*-class battleships. Line officers dominated the board. They set the tone for discussions about the new battleships' armament, the arrangement of which determined the parameters of the new class's design. 'Among the eighty commentaries received regarding the Connecticut gun arrangement was one that called for a total reorganization of the process of battleship design – under line officers.'[13] Hitherto, the Bureau of Construction and Repair had been responsible for the design of warships. It was at this point that an epistle from France added to the fray.

The naval attaché in France, Lieutenant William Sims, sent in a report on French warship design methods. In his fifty-nine-page paper he drew attention to the practice in France where constructors followed the orders of sea-going officers. Sims argued that this was a practice that the United States would do well to emulate. This notion gained currency and as the control of the line officers increased in the General Board, the control of the Construction Bureau over ship design waned. In 1905 the decisive blow fell and the power of the bureau to design warships was broken.

In October 1905, in accordance with its charter, the General Board recommended the types of ships to be included in the building program for Congress. However, the Board also specified the number and caliber of main guns; the freeboard (the distance between the waterline and the main deck) – something well within the province of naval architects – and the armor protection for the proposed battleships.[14]

The power of the Construction Bureau and the engineers that populated it had been broken and from now on it was line officers who would have the commanding voice in warship design. By 1907 their encroachment into warship design had progressed so far that a line officer, Rear Admiral Converse, headed the Board of Construction. With the autonomy of the engineers circumscribed, the naval officer corps was mired in conservatism over warship design. A critical reform occurred in 1940 when the Bureaus of Construction and Repair and Engineering were merged to form the Bureau of Ships. This bureau was then the omnibus bureau for the design, construction and repair of ships.[15]

In 1909 Naval Secretary Truman H Newberry ordered the membership and influence of the General Board increased as part of a larger reorganisation of the Navy Department. Eventually, President Taft's Navy Secretary, George von Lengerke Meyer, abolished the Board of Construction and charged the '"General Board with the determination of purely military details of all new ships."'[16]

The naval reformers, led by Sims, had hoped to concentrate all power in the hands of the General Board, but in this they failed. A commission authorised by the president to reform the naval hierarchy had recommended such a scheme in a 'Naval General Staff'. When this was presented to Congress, it was shelved. The power of the General Board in warship, especially battleship, design was 'absolute'. Although the General Board was now onboard with the technical changes wrought by adopting the all-big-gun battleship, they were not progressive in their outlook on technology. 'Technology was to be used for Anapolite purposes and strictly in according to a clearly determined set for cultural prerequisites.' The reformers had hoped that with the consolidation of power over ship design in the General Board, more progressive attitudes would prevail. This is not what happened: 'they had overlooked the general drift of naval administrative tradition and the subtle but pervasive influence of George Dewey ... Consequently the board became, among other things, a synod dedicated to the maintenance of naval orthodoxy and the suppression of heretical innovation.'[17]

One of the consequences of this conservatism in outlook was the minimising of the submarine threat to capital ships: 'Sims and most of his colleagues perceived the submarine threat to be minimal and easily countered by the battleship's higher speed and the new anti-torpedo modifications incorporated into battleship hulls.'[18] The submarine survived by serving the battle fleet as a scout: submarines would precede the battleship force and report enemy movements and attack capital ships as opportunities arose. However, the First World War changed this perception and caused some new thinking about submarines and how commerce should be protected.

Doctrine development

For the United States Navy, the principal means whereby doctrine was tested was at the Naval War College. Secretary of the Navy William E Chandler founded the college on 6 October 1884, with order number 325. This order simply read: 'A college is hereby established for an advanced course of professional study for naval officers, to be known as the Naval War College.' The college was housed in a former asylum for the poor at Newport, Rhode Island, and its first president was Commodore Stephen B Luce.

Luce was chosen because it was his insight and initiative that had brought the need for the college to the forefront of the navy adminis-tration's thinking. He had been assigned as an instructor at the Naval Academy when it was displaced from Annapolis, Maryland, to Rhode Island during the Civil War. He felt that there was little systematised higher education throughout the navy. He found that there was no standard for exercising tactics, nor a means to synthesise any lessons gleaned from exercises. In short, he felt that: 'war is the *central issue* around which the profession of arms exists and there was then no existing institution where a naval officer could study it. It was his prodding that led to the creation of the College.'[19] Luce felt that the proper under-standing of war fighting required scholarship, especially of an historical nature. To this end he made the social sciences central. Pride of place went to the study of politics, history, management and international law. An innovation that he fostered was the utilisation of war-gaming as an analytic tool; he also integrated both officers and civilians as faculty.

In the twentieth century the school blossomed and became the source for operational doctrine. Under the tutelage of Rear Admiral William S

Sims, the Naval War College began to address how to best use submarines and aeroplanes. Sims served as the college's fifth president in 1917; his presidency was interrupted when he was dispatched to England to co-ordinate the United States' entry into the First World War and resumed in 1919.

On 11 November 1912 Captain William Sims addressed students at Annapolis and made the case for a Naval War College's practicality. His major themes were:

- The value of a systemic method of problem solving.
- The real business of the Navy is preparation for war.
- The necessity of war games for perfecting doctrine.

The thrust of this lecture was to expound the utility of war games as a tool for the development and perfection of doctrine. Sims stated that the 'qualities of mind and military character can be acquired no other way than by constant and intense competitive practice – constant and intense training of the mind and the will through handling the various types of situations in competition with alert minds that are handling the forces on the other side.'[20]

Sims's argument was that by using war games, a nimbleness of decision-making can be inculcated in the minds of high-ranking officers. He said elsewhere that training while afloat could help to perfect tactical operations, such as manoeuvring a ship or perfecting gunnery. According to Sims: 'The peace duties of junior officers, gun-division officers, navigators, first lieutenants, engineering officers, gunnery officers, and executives are most excellent training for the principal duties they will have to perform in time of war.' His argument was that using ships and the fleet to explore operational and strategic questions was impractical, 'due to the simple fact that it is not possible actually to use great fleets to play a sufficient number of war games to provide its officers with adequate mental training in strategy and tactics.' The Fleet could not be moved around like on a game board. It would be expensive, laborious and time-consuming to use the fleet to thrash out potential solutions to doctrinal and strategic issues. Ultimately, a synergistic relationship would develop between war games played at the college and testing those 'gamed' solutions by the Fleet. These would become institutionalised as fleet problems, begun in 1923 and the last played in 1940. These fleet problems would explore strategic questions such as the attack and defence of the Panama Canal, the

Caribbean, and the Hawaiian Islands. At the heart of how the navy developed doctrine and theory of war fighting was the war game. In the same speech at Annapolis Sims said:

> The war games – the tactical game and chart maneuvers – bear the same relation to efficiency in handling a fleet as dotter and caliber practices bear to efficiency in handling a ship's battery, or as practice on the field bears to efficiency in handling a football team.[21]

For Sims, war games acted to hone the minds of officers. Through repeatedly playing simulations, the officers involved would develop decision-making habits, 'almost automatically from the war doctrine developed by the training itself.' A benefit of the tactical games, the simulations of fighting forces in conflict situations, is that fighting tactics can be tried out. The 'tactical game demonstrates the necessity for new or modified types of vessels, or new or modified uses for those already built.'[22] In short, war games are the next best thing to having the Fleet at your disposal to try out thought experiments. By constructing rules that most closely approximate the conditions for the forces to be engaged, in other words, to have the most accurate 'control' for the experiment, a realistic test for assumptions and ideas can be uncovered. The results from these 'experiments' could then be used to modify the materials, doctrines and tactics used by the Fleet.

The first modern naval war game was created by the celebrated Fred T Jane (of *Jane's Fighting Ships* books). He published a set of rules so that the capabilities of various warships could be compared. He marketed these rules as a means to enhance the attraction of his books. In Jane's game, ship models were set up and the rules would dictate movement, fighting and communications. Players would represent individual ship captains and a player would be assigned to act as fleet admiral, who set standing orders.[23]

For the navy as an institution, war-gaming did not become established until it was adapted at the Naval War College in 1894. The adoption of war-gaming at the college can be attributed to William McCarty Little, a civilian. Little had been a lieutenant in the navy, but by 1887 he had retired. However, Sims was impressed with Little's zeal for gaming and he was kept at the college as a lecturer. He delivered lectures on the utility of war games from 1887–93. In 1894 war games were adopted as a normal part of the college curriculum.[24]

As the system of game design, play, analysis and academic research matured, it became systematised. By 1900 the navy adopted a process called the 'applicatory system'[25] for planning as the means for the navy to solve problems and perfect doctrine. The heart of this process was the idea that learning is best done when principles are applied through practice: 'It consisted of three parts: the estimate of the situation, the writing of orders, and the evaluation through gaming or maneuver board exercises. Its purpose was to permit officers in command situations to exercise intelligent options for the resolution of problems rather than to be slavishly bound to a method conceived at a higher level.'[26] This applicatory system would serve the navy well. It provided a system for analysis, acting upon this analysis and then scrutinising the results. By the time William McCarty Little died on 12 March 1915, the tri-level war game (strategic, tactical and single-ship combat games) and conventional academic analysis made for a robust infrastructure to research, test, adopt and perfect doctrine for the US Navy.

When Little died, the direction of war-gaming at the Naval War College was left to the stewardship of William Sims, who had taken the presidency again in December 1918. He focused the games on strategic problems. When Rear Admiral Harris Laning commanded the college from 16 June 1930 to 14 May 1933, he shifted emphasis to perfecting tactics.

Anti-submarine forces

The ship type that was most responsible for combating the U-boat was the destroyer. As a ship type there had been little evolution in the thinking of what a destroyer's function should be from the time the class was developed in 1905 through to the First World War. They were expected to: 'protect the fleet from enemy torpedo boat attacks and to attack offensively with their own torpedoes.' The primary qualities for a destroyer were therefore speed and good seakeeping. They needed to be able to keep pace with the battleships regardless of weather. However, by the 1920s the navy began to reconsider the role and attributes it needed in their destroyers and in 1927 the type's design was reconsidered. By 1931 a final set of specifications and performances were codified. They wanted a ship of 1,500 tons, increased speed and seaworthiness, and able to deliver a torpedo attack in anything but the worst weather. There was little attention given to anti-submarine warfare, and depth charges remained the same as when developed in the First World War. They were either rolled off the ship's stern or shot away from the ship by centreline Y-guns.[27]

At the time of Operation Drumbeat, destroyers were attached to the navy's three fleets: the Pacific, Asiatic and Atlantic fleets. The Atlantic Fleet was under the command of Admiral Ingersoll as of 1 January 1942. The destroyers attached to the Atlantic Fleet were designated DesLant (Destroyers, Atlantic). These type commands were administrative only.

> DesLant was responsible for maintenance, basing facilities, and the dispatch of DDs. They kept track of the destroyers attached to the various fleets. And from the 'ship pool' they furnished destroyers when wanted for such operations as convoy escort duty, a 'hunter-killer' campaign, or service with the local defense forces of a sea frontier ... They were in over-all charge of all DD personnel. They advised on strategy and tactics. They recommended new battle gear and improvements of old. They requisitioned facilities and were in charge of training new DDs and of 'refresher' training for veteran ships. 'They pushed construction.'[28]

The purpose of this organisation was to maintain these ships in fighting formations, crewed and supplied appropriately, and with a means to harvest the experience garnered afloat, so that experience could be systematised and translated into exercises and thus eventually tailored into doctrine for these units.

In practice, destroyers were organised into flotillas. A flotilla was a formation of destroyers used at the discretion of the fleet commander. An effort was made to keep flotillas intact so that a body of experience and familiarity could be cultivated. These flotillas were composed of two or more squadrons. These squadrons, in turn, were comprised of two or three destroyer divisions (DesDiv). There was no formal size to these groupings. However, typically, a division was composed of four destroyers, although some contained up to six. A commander or a junior captain typically commanded a DesDiv.

When the United States entered the war, there was no formal A/S (anti-submarine) doctrine and there was no effort to study after-action reports of encounters with submarines: 'The A/S vessels at sea lacked specific methods, no new doctrines had been formulated for A/S operations; the results obtained by current A/S measures had not been carefully assembled and scientifically studied since the Battle of the Atlantic began.' Commerce protection had been a preoccupation of naval theorists since the advent of steam engines. However, the object of consideration was the surface raider. It was only towards the end of the First World War that submarines were considered as the primary threat to commerce: 'The classical answer formulated by Mahan above all others but echoed by many, was that command of the sea, achieved by the decisive battle, would enable the victorious fleets to so dominate ocean as to drive away the majority of potential raiders.'[29]

According to studies by the Royal Navy, the best means of combating this raiding was to concentrate forces in the areas of the greatest threat, namely the approaches to Britain. Convoying was not considered a necessary measure prior to the First World War. Although convoys had been used very effectively during the Napoleonic wars, they were considered anachronistic in the age of steam power. It was felt that steamship companies would balk at the restrictions and naval officers were not in favour of this mode of action, as they perceived convoying as defensive and passive, and therefore contrary to the Service's tradition and the expectation of the nation for offensive action.

For the US Navy in the Second World War, the first attempt to systematise anti-submarine warfare for destroyers was not made until February 1942. In Boston, a group of destroyer men and others concerned with anti-submarine warfare met at the navy yard. The outcome of this meeting was the creation of the 'Atlantic Fleet Anti-Submarine Warfare Unit – a body to study the ways and means of A/S warfare, devise methods for combatting the U-boat, and train instructors for the Atlantic Fleet Sound School.' This unit was established in Boston on 2 March 1942 with Captain W D Baker as commanding officer.[30]

The predominant ASW tactic was the 'hold down'. Generally, a destroyer or an ASW vessel would engage a submarine by using this tactic, which was intended to hold a submarine underwater to the point where its air supply or batteries became exhausted. Once the submarine was exhausted, it would be forced to the surface, at which point the escort's superior guns and the submarine's vulnerability would ensure the sub's destruction.

The other critical component in ASW warfare was aircraft. From the inception of the military use of aircraft there had been friction between the army and navy over how aircraft assets would be managed. This friction came to a head over anti-submarine warfare.

> To the Army, control of land-based aircraft whether operating over land or water should be its responsibility. To the Navy, it seemed equally natural that operations over water, against seaborne targets, should be a naval responsibility.[31]

In 1920 Congress passed a law which stated that the army would control all aerial operations which originated on land, and all aerial activity connected with the Fleet would be under the navy's suzerainty. This demarcation was codified by regulation in 1935. The Joint Action by the army and navy, 1935 (FTP-155) stipulated that the navy 'was also given responsibility for all inshore and offshore patrol for the purpose of protecting shipping and defending the coastal frontier.' This was relatively clear. However, the army grew fearful that this might provide a wedge for the navy to encroach onto the army's area of operation. The navy argued that since it was responsible (in effect) for coastal defence, it should have sway over all aircraft assets on the coasts. The army argued: 'the Navy would, according to this argument, gain control of the Army air forces.'[32] Certainly, the army was not willing to cede to the navy what would, in effect, amount to their control of all military combat air assets on the coasts.

Operationally, this meant that the army refrained from practising reconnaissance flights more than a hundred miles off the coast. The Army Air Force used B–18s and B–24s for medium and long-range patrols. The army used three broad search/patrol anti-submarine patterns: first, routine patrols over water where there was a suspicion of submarine activity; secondly, air escort was used over convoys going through areas where submarines were expected; and thirdly, the operation that aircrews most preferred was what the Army Air Force called 'killer-hunts' in an area where there was considerable evidence of U-boat activity, such as sightings of submarines and reports by torpedoed ships. The Army Air Force considered itself to be more 'offensive-minded' than the navy. The army's anti-submarine culture was oriented towards hunting submarines, while the navy was more invested in protecting commerce.[33] By the eve of the

Second World War it had been established by legislation and practice that the navy would be responsible for the protection of coastal shipping and conducting patrols 100 miles off the coast.

The navy did precious little to shoulder this responsibility for coastal shipping defence. Although FTP-155 had clearly demarcated the navy's responsibility, little assets and no training had been assigned to this task. Despite all of the bureaucratic fighting, it fell to the army's First Bomber Command to conduct the patrols for submarines when the war came to the East Coast.

FTP-155 had considered enemy activity at the coasts, including an incursion by submarines: 'nothing had been planned specifically to counter a campaign by enemy submarine forces. Training exercises off the Atlantic coast had apparently envisioned a surface task force, supported by carrier-based aircraft, as the only likely form of enemy action.' The British had also neglected a coastal anti-submarine air command. They responded by creating Coastal Command, which was responsible for the defence of local, English waters. This was an RAF division, but was under the effective control of the Royal Navy. "No such plan had been laid or agencies established in the United States."[34] For the United States' East Coast, no effective air patrols were instituted until the U-boats struck coastal shipping. It took the pressure of sinking ships and dead crews to push the armed forces to create an effective ASW patrol doctrine.

Conclusion

When the US Navy was confronted by Dönitz's U-boat assault, there was no formal anti-submarine warfare doctrine. Escort vessels had a tactic when they attacked a submarine – the 'hold-down'. However, there was no training or doctrine for units above the individual ship. How were patrols to be established? How were convoys to be formed? What formations were dedicated for anti-submarine warfare? None of these questions had been completely considered prior to the assault.

The navy had effective tools to develop doctrine. Since the turn of the century the Naval War College had been able to refine operational questions through the use of war games. In Morrison's *History of United States Naval Operations in World War II*, he emphasises the importance of the Naval Academy and the War College: 'The Naval Academy had long been an important influence upon the capabilities, spirit and cohesion of the general body of officers. In later years the Naval War College, founded by Admiral Luce and supported by Mahan, had effectively indoctrinated and trained senior officers in the essential art of higher command.'[35]

However, little consideration had been given to the protection of commerce. The entrenched conservatism of the dominant line officers retarded the evolution of ship design and their jealousy regarding the incipient encroachment by engineers into their prerogatives crippled technical innovation and education for officers. The navy was thereby ill-equipped to recognise the potential threat of submarines as commerce raiders.

There was a failure of imagination prior to the German assault. 'Admiral King never appreciated the strategic value of the submarine.' Neither he, nor 'Hap' Arnold, the commander of the Army Air Force, sufficiently considered how and what forces should and could be brought to bear against the threat from submarines. There was scant consideration of a U-boat assault on coastal traffic off the eastern seaboard. Admiral Sims had written *The Victory at Sea* about the tactics and equipment that defeated the U-boats in the First World War. He wrote of: 'the techniques for tracking U-boats, the value of communications intelligence, and successes of the airplane ... German Admiral Karl Doenitz made no secret of his ideas either.' These available resources made this failure of imagination all the more egregious.[36]

When the U-boats of Operation Paukenschlag struck, the navy had no body of literature, no habit of practice and no theory of how to defend shipping against these submarine depredations.

2

Atlantic War Mobilisation

The world was sliding towards another world war. As events unfolded in Europe, Franklin Roosevelt sought to draw the United States closer to Great Britain. 'Between September 1939 and December 1941, the United States moved from neutral to active belligerent in an undeclared naval war against Nazi Germany ... With America's isolationism, disillusionment from its World War I experience, pacifism and tradition of avoiding European problems, President Franklin D Roosevelt moved cautiously to aid Britain.'[1] This was the great project that FDR shouldered. He understood and accepted that the United States would have to become embroiled into the war. However, he also comprehended that he had to pull the American public into this same appreciation. From the start of the war to America's entry, FDR had to walk a tremulous path between accelerating involvement and allaying fears of destruction and dislocation from war.

The diplomatic tide that had flowed from the end of the First World War was ebbing. The international diplomatic regime ushered in by the Washington Naval Arms Limitation Treaty negotiations of 1922 had run its course. Concomitant with the waning of the Arms Limitation regime was the increasingly tenuous international environment:

At Geneva the exhaustive search for European disarmament died, and at London in 1936 naval limitation expired. Italy's conquest of Ethiopia in 1935–36, and the United States Senate rejected even a highly conditional membership in the World Court ... One by one the symbols of post-war accord and the Wilsonian New Diplomacy collapsed.[2]

The international order between nations that was a product, substantially, of American prowess and statesmanship was breaking down. The global economic catastrophe of the Great Depression collapsed governments, supplanting capitalist democracies with Fascist governments in Italy and Germany. The armed forces of these Fascist governments were dynamic. They were also expansive and a new and catastrophic arrangement of the international order was imminent. Once Italy had shown the fecklessness of the League of Nations when the former conquered Ethiopia without substantial recrimination, the Axis alliance was inaugurated between Germany and Italy.

By 1938 Japan was well on its way to digesting the best parts of China; Germany had consumed Austria and was setting the table for Czecho-slovakia. The winners of the First World War, France, Britain and the United States, seemed powerless to thwart these aggressors. The League of Nations had failed; the series of naval arms limitation treaties had failed. For the US president, remilitarisation and rearmament seemed to be increasingly the inescapable requirement, excluding appeasement and capitulation. However, for a segment of the American population, confrontation with Hitler and the aggressive powers was unpalatable. 'By 1938 the United States was strongly committed to isolationism.'[3]

The president was focused on passing his 'New Deal' legislation and the threat to the United States from Japan and Germany seemed remote to the general public. A cornerstone of his New Deal was the National Industrial Recovery Act. This bill was signed into law on 16 June 1933 after being introduced on 17 May, creating the Federal Emergency Administration of Public Works in the process. Among the powers afforded the president were the following:

> ... if in the opinion of the President it seems desirable, the construction of naval vessels within the terms and/or Limits established by the London Naval Treaty of 1930 and of aircraft required therefor and construction of heavier-than-air aircraft and technical construction for the Army Air Corps and such Army housing projects as the president may approve, and provision of original equipment for the mechanization or motorization of such army tactical units as he may designate ...[4]

Thus Roosevelt could authorise increased military preparations by fiat.

Once war was declared by Britain and France, attention began to turn to European affairs. After seven months of 'phoney war', Germany invaded Denmark and Norway on 9 April 1940. The administration used this as a spur to repeal the arms embargo against belligerents. Britain and France could now buy American arms and munitions. However, they would have to take title to these products in American ports and transport them to Europe in their own shipping.

The country began to gird for war. The navy had some valuable assets as a consequence of the Depression:

> The service enjoyed high-quality personnel because the Great Depression allowed its recruiters to exercise an unprecedented selectivity. For example, between July 1938 and June 1939, 159,409 volunteers were examined but only 14,512 – 9 per cent – were accepted ... Re-enlistment rates were extremely high – 72.2 per cent in 1938, 80.8 per cent in 1939, and 73.0 per cent to the middle of 1941; desertions were negligible, averaging only about sixty a year. The result was an experienced, thoroughly professional service.[5]

In 1940 nine battleships were ordered, as compared with eight ordered between 1937–40. Also, eleven aircraft carriers, three battlecruisers, eight heavy and thirty-one light cruisers, and 189 destroyers were ordered. In addition, Roosevelt set an annual production goal of 50,000 aeroplanes for the military.[6]

Aid to Britain was deemed vital by the Roosevelt administration. Once France and the Low Countries had been conquered in June 1940, Britain was all that stood against Hitler's control of Western Europe. Roosevelt agreed to the 'destroyers for bases' deal. In return for fifty First World War-era US destroyers, the British ceded the navy ninety–nine-year leases for bases at Antigua, British Guiana, St Lucia, Bermuda, Trinidad, and three bases at Newfoundland. Prime Minister Churchill also gave an assurance that no matter what befell the United Kingdom and Empire, the Royal Navy would never scuttle or be surrendered. The problem that was developing was a drying-up of available British funds. Although Britain could now buy American arms, they were running short of the money to do so. While the president was cruising in the Caribbean, he came upon the expedient of not selling munitions to Britain, but instead, lending them. Lending war materials was not prohibited by the neutrality laws. On 17 December President Roosevelt addressed the nation by radio. He used another of his bromides to garner support for a policy he preferred. He said that giving arms to Great Britain as an outright gift would stoke war production at home. This would be good business. He argued that by eliminating the dollar sign, the law would not be violated. He used a homily as an argument. He said: 'Suppose your neighbor's [Great Britain] house catches fire. You [the United States] lend him your garden hose.'[7] Two weeks later, on 29 December, he followed-up with a fireside chat. He said:

> If Great Britain goes down, the Axis powers will control the continents of Europe, Asia, Africa, Australia, and the high seas – and they will be in a position to bring enormous military, and naval resources against this hemisphere. It is no exaggeration to say that all of us, in all the Americas, would be living at the point of a gun – a gun loaded with explosive bullets, economic as well as military ... The experience of the past two years has proven beyond doubt that no nation can appease the Nazis ... We must be the great arsenal of democracy ... We must apply ourselves to our task with the same resolution, the same sense of urgency, the same spirit of patriotism and sacrifice as we would show were we at war. We have furnished the British great material support and we will furnish far more in the future ... We have no excuse for defeatism. We have every good reason for hope – hope for peace, yes, and hope for the defense of our civilization and for the building of a better civilization in the future.[8]

In his typically congenial fashion, Roosevelt 'chatted' with the American people. His skills as a rhetorician were put to good effect. He laid out his arguments why appeasement was not viable. He gave cause for hope and argued that the defence of Great Britain was both heroic and in the nation's self-interest. Finally, he made the fight one of the defence of human civilisation against the foreboding forces of barbarism. A tidal wave of laudatory telegrams and letters were received at the White House.

In January 1941 the president asked Congress for legislation to lend war goods to the Allies. This was the Lend-Lease Act. It was approved and signed into law on 11 March 1941. The law was a significant step down the path to belligerency and opened a pathway whereby the president could export munitions to Great Britain. It enjoined the president to certify, through the Secretaries of War and Navy, that the munitions in question were not vital to the defence of the United States. Section 3, (4) (d) prohibited 'convoying of vessels by naval vessels of the United States'; (d) maintained the prohibition of US-flagged vessels to enter a combat area. To allay any reluctance in case that, due to a defeat of Britain, the weapons would fall to the Axis, Section 4 explicitly stated: 'the foreign government undertakes that it will not, without the consent of the President, transfer title to or possession of such defense article or defense information by gift, sale or otherwise, or permit its use by anyone not an officer, employee, or agent of such foreign government.'[9] Once Britain or Canada had bought munitions from the United States they 'had to be paid for with cash, and carried in their own ships ... The United States, by enlisting private enterprise and building new government plants, would embark on an all-out military and naval defense programs, but lend or lease as much production (including food) as could be spared to Great Britain and other countries that were fighting the Axis.'[10] The matter of cash to carry the munitions would surface, but for this legislation, FDR was able to support the British, short of compromising the country's neutrality (such as it was).

Although the Allies had the largest pool of merchant shipping, the United States' portion was not that significant. The US Merchant Marine was flagging: 'In 1940, only 1,550 out of 6,714 vessels arriving from the other continents flew the American flag ... from Europe, 172 out of 2,850. Most extreme, only one of the 1,495 incoming ships from war-zone Britain flew our flag.'[11] Of the Allies' merchant marines, the three most important fleets were those of the British Commonwealth, as having the world's largest extant merchant fleet; Norway, which had considerable numbers of ramp steamers and tankers; and then the United States.

The debate over Lend-Lease was the last stand for the Isolationists:

Senators Burton Wheeler, Arthur Vandenberg, Haram Johnson, Robert Lafollette, Jr, Bennet Champ Clark, their allies in the House of Representatives, and their spokesmen outside, in particular Charles Lindbergh, were on the defensive, themselves increasingly isolated ... On March 11, 1941, the Lend-Lease bill, skillfully amended to enlarge the majorities but safeguard the intent, passed the Senate by a vote of 60 to 31 and the House by 317 to 71.

Ultimately, all of the allies of the United States received Lend–Lease aid, which totalled $50 billion through the war. Of these monies, the United Kingdom received the greatest amount, $31 billion, and next was the Soviet Union, which received $11 billion.[12]

Conditions in the United Kingdom were deteriorating: 'A million to a million and a half tons of shipping lay over in British yards awaiting repair.' There had been a considerable decline in the imports to the United Kingdom: 'total imports to the British Isles continued to fall sharply, from about 60 million tons in 1939 to about 45 million tons in 1940 to an uncomfortable and worrisome rock-bottom 31 million tons in 1941. By the end of that year, almost all consumer goods and food in the British Isles were rationed and "Victory Gardens," begun as patriotic gestures, had become virtual necessities.'[13]

There was a sense of urgency that motivated the American administration. Roosevelt appreciated that the defence of the United States was intimately entwined with the survival of the United Kingdom. If Britain either surrendered or was conquered, the Atlantic would no longer constitute the country's moat for defence, but would instead become the pathway for invasion. March 1941 was a difficult month. The British were 'losing ships at the rate of over 500,000 tons a month and losses were on the rise ... New building in shipyards now under the blitz would replace at best only 30 per cent of the losses. At this rate Britain would import for the year 14 per cent less than its required minimum.'[14]

Roosevelt was sensitive to the threat that was building in Europe. He could not organise the nation's economy for wartime; that would require new legislation. However, he could issue orders to the country's military. On 15 March Roosevelt, at the annual White House Press Corps dinner, gave a speech hoping to shift the focus of the nation's attention from the debate over Lend-Lease to getting munitions to the battlefronts. On the same day, orders were issued to the Atlantic Fleet by Admiral Stark, the Chief of Naval Operations that they were to return to port on the East Coast and 'strip ship of inflammables and peacetime conveniences, undergo overhaul, apply camouflage paint, and prepare for active duty. A squadron of destroyers due for transfer to the Pacific was to remain. Except in the

Caribbean, neutrality patrols ended. Admiral Stark told Admiral King that this was in effect an Atlantic war mobilization.'[15] The Atlantic Fleet was girding for war. The president was setting the navy in place as the bulwark against aggression into the Western Hemisphere. However, in doing so, ships and the men that sailed them were being placed into a war zone.

Developing plans

The plans for involving the United States in the war were now to be referenced as the Rainbow plans. On 30 June 1939 War Plan Orange, the guiding plan hitherto, was shelved and in its stead the Rainbow plans were formulated. Rainbow 1 was the plan for the defence of the western hemisphere from the 'bulge' of Brazil into the north Atlantic. Rainbow 2 was a war in the Pacific against Japan and in alliance with Great Britain and France. The American military focus would be almost entirely on the Pacific, with token participation in the Atlantic and Europe. Rainbow 3 anticipated a war in the western Pacific without allies, basically the Orange plan. Rainbow 4 was the United States' unilateral defence of the western hemisphere, extending south past the 'Brazilian bulge'. It assumed an alliance with Britain and France. The United States would send its navy to the eastern Atlantic and an expeditionary force to Europe.[16]

For Roosevelt, the highest priority, after hemispheric defence, was the maintenance of Britain's viability as an ally: 'At a meeting of his defense advisors on January 17, 1941, Roosevelt concluded that the primary objective must be the maintenance of supply lines to Britain and ordered the navy to prepare for escort of convoys ... The new strategic emphasis on Europe was embodied in the individual and joint plans of the armed services entitled RAINBOW 5.'[17] The implementation of Rainbow 5 was effected by the increasingly intimate co-ordination between British and American military planners. This culminated in March 1941, in the ABC-1 (American-British-Canadian) plan. This plan stipulated that if the United States was drawn into the war, a three-stage strategy would be followed. The first stage was to secure sea-communications between the US and Britain. Secondly, forces would be accumulated in the United Kingdom, and lastly, those forces would invade the European mainland and thereby defeat Germany.

In order to prepare the navy to put the plan into effect, it was decided to transfer units from the Pacific Fleet to the Atlantic as expeditiously as practicable. The Atlantic Fleet was evolving from a patrol force into a formidable fighting formation which 'consisted of three battleships, five heavy cruisers, four light cruisers, two aircraft carriers, and fifty-nine destroyers. The Pacific reinforcement would add three battleships, one aircraft carrier, four light cruisers, and eleven destroyers.'[18]

The Atlantic Fleet was now charged with the mission of enforcing America's neutrality. This entailed protecting outbound convoys from German surface raiders, like *Bismarck* and *Tirpitz*, despite the fact that the German ships easily outclassed any battleships the US had available. The fleet was also charged with protecting convoys against U-boats:

> The navy had already established a force of three destroyer squadrons, nine ships to a squadron, for this assignment ... These twenty-seven destroyers, gathered at Newport, Rhode Island, with additional patrol planes and Coast Guard cutter, formed what the navy designated enigmatically as the Support Force. It was to be ready for action by mid-May 1941 after six weeks of intensive antisubmarine warfare training, alterations, and trials.[19]

They were expected to operate from bases in Northern Ireland, Scotland and, eventually, Iceland. An additional squadron of destroyers was assigned in July and a fifth was planned. The aircraft carriers *Ranger* and *Hornet* would form an anti-raider striking force based out of Bermuda. A third carrier would relieve either of these two for maintenance. Four light cruisers would protect the carriers, and two heavy cruisers would form a striking force based from Iceland. Four older light cruisers would form a patrol squadron that would operate between Africa and Brazil, protecting the southern Atlantic.

The Atlantic patrols were becoming increasingly embroiled. In January 1941 there were 2,005 vessels brought under observation by US warships or planes. By March there were 3,420 contacts and the next month, 3,647.[20]

On 7 April 1941 Roosevelt ordered the Pacific Fleet to send the ships earmarked as reinforcements to the Atlantic Fleet. Three days later he informed his advisers that he wanted to extend the American defence zone to include the Azores, some of the Cape Verde Islands and Greenland. America was flexing its muscles and relieving pressure on the hard-pressed Royal Navy. However, he was not looking to displace the Royal Navy from eastern Atlantic waters. Instead, he wanted the flag flown in these waters

25

as a warning to the Axis that the US was not sanguine about events, was taking cognizance and would rise to any challenges. It was a signal to Hitler that Roosevelt did not intend to balk at aggression in the Atlantic.

So as to accommodate the president's directions, the navy developed doctrine for its expanding responsibilities. Western Hemisphere Defense Plan One was the result: 'According to this plan, the six battleships of the reinforced fleet, comprising Task Force 1, would individually patrol set course running east of the latitude of Philadelphia to fifty degrees west longitude (the line of the west coast of Greenland), then north-east to the twenty-sixth meridian and the edge of the war zone declared by Germany and back.'[21]

Task Force 2 was composed of the aircraft carriers. They would patrol the unfrequented waters east of Bermuda, approaching the Azores. Task Force 3, four old cruisers, would patrol from Puerto Rico or Trinidad to the southwest towards Africa, then to Brazil and return to the Caribbean. Task Force 4 was designated the Support Force and detailed to stand ready for deployment to 'higher latitudes', meaning that it would patrol a block of the central Atlantic. These forces operated under the strictures that if they sighted Axis vessels in their zones, they were to trail them and broadcast their positions. In effect, the US Navy was extending the patrolling area covered by the Allies. This was a great benefit for the Royal Navy, as they would no longer be burdened with patrolling the entirety of the Atlantic and could thereby concentrate their forces in the Western Approaches, the critical area of the war in the Atlantic. Portentously, for the first time, the use of force was sanctioned. The patrolling ships were under orders to 'prevent interference with American flag vessels in the expanded defense zone. Furthermore, in waters close by – the Gulf of St Lawrence, the Caribbean, Bermuda, and otherwise within twenty-five miles of Western Hemisphere territory – patrols should warn away Axis ships (technically, vessels of nations having no territory in the Western Hemisphere) and attack them if they failed to heed the warning.'[22]

Growing belligerency
In addition to extending American warship patrols into the Atlantic, Roosevelt made US shipyards available to the Royal Navy. In February, the British asked if their aircraft carrier, *Illustrious*, could be repaired in American yards; German dive-bombers in the Mediterranean had

damaged her. Roosevelt approved this request without hesitation. The British went, on the claim that their shortage of dry-dock space was critical and they needed extensive access to American yards. Roosevelt sent the Assistant Secretary of the Navy, James Forrestal, to London. Between the wars, due to economic strictures British shipyard capacity had eroded from 3,500,000 tons in 1930 to 2,500,000 by 1937. Forrestal worked out a long-term schedule for the repair of British ships in American yards. By the end of March, there was a pervasive sentiment in the US Navy that aid to Britain was vital. A schedule to repair eight Royal Navy warships in US yards was in place and Congress provided $200 million for repair work under Lend-Lease. The commitment of the US for the use of yards to repair Royal Navy ships was of no small moment. By August 1941 eight out of fifteen British capital ships were unavailable for operations due to a need for repairs or refitting.[23]

On 29 March the president ordered the seizure of sixty-five ships from Axis or Axis-controlled countries in US ports. On 2 April funds for 200 merchant ships were appropriated to be built for the British, and US repair yards were made accessible for the ships of the British merchant marine. 'In the last nine months of 1941, British shipping under repair in American ports averaged 430,000 tons a month.' On 30 March 1941 the Coast Guard was authorised by Congress to take certain Axis vessels into 'protective custody', including 'twenty-seven Italian, two German and thirty-five Danish ships.'[24]

The situation was particularly sensitive regarding French North Africa. The Vichy government had intimated to the Americans that they were considering strengthening their defences in North Africa, with an eye towards defending their territory against incursions by either US or British forces. However, the US envoy to French North Africa, Robert Murphy, sent a cable on 19/20 May. He wrote that he had received assurances from General Weygand, the French regent in North Africa, that the Germans had not penetrated French possessions in North Africa and that they had only two divisions in Libya.

Despite Murphy's assurances, Roosevelt was growing skittish about the potential German seizure of Dakar and the Azores, which would give them access to the mid- and southern Atlantic. On 22 May he ordered 25,000 troops be readied for deployment to the Azores by 22 June. He had sent a note to the Portuguese government asking if they would accept US protection of these islands, but did not wait for the reply before ordering these preparations. Roosevelt was starting to hedge. He was considering that the Atlantic was both the highway to maintain Britain and the threshold of the United States' own defence. The navy balked at this preparation. Admiral King estimated that invading the island group would require two battleships, most of the modern cruisers and eighteen destroyers and the commitment of these forces would prohibit the continuation of patrolling. The army and the navy did not have adequate troop transports, but to lift the expeditionary force to the Azores would require an additional twelve transports, which would have to be acquired or converted from existing merchant shipping. Nevertheless, planning for the islands' seizure proceeded.[25]

Commissioned for the Robin Line of New York in 1919, SS *Robin Moore* was a 5,000-ton American freighter. On 21 May 1941 she was en route from New York to Cape Town, South Africa, about seven hundred miles east of the Brazilian bulge into the Atlantic, and flying an American flag at her masthead, when *U-69* found her. The submarine's captain, Kapitän-leutnant Jost Metzler, ordered the ship to stop, cease using her wireless and to send the ship's papers over in a boat to the submarine. The papers revealed the ship to be carrying steel rails, trucks, a tiny number of small-calibre rifles and a tiny amount of ammunition for them. This cargo was considered contraband and was accepted as a legitimate target for confiscation and/or destruction by the German naval command. Metzler warned the crew that they had twenty minutes to abandon ship. Once the crew of thirty-eight, together with eight passengers, were in lifeboats, he then sank the ship by torpedo.[26] *Robin Moore* entered history as the first American-flagged ship to be sunk in the Atlantic by a U-boat in the Second World War.

On 27 May Roosevelt spoke to the American people. This speech was a statement of his justification of preparing for war. He asserted that Hitler would not be content with the conquest of Europe. He said that if Hitler should conquer or ally with Spain and Portugal, he would gain access to the Cape Verde Islands and northwest Africa. This would place German forces within seven hours' flying time from Brazil. In short, the moat of the Atlantic, which had hitherto protected the western hemisphere, would be breached. He concluded the speech by saying that the world was now divided between slavery and freedom. To safeguard American freedoms, the nation's armed forces were being mobilised and placed into strategic positions so as to be ready to repel any assault. The speech ended with FDR declaring a proclamation of unlimited national emergency. The president could now mobilise communications, public utilities and transportation. Roosevelt's popularity rose from 73 to 76 per cent by June. Public opinion favouring escorting convoys to Britain rose from 41 per cent in favour on 15 April to 55 per cent by 9 June.[27] Roosevelt ordered all Axis consular and propaganda offices closed and the personnel to return to Germany.

A further non-neutral act was made on 14 June when the United States froze all German, Italian and some neutrals' (including the Soviet Union) assets in America. However, once Germany invaded the Soviet Union, these assets were unfrozen.

The war was creeping westward. The German conquest of Denmark created apprehensions in Britain that the Germans might cast avaricious eyes upon Iceland, a Danish colony. It could be used by the Allies to either refuel escorts convoying merchants across the Atlantic, or by the Germans to extend the U-boat patrols further into the mid-Atlantic. On 25 March 1941 Hitler proclaimed an extension of the blockaded zone. He extended this to include all of Iceland, and further to the west to the three-mile territorial limit of Greenland. He ordered that any merchant ships found therein could be sunk on sight. Churchill, however, had beaten Hitler to the punch. A joint British-Canadian force had occupied Iceland on 10 May 1940. However, the population of the island had found the occupation annoying.

The British were hard pressed to meet their global requirements, as the war in the Mediterranean was straining Commonwealth resources. The British prompted the Icelanders to approach America and request an American garrison for the island. Since the US was still neutral, it was felt that their occupation would both insulate the island and make the occupation less burdensome. The carrot of a favourable trade relationship with the United States was an inducement that the Icelanders could ill afford to refuse. On 14 April the Icelandic Consul General in Washington, DC, opened secret negotiations towards this end and Roosevelt grasped the opportunity with alacrity. Planning for the seizure of the Azores was terminated on 13 June and plans went ahead for the garrisoning of Iceland. The plan that was generated for this occupation called for the landing of nearly thirty thousand troops and 231,554 tons of equipment onto Iceland: 'The Navy Department gave assurances that on five days' notice three naval transports with a total capacity of 4,000 men could be provided for the Iceland movement, that on or about 20 June four Army transports being converted by the navy and with a capacity of about 6,000 men could be made available; and that by 28 June transportation for the entire Iceland force could be provided.'[28]

A vital step in making these plans was to survey the island and this brought the first incident that could have caused war. The survey of Iceland was assigned to the destroyer USS *Niblack* with the division commanding officer, Commander Dennis L Ryan, aboard. On 11 April 1941 *Niblack* was five hundred miles southwest of Iceland as part of the forward screen for a convoy delivering personnel to Iceland. The ship was steaming towards the island when she spotted survivors from a torpedoed Dutch freighter. The ship slowed to retrieve the shipwrecked sailors. As these victims clambered aboard, sonar made contact with a submarine. The contact was approaching from the starboard beam at a range of 1,400yds – the ship was a veritable 'sitting duck'. The division commander agreed to an attack. Although there was little chance of damaging the submarine, an attack might disrupt any torpedo set-up. Once the survivors were aboard, the warship went into action at 28 knots. Within five minutes of the first contact, three depth charges, at five-second intervals, were dropped. Although the depth charges caused no damage (or consternation to the Germans as the depth charges were very wide of the mark), the submarine retired.[29] Thus was the first warlike act by a US warship in the Battle of the Atlantic.

Germany attacked the Soviet Union on 22 June 1941, changing the focus of the war. The pressure in the Atlantic slackened and fear of an invasion of Britain subsided. By July it was becoming clear that the Germans were not going to have an easy time defeating the Soviets. Secretary of War Stimson urged the president to seize the initiative in the Atlantic. Officials from Vichy France told FDR in confidence that they thought the German attack on Russia was an admission of weakness, that Germany could not extort from the Soviets what they wanted. They felt 'that Germany feared American participation, even that it had lost the war. Now was America's chance to act, said one French official.'[30]

The strengthening of the Atlantic continued. Over six weeks from

9 June, the battleships *Idaho, New Mexico, Mississippi, Texas, New York* and *Arkansas* were transferred from the Pacific to the Atlantic. This meant that, as of July, there were always at least two battleships on patrol between the Grand Banks and the German-declared blockade zone abutting Icelandic waters. In addition, three aircraft carriers patrolled out of Bermuda. These were *Yorktown, Wasp* and *Ranger* (when *Ranger* was undergoing maintenance, the escort carrier *Long Island* took her place).[31] By August the light cruiser escorts for the carriers were released from their troop transport escorting duties and joined the aircraft carriers. Despite the allocation of these considerable resources, no German raiders were encountered. Submarines, however, did encounter one of these patrols.

On 19 June the battleship *Texas* steamed on patrol at the edge of the Iceland-German blockade zone. It had been an uneventful cruise for the twenty-five-year-old ship. She had reached the eastern extremity of her patrol zone and had turned to repeat her cruise, homeward-bound. Unbeknownst to the American crew, the ship was being stalked by *U-203*. The German submarine strained to find a firing position, but the zigzagging ship was not an easy prey. When the U-boat returned to base, Hitler exhibited anxiety that a confrontation had only been narrowly missed; he was concerned about any possible confrontation with the United States that might give the Americans an excuse to enter the war. From that date, Hitler ordered that no American ships were to be attacked, at least until the Soviet Union was subdued.

On 1 July the government of Iceland placed the island's defence in the hands of the United States. Task Force 19 arrived in Reykjavik on 7 July after an uneventful passage. The task force landed the 1st Provisional Marine Brigade. They were escorted by two battleships *(Texas* and *New York)*, two cruisers and thirteen destroyers – a considerable part of the US forces in the Atlantic. While the task force was completing its offloading and refuelling, it received a notice that the German battleship *Tirpitz* was preparing to sortie and assault the American force. The two First World War-era ships would have stood no chance against the modern German state-of-the-art battleship. Fortunately, British reconnaissance flights correctly identified the German ship safely in Kiel.[32]

By June 1941 the transatlantic convoy system that would endure for the remainder of the war was largely in place. United States escort groups were composed of a destroyer and several corvettes. They would shepherd a convoy of approximately fifty merchantmen to the mid-ocean meeting point (MOMP). The escort groups originating from North America would be relieved by a group at Iceland. As of 9 July there were fifteen destroyers available for escort duties. By the end of October this force had been increased to fifty-four destroyers, the designated quantity. In July an American escort base was made operational in Argentia, Newfoundland, the latter having been one of the bases gained by the US Navy from the destroyers for bases deal.

The Atlantic force's capital ships were concentrated at Newport, Rhode Island. The role of the Atlantic Fleet was ephemeral. For Admiral Stark, the fleet was expected to act as a 'trip-wire' for war. Once combat operations were begun, Stark expected the Atlantic Fleet to operate much as it did during the First World War – integrated into the Royal Navy's North Atlantic operations.

President Roosevelt, on 9 July, set broad policy for the Atlantic Fleet. He ordered that American escorts would accompany convoys, which included American and/or Icelandic merchant ships and those British ships that joined en route. To implement this plan, Admiral King negotiated with the Canadian navy to alternate escorting functions, reaching agreement on 22 July. Both the US and Canadian navies would contribute thirty escorts. However, Roosevelt rejected the scheme as both politically and legally dubious. He 'rejected the agreement on the grounds that it was impossible to enter into formal undertakings with foreign authorities for the operation of American naval forces, and so when Plan Four went into effect on July 24, provision for combined convoys was withheld.'[33]

The US Navy and Royal Navy's growing intimacy

From 9–12 August 1941 FDR, Churchill and their staffs met at Argentia, Newfoundland. For Roosevelt, Argentia established the political basis for escalating war planning and preparations. This basis was codified as the Atlantic Charter, a statement of Wilsonian-like principles for peace. FDR expected this charter to be used to rally anti-Axis forces. These principles were: 'non-aggrandizement, self-determination (with the "wish for restoration of sovereignty and self-government to peoples forcibly deprived of them"), freedom of the seas, abandonment of force, disarmament, and ultimately, in some form, a world security organization.'[34] The charter was also a useful propaganda and foreign policy tool as it drew a clear contrast with the Axis powers. The anti-Axis forces were fighting (or pledged) to a multilateral world of independent nations, defined by expressions of popular will. The implication was that the Axis were fighting to impose their will forcibly on others and for their own good at the expense of those they subordinated.

Churchill's purpose at Argentia was to graft American aims and intentions increasingly to Britain. He also argued (successfully) that the Royal Navy needed to withdraw their fifty-two escorts from the western Atlantic and transfer them to an all-British convoy route to Murmansk, which would open a supply route to Russia.[35] These escorts would also be used to bolster convoy escorts on the lanes to Gibraltar. Roosevelt committed the navy to escort convoys in the western Atlantic as of 1 September. He ordered that US destroyers escorting convoys could attack any U-boat encountered, regardless of the range from the convoy.

Admiral Harold Raynsford Stark was made Chief of Naval Operations (CNO) on 1 August 1939. He was replacing Admiral William Daniel Leahy, who had served as CNO from 2 January 1937 to 1 August 1939. Stark was at sea as the commanding officer of Cruiser Squadron 3, when Roosevelt appointed him as CNO.[36]

The strategic orientation that codified this emphasis on the Atlantic was made coherent by a succinct document that Admiral Stark had laid before FDR the week after the president was re-elected in 1940. This was the 'Plan Dog' memorandum. Stark laid-out the broad strategic possibilities as he saw them. He labelled them options A to D (hence Plan D, for 'dog'). In option A he proffered the main US effort to be the defence of the hemisphere. In B he proposed a defence in the Atlantic and a full offensive against Japan, in alliance with the British and Dutch. Plan C was an equal effort in both oceans, additionally supporting the nationalist Chinese. Plan D called for the defeat of Germany first, a strong offensive in the Atlantic and a defence in the Pacific. He argued that defeating Japan was secondary as Germany was the strongest of the Axis powers and posed the greatest threat to the US. In this memo, Admiral Stark argued succinctly that American security depended upon the fate of Great Britain, especially her fleet. Stark wrote:

if Britain wins decisively against Germany we could win everywhere, but that if she loses the problems confronting us would be very great; and while we might not *lose everywhere*, we might possibly, not *win* anywhere.

Plan D was accepted by the Joint Board, which endorsed Admiral Stark's Plan Dog on 21 December, 1940.[37] This became the basis for the 'Germany first' orientation that underlay all Anglo–American planning throughout the war.

Although the navy was starting to gird itself for the conflict, it was still dependent upon the British. Admiral King lamented to a subordinate:

> American escort operations entirely depended on British experience and sophisticated facilities, on the ULTRA decryption work at Bletchley Park, on the Operational Intelligence Centre, Trade Plot, and the Submarine Tracking Room at the Admiralty, and on the Western Approaches Command at Liverpool. ... American command in the western Atlantic had to be instituted and escort units inserted without disrupting the schedule of convoys, six to eight of which at regular intervals were passing back and forth across the ocean on any given day.[38]

The US Navy was rousing for the fight, Roosevelt was inching towards belligerency and Churchill was encouraging the president ever more towards a declaration of US co-belligerency. However, FDR knew that the American public was not ready to accept a declaration of war and the isolationist fire was not yet completely doused.

Admiral King moved the Atlantic Fleet's support force from urbane Newport, Rhode Island, to rustic Casco Bay, Maine. He wanted the replenishment forces as close as possible to the routes the convoys were taking across the Atlantic. Destroyer tenders, repair ships and oilers either remained at the new base in Maine, or made the trek to the cusp of the war zone, and anchored at Iceland. King further took the step of establishing a 'destroyer pool' in Maine. This had the effect of eroding the destroyer squadron and division cohorts. This step made destroyers available for deployment as escorts as needed. However, it also broke up teams of ships that had trained, or at least were organised, together.

The Atlantic escort force was evolving and by September:

> ... thirty-three destroyers, every one the Atlantic fleet commander could get his hands on, and the Coast Guard cutter *Campbell* were ready for merchant

vessel escort at the northern bases. Another sixteen were due at the end of October and six more by the end of the year, leaving a bare minimum to escort warships, one division (four ships) to patrol the Caribbean, and a sonar training division at Key West which Admiral King coveted.[39]

King was now able to deploy six escort groups of five destroyers each to meet the American obligation to escort convoys. His vision was to have a total of seven escort groups of six destroyers each. This would afford one group at a time to lay over in Boston for maintenance. The strain of incessant voyages across the Atlantic precluded maintaining all the ships in operations, so he was not able to sustain these numbers of ships at sea continuously. Of those that were mobilised, few were up to peacetime standards of efficiency. Few ships were equipped with radar and those that did have radar installed were rushed into activity without adequate training in the new equipment.

However, the Germans were not idle. As the navy frantically deployed escorts, the Germans also fielded increasing numbers of U-boats. The total number of submarines in commission increased from sixty-five in July to eighty in October, and the numbers of submarines that could be maintained on station was increased to thirty. Dönitz was about to let loose the soon to be dreaded wolf packs. The first wolf pack of fourteen boats, named Group Markgraf, was formed. It prowled the waters between Greenland and Iceland. As Markgraf was deploying towards the latter part of August, German naval intelligence enhanced the encryption of submarine communications with the shore: just as more U-boats were being deployed, the British ability to read their radio traffic was degraded. The German high command had begun to super-encipher U-boat locations within enciphered messages. Masking U-boat deployments, this delayed the British being able to act on intelligence – there was now a lag of up to four days in reading signals between the boats at sea and command ashore.

Combat not war

On 4 September 1941 the inevitable came to pass: USS *Greer* was 125 miles southeast of Iceland, steaming to deliver mail and some officers to the garrison. She was sailing without other allied ships, though she was not alone for she was stationed at the northern extremity of Group Markgraf. The area had been assigned to *U-652*. At approximately 10:30 in the morning, a roving RAF bomber spotted the U-boat on the surface a few thousand yards in front of USS *Greer* and radioed the contact to the American ship. The commander of the escort group, Commander Johnson, was aboard and he authorised the search for the submarine, in accordance with FDR's orders that Axis warships within the American defence zone should be tracked and reported. Johnson then authorised an attack on the submarine, reasoning that this was a natural extension of the standing orders, although the condition was that they would have to be fired upon first. The destroyer gained sonar contact and pursued the submarine, keeping her submerged for hours. Hitler had forbidden his submarines from attacking US warships, so there was no way for *U-652* to assault its pursuer. *Greer* had been maintaining contact for an hour, making occasional depth-charge attacks but causing no serious damage. It became manifest to Oberleutnant Fraatz that the American's tactic was the hold-down and eventually his air and electricity would become exhausted. The submarine commander, Oberleutnant Georg-Werner Fraatz, decided that his crew was in imminent peril and took the decision to defy the Führer's orders. After four hours of being dogged by the US ship, *U-652* fired a torpedo, but an unexpected turn to starboard threw off the German's aim. Ten minutes later a second missile was fired, also missing. The US ship rolled off her last depth charges at 12:56, causing minor damage. *Greer* then quit the now manifestly deadly game and continued to Reykjavik, Iceland. Fortunately, there was no loss of life, in this, the first shooting incident of the Second World War between US escort forces and Nazi submarines.[40]

The next day, 5 September, President Roosevelt met with Admirals King and Stark. At the conclusion of the discussions, the president authorised escort of convoys to and from Iceland. This escorting could be done without the presence of American or Icelandic-flagged merchant ships in the convoy. He also permitted the escorting of American-flag merchant ships by the Royal Navy and the Royal Canadian Navy, and as far as Iceland. A few days later, Roosevelt authorised the shooting on sight of German and Italian warships anywhere within the American defence zone (Iceland and the rest of the Atlantic Ocean to the west). 'By September 16, when the first American escort group, Task Unit 4.1.1, met the American-escorted convoy, HX 150 out of Halifax, the United States Navy was in a state of full belligerency in the Western Atlantic.'[41]

On 11 September Roosevelt addressed the nation by radio. This was a defence for US intervention into the Battle of the Atlantic:

The *Greer*, he insisted was on a 'legitimate' mission to Iceland, an American outpost *protecting* waters through which passed ships of many flags carrying food and war material provided by the American people as an essential part of their own defense. If the U-boat had been unable to identify the destroyer, as the Nazis claimed, and still fired, this reflected a policy of indiscriminate violence, as proven by such other attacks as the sinking of the *Robin Moor* and the stalking of the USS *Texas* in June, and the recent sinking of the Panamanian freighter *Sessa* and the American freighter *Steel Sea Farer.*

The next day the *New York Times* headline read: 'ROOSEVELT ORDERS NAVY TO SHOOT FIRST'. According to a Gallup poll, 62 per cent of those interviewed approved of FDR's new policy.[42]

On 17 September the Admiralty recommended that the US Navy assume responsibility to patrol the Denmark Strait, so that British ships could transfer to the Mediterranean. Admiral King consented to this and ten days later the US Atlantic Fleet was concentrated in northern waters. The navy deployed one old and two modernised battleships (with the newly commissioned battleship, *Washington*, as a reserve stationed in Rockland, Maine); three heavy cruisers and an aircraft carrier were patrolling from Hvalfjörður, Iceland. There were one modernised and two older battleships and a carrier and two light cruisers at Argentia, and another carrier and a light cruiser ordered there. Fifty American destroyers were now either stationed in the northern Atlantic or engaged in escorting operations. By October the forces in the Atlantic were equivalent to the navy's strength in the Pacific.

Roosevelt was moving increasingly towards making the United States a belligerent and the nation towards a war footing; he understood that the economic preparations for war would be one of the most critical fronts for war readiness. On 30 August FDR ordered Secretary Stimson to submit by 10 September recommendations on how war production could be allocated for the United States and the Allies to attain victory by June 1942.

In 1941 US war production was less than 10 per cent of the whole economy, and less than 65 per cent of the war production of Britain and

Canada. War production in the US was not expected to exceed the British-Canadian production until the last quarter of 1942. The US was projected 'to produce 230,000 tons of shipping in the same quarter [it was] calculated that defeat of Germany would require 10.8 million already planned through 1943 and an additional 13.1 million tons.'[43]

By the end of 1941 there were clear indications that events were speeding towards a confrontation in the Atlantic. On 17 October USS *Kearny* was torpedoed by *U-568* while assisting a convoy approaching Iceland. On 17 October a Canadian convoy was 400 miles from Iceland when they encountered a wolf pack. The escort of four corvettes and a destroyer found themselves overwhelmed. Three freighters were sent to the bottom during the night and the convoy transmitted an urgent call for help. In response four American destroyers, a Royal Navy and Free French escort responded to the call. When the US destroyers arrived the next night, *Kearny* commenced rescue operations for a burning freighter. While she was assisting the stricken ship she received a single torpedo from a salvo of three which were fired at her. Damage was extensive. All internal communications and electricity were knocked out. She had taken water forward and her bow settled 4ft deeper. Although the ship was able to sail to Reykjavik on her own power, she had sustained considerable damage and eleven sailors were killed and twenty-four were wounded. These were the first US combat casualties of the Second World War.[44]

Franklin Roosevelt took to the radio to address the nation on 27 October 1941. He used this address to demonise Hitler and used considerable hyperbole to justify increasing the country's participation in the war. He used the address to call for the arming of merchant ships. He said that:

> The U.S.S. Kearny is not just a Navy ship. She belongs to every man, woman, and child in this Nation ... The purpose of Hitler's attack was to frighten the American people off the high seas – to force us to make a trembling retreat. This is not the first time that he has misjudged the American spirit. That spirit is now aroused.

FDR then took the opportunity to isolate the Isolationists that remained.

> And some Americans – not many – will continue to insist that Hitler's plans need not worry us and that we should not concern ourselves with anything

that goes on beyond rifle shot of our own shores ... The fact is that Nazi propaganda continues in desperation to seize upon such isolated statements as proof of American disunity.[45]

A U-boat sank USS *Reuben James* on 31 October. She was part of the screen of five US destroyers escorting a thirty-four-ship convoy towards Ireland. *Reuben James* was stationed 2,000yds off the port beam of the convoy. At about dawn she had turned to investigate a radio–direction bearing contact indicated by the ship's radio direction-finder. She was then struck under the no. 1 stack by a torpedo. The resulting explosion blew the bow of the ship off and holed her under the no. 3 stack. She floated for about five minutes; 115 American sailors were killed from a crew totalling 160.[46]

The United States was not exclusively on the receiving end of the violence. The cruiser *Omaha* and the destroyer *Somers*, off the bulge of Brazil on 6 November 1941, arrested the German raider *Odenwald*. The German ship, a freighter that had been stranded in Japan since the start of the war, had escaped as far as the southern Atlantic when she ran into the US patrol. The freighter flew an American flag and had a home port of Wilmetto, Delaware, painted on her transom, adopting the guise of a legally registered US ship. However, the executive officer on the cruiser noted that the ship's stern was dissimilar from the freighters that were built near Philadelphia, on Hog Island, during the First World War (the 'Hog-Islanders', named after the island they were built on). When the Americans challenged them by megaphone, the German accents gave them away. A boarding party was sent over and the ship was taken to San Juan, Puerto Rico, after the Americans repaired the ship, which the German crew had tried to scuttle. Then seizure was challenged by Germany and a court in Puerto Rico upheld the capture and awarded the US government $124,211 in damages. This was the first 'prize money' granted since 1839 to an American warship. In response to this seizure, Hitler ordered on 13 November 1941 that any German ship that found herself being 'shadowed' or otherwise endangered was authorised to use her weapons.[47]

These confrontations at sea pushed Congress towards greater sympathy towards war. On 13 November the remaining neutrality laws were rescinded. Arming of merchant ships would commence and on 6 November the Admiralty received notice from the US Navy that any raiders that broke into the Atlantic would be pursued, wherever it was in the ocean.[48]

For Germany, the U-boat campaign against British shipping in 1941 was inconclusive. Through 1941 there were 291 merchant ships sunk in convoys totalling 5.3 million tons. In addition, USS *Reuben James* was sunk; USS *Kearny* and USS *Salinas* (a USN tanker) were damaged, which brought the US closer to belligerency. FDR was able to get weakening amendments to the Neutrality Acts passed. Admiral Stark wrote to Admiral Hart (commander of the Asiatic Fleet): 'The Navy is already in the war of the Atlantic, but the country does not seem to realize it ... Whether the country knows it or not, *we are at war*.'[49]

The hesitation and hiccupping progress towards war all changed on 7 December when the Imperial Japanese Navy devastated the Pacific Fleet at Pearl Harbor. Hitler, seeing America weakened, took the opportunity to gratify his admirals and declared war on the United States on 11 December. Given the scope of the friction in the Atlantic already evident, he felt that the declaration of war made little effective difference. Italy immediately also declared war on the US and the United States' response was to return the declaration. The United States was now completely engaged in the world war. In the following month, the full force of the war would be graphically brought home to the United States as Admiral Dönitz unleashed Operation Drumbeat against the US East Coast.

3

Rearmament: The Navy and Public Relief

The Great Depression had shaken the western world. Both Britain and the United States looked to retrench naval expenditures and the succession of naval arms limitation treaties were motivated, in part, to curtail spending. Franklin Roosevelt, however, had other ideas about what the relationship of naval spending to economic recovery should be. One of the means that the new Roosevelt administration used was to increase government spending to spark the economy. Hitler came to power as the chancellor of Germany on 30 January 1933, one month and five days after Franklin Roosevelt was sworn in as president of the United States.

The economic crash of 1929 led the Hoover administration to cut back on naval appropriations: 'Since the early 1920s, Congress had been reducing shipbuilding appropriations substantially, and it seemed unlikely that the unsympathetic seventy-second Congress would reverse the precedent of these earlier decisions.'[1] There was discussion about both curtailing new construction and closing navy yards. In October 1931 the Chief of Naval Operations, Admiral William Pratt, proposed that the naval yards at Boston, Massachusetts, and in Charleston, South Carolina, be closed. The Chief of the Bureau of Construction and the Navy General Board recommended these yards as supernumerary. The Navy Department was under stress to have a net reduction in its budget. No savings from base closures would be transferred to another bureau. A press leak of the plan to close the bases resulted in a public uproar, so when President Hoover presented the draft budget for the navy in 1933, there was no mention of base closures. During the budget debates, Congress made it clear that it would not permit substantial replacements or additions to the

Fleet. Nevertheless, Work Relief Funds were used as part of the funding for new ship construction, authorised by presidential fiat.

The National Industrial Recovery Act (1933) was enacted on 16 June 1933, to use the resources of the federal government to stimulate industrial expansion; it was 'An Act to encourage national industrial recovery, to foster fair competition, and to provide for the construction of certain useful public works, and for other purposes.' President Franklin Roosevelt used this legislation to justify using these funds on warship construction. Section 202 of the law provided for 'the construction of naval vessels within the terms and/or limits established by the London Naval Treaty of 1930 and of aircraft required therefore and construction of heavier-than-air aircraft ... as the President may approve'.[2] FDR needed no great prompting – his view of how to restart the economy from the Great Depression envisioned using the power of federal spending to 'prime' industrial revitalisation.

The Chief of Naval Operations under Herbert Hoover was William Pratt, who was appointed CNO on 17 September 1930 and was replaced on 30 June 1933. Pratt became a divisive figure for the naval officer corps. He was frequently considered as siding with the president against the navy. This was most manifest when it came to the naval budget. When Pratt was invested as CNO, Hoover made it clear that he wanted big cuts to the navy's budget. This conflict over the budget came to a head between Pratt's office and the General Board. The latter was tasked (among other things) to prepare 'worst case' estimates of potential conflicts. It was this planning around other nations' capabilities that impelled the board to plan for conflicts regardless of their plausibility: 'For this reason, the General Board continued in the late 1920s to plan for war with Great Britain. By contrast, Pratt relied more heavily on analysis of national *intentions* and came to the not illogical conclusion that a war between the United States and Great Britain was virtually impossible.' Pratt was required to acclimatise the navy to a fiscal environment of curtailment and austerity, and presided over a navy that was contracting. Monies allocated to the navy went from a high of $403 million in fiscal year 1931 to $333 million in 1933. What was worse for the navy's officer corps was the contraction in personnel and ships. There was a planned reduction of 4,800 men and the mothballing of one battleship, sixteen destroyers, twenty-five submarines and five miscellaneous light vessels.[3]

Prior to Franklin Roosevelt's assumption of office, the navy General Board was considering the 1933 building programme. Ultimately the board proposed the following programme: one 10,000-ton, 8in cruiser, two 6in cruisers and two aircraft carriers of 13,800 tons each (these carriers became *Yorktown* and *Enterprise*), one large (leader) destroyer and three destroyers and six submarines. The total bill for this construction was estimated at $400 million. When Congress was presented with this proposal, it was not approved. Instead, Congress ordered a cut of the navy's extant budget of $50–60 million, which would have resulted in the decommissioning of approximately one-third of the fleet.[4] By the time that President Herbert Hoover was voted out of office in 1933, there had not been one naval vessel authorised under his administration, but the passage of the National Industrial and Recovery Act (NIRA) of 1933 was to save the navy.

In March 1932 Senator Wagner introduced a bill for $1.1 billion to be used for his Employment Stabilization Act. The act provided for expedited planning and streamlined budgeting for efforts to relieve economic distress. The navy was apportioned some of these funds to help with its six-year construction goals. This was to fund six destroyers that had hitherto been authorised. However, once Congress had completed its deliberations, the navy's share had been truncated and the total monies allocated had been halved to $500 million by 21 July 1938.[5] The navy was allocated a further $10 million for shore construction.

The overall vitality of ship construction was declining. The value of construction contracts at the seven largest naval shipyards had fallen by approximately 55 per cent from 1931 to 1932 for all shipping construction, both naval and commercial. These private yards were facing lay-offs and bankruptcy. Naval construction required a considerable technical proficiency to design, build and repair ships: if the workforce were to be laid off, the skills needed to maintain the Fleet would atrophy. So as the summer of 1932 unfolded, there developed a threat that the private shipyards might be broken up. Following the First World War, there was a superfluity of naval and merchant ship construction capacity, and the shipyards had had over-capacity from the end of the war through to 1929. The 'mail subsidy and construction loan provision of the Merchant Marine Act of 1928 were felt ... Ironically, private shipyards entered the depression with firm work commitments for at least three years.'[6] In the summer of 1932 shipping construction peaked, with a national workforce of 30,000. The ships built under this act would be completed in 1934, and then the shipyards would have no new contracts. However, with the election of Franklin Roosevelt, the navy had a champion in the White House. The 1934 naval budget amounted to $266 million. Of this amount $238 million was provided through NIRA. Allocations through NIRA could be provided by executive order, so any scuffles in Congress were avoided. This disbursement enabled construction to begin on thirty-two ships funded by NIRA and five through the navy's conventional appropriation.

Although Pratt had been associated with reductions in ships, personnel and budgets, on the eve of his replacement as CNO he wrote a paper entitled: 'For the Equalization and Limitations of Armaments'. He sent a copy to Secretary of State Cordell Hull and the Secretary of the Navy, Claude Swanson. In this document he reviewed the aims, intentions and the prospects for negotiating reductions of the armaments of the major naval powers. He described Japan and Germany as aggressive. His conclusion was:

> that in the final analysis the best hope of peace ... is that the United States and the United Kingdom must stand firmly side by side, shoulder to shoulder, 50-50 in all things; and in the case of a break [ie war] the mutual interests of Great Britain and ourselves in sea power will draw us inevitably closer together provided we take care not to let economic or other matters drive a rift between us.[7]

Economic strictures grew so dire under Pratt that he proposed a 'rotating reserve system'. He proposed that all vessels would be tied to a dock for one-third of their time and be manned by only 60 per cent of the established crew. However, there was such an outcry that the plan was not implemented. Pratt served as CNO until 30 June 1933: he was not popular.

Rebuilding the Fleet and public relief

The sixth CNO, William Harrison Standley, assumed office on 1 July 1933. Immediately, there was a sense that the recent austerity was to become a thing of the past. The first evidence of this new leaf was the passage of the Vinson–Trammel Act.

Congressman Carl Vinson was to become as a great a champion for the navy as any in its history. The father of the two-ocean navy, he was born on 18 November 1883 on a farm in Georgia, the fifth of seven children, to Edward and Annie Vinson. He attended the Middle Georgia Military and Agricultural College and completed law school by 1902. He was elected county court solicitor and at the age of twenty-five was elected to the state assembly (the lower house of the state legislative branch). Eventually, Vinson was able to win election as the representative in the United States House of Representatives for the tenth district of Georgia (landlocked in mid-state) on 3 November 1914, and when he eventually retired from Congress in 1955 he was by then the longest-serving representative in history.

In 1917 a number of vacancies opened in some committees. Vinson chose to sit on the House Naval Affairs Committee and became a stalwart for US naval expansion. During the debates on the 1922 Washington Naval Treaty, Vinson was critical. He said that the eleven ships that the US was going to scrap were 35–45 per cent complete and had already cost $350 million, so their scrapping would be an affront to American taxpayers. By 1923 eight Democratic members on the committee had resigned so Vinson became the ranking Democratic member.[8]

Vinson's first attempt to pass a considerable increase for the navy came in 1932, when he introduced legislation to build 120 ships at a cost of $616 million. This funding, he argued, was an attempt to rebuild the nation's shipyard capacity. By 1942 three aircraft carriers, nine light cruisers, eighty-five destroyers and twenty-three submarines would join the Fleet. The bill was passed by his committee and passed the House of Representatives. However, President Hoover was opposed to large-scale spending on the navy. The bill died for lack of his signature.[9] Vinson bided his time until the new president was elected.

Vinson was attracted to FDR early. In Georgia, Vinson organised the Baldwin County Roosevelt Club. Once FDR was elected, the president-elect took a trip for his health to Warm Springs, Georgia. This was less than one hundred miles from Milledgeville, and Vinson and FDR met there on 29 November 1932. Both men agreed on the need to strengthen the navy. However, instead of $616 million as Vinson had wanted, FDR agreed to $100 million less and an annual maximum of $30 million for shipbuilding through to 1937. To justify this expenditure, they agreed to couch the requested appropriation as part of a public works programme. They were not making ships, they were making jobs, was the rationale.

Behind the scenes, Vinson worked successfully to line up the support of unions, Secretary of the Navy, Swanson, and the Speaker of the House of Representatives, Democrat Henry Thomas Rainey. At a news conference on 1 May, Secretary Swanson told reporters that the president had agreed to support a bill that would include $46 million to start work on thirty warships, as part of a public works programme. This bill was passed into law as the National Industrial Recovery Act on 16 June 1933. One month later, bids were entertained and awarded to private shipyards.[10] The navy considered seven private yards to be critical: Bethlehem, New York Ship, Newport News, Bath, Federal, United and Electric Boat, as they had the capacity and experience that the service deemed vital to maintain; these yards submitted bids for the new ships.

Concurrent with the efforts to have new legislation enacted, the shipbuilders were not idle. The National Council of Shipbuilders was organised as their trade association. This represented nearly 90 per cent of the country's shipyard capacity, but only 50 per cent of the companies building and repairing ships. The navy started to make allusions to a preference for bids from yards from the new trade association. A navy spokesperson was quoted as saying: 'it is much more satisfactory to have these contracts placed with facilities that are familiar with the Navy Department work, Navy Department classifications and so on.'[11]

Comprehensive military procurement planning was initiated in June 1922, with the creation of the Joint Army and Navy Munitions Board. The Assistant Secretary of the Navy was the board chairman. 'The duties outlined for the Board were the coordination of the planning for acquiring the munitions and supplies needed by the Army and Navy for war and the preparation of suitable plans to make it possible to put the procurement plans into effect. The latter meant the preparation of an Industrial Mobilization Plan.'[12] The navy embraced the need for planning. Selected officers were sent to the Harvard School of Business for a two-year course in business administration. In 1924 the Army Industrial College was opened in Washington, DC, to which the navy sent officers; the first class entered on 21 February 1924. The mission of the school was to study and enhance the relationship between military logistics and industrial mobilisation. The facility was modest: there was a director and five officer-instructors (one from the navy). The student body grew to forty army and fourteen navy/marine corps officers by the 1930s.

Although there developed a small cadre of business-literate officers, procurement and contracting was still dominated by private industry. The spectre of military-private collusion brought the Department of Labor into the mix for military contracting. The Department of Labor determined in June 1933 that a programme of full employment for skilled shipyard workers was required. The National Council estimated that a forty-hour work week would enable a growth in the target labour force of 15 per cent over the 1923–33 figures. Through the course of negotiations in Congress, it was determined that a thirty-two-hour week should be standard in naval shipyards, and forty hours for merchant shipbuilding and repair work. However, on 26 July the Navy Department announced that it would impose a five-day, forty-hour week as its standard. This meant that forty hours' worth of work would be paid as though it was thirty-two hours. The Comptroller General ruled that this would violate federal law, so the navy withdrew its proposal. In August the president reiterated that the navy must conform to federal law in making its purchases. The relevant codes for shipbuilders only delineated the wages for unskilled labour; private yards framed their bids using this lower standard and the navy accepted the bids. The contracts created downward pressure on wages. and by March 1934 labour strife was brewing in the yards. At the New York Shipbuilding Company, located in Camden, New Jersey, one of the largest, which went on to produce some of the most successful ships of the war, a strike erupted. The navy immediately claimed that it had no jurisdiction in the dispute, arguing that the contracts were fixed-price agreements: awards were made to the lowest bidder. 'The navy had no authority to increase the contract price unless it made changes in design specifications which caused an increase in costs.'[13]

By 1917 the New York Ship Company was the largest shipyard in the world, and in 1921, 30 per cent of all the battleships in the US Navy were constructed there. By the summer of 1933 wages and conditions at the shipyard had deteriorated. As the stresses at the yard evolved, the Industrial Marine and Shipbuilding Workers of America (Marine and Shipbuilding Union) incorporated in 1934 at the yard.

A strike was declared and work on navy ships was halted. The construction of three light cruisers and four heavy destroyers was now suspended. Eventually, the union encompassed the nation and reached a membership of a quarter of a million. The yard went on after the war to build the world's only nuclear-powered cargo ship, USS *Savannah* (1959), and eventually closed in 1967. When the federal government, through the offices of the Shipbuilding Code Authority, sent a negotiator to Camden, the strike was resolved. The terms of the agreement compelled the company on 11 May to increase the salary of all workers. This agreement was used as a model for the shipbuilding industry and on 1 July 1934 a presidential order imposed a flat rate of pay for all naval shipbuilding at private shipyards.[14]

After the resolution of labour disputes at New York Ship, Assistant Secretary of the Navy, Henry Roosevelt (cousin to the president), forwarded a budget proposal of $77.5 million. Most of these monies were targeted for the modernisation of five older battleships. The boilers and engines were replaced, anti-aircraft defences were stiffened and main gun elevations were increased.

The Bureau of Yards and Docks also added its estimates and requests. This estimate enumerated 137 projects at a projected cost of $137 million. The monies for these projects were expected to come from the Public Works Administration (PWA), as they were earmarked for base improvements, and in November 1934 funds had been secured through the PWA. The monies were justified for the purpose of 'building up the U.S. Fleet within treaty limitations and the improvement of facilities necessary for its development and maintenance.'[15] Not only were ships built, jobs were also. Over two years the NRA was able to spend $25 million on the behalf of the Bureau of Yards and Docks. This allowed for the maintenance and improvement of shore facilities; it also kept the navy's funding intact and accustomed legislators to using the NRA for shipbuilding.

Although there was funding available for ship construction, there was a bottleneck at the design end. The navy design staffs were not equipped for the volume of work that was now made available after the strictures of the Hoover years. By 1930 only three private shipyards maintained their own design staffs. These were Bethlehem Shipbuilding Corporation, Quincy, Massachusetts; New York Shipbuilding; and Newport News Shipyard and Dry Dock Company, Virginia. Plans were in hand for heavy cruisers only. A new class of destroyers was close to complete. Aircraft carriers, light cruisers and submarines had to be drafted in their entirety.

The class of destroyers that were funded was the *Mahan* class. The initial contracts for these destroyers were let to three yards: Bath Iron Works, Federal Shipbuilding and Dry Dock Company, and United Shipyards, Incorporated, were each awarded two ships. These three turned to the eleven-year-old naval architecture firm, Gibbs and Cox of New York City. Although the firm had not designed a warship before, they had made the plans for passenger-liner cargo ships. These ships, for the Grace Line, used superheated steam boilers, high-speed turbines and double reduction gears. This engineering plant represented something more advanced than hitherto used by the navy. The new destroyers were expected to make use of this new system: these ships proved very successful, and the navy ultimately ordered sixteen ships for this class.[16]

Due to the inability of the navy to get ships designed and built expeditiously, when the navy sent a list of projects it hoped to have paid for through PWA, funding ran dry. The following items were sent for funding in the 1936 budget, the priorities being '(1) ship repairs and improvements; (2) machine tools; (3) shore construction; (4) airplane parts and accessories and (5) radio communications and compass equipment and facilities.' The Emergency Relief Appropriation was passed in April 1935 and this all but shut off the PWA. The Act required that only projects related to housing and hospitalisation and the storage of supplies at existing facilities could be accommodated under PWA.[17] Once the Vinson–Trammel Act was passed, all other sources of funding became superfluous.

Rebuilding the Fleet: Vinson opens the sluice

In the decade after the 1922 Washington Naval Treaty, Great Britain had laid down 134 new warships (thirty-six destroyers), Japan 130 (forty-three destroyers), France 166 (fifty-five destroyers) and Italy 115 (thirty-nine destroyers). Under the Hoover administration, not one warship was laid down. Carl Vinson would not tolerate this situation: on 9 January 1934 Vinson introduced HR6604 (the Vinson Bill). The intention was to build the fleet up to the strength authorised by current treaties. He proposed authorisation of a 15,000-ton aircraft carrier to replace the aged *Langley*, 99,200 tons for new destroyers and 35,530 tons of submarines and auxiliary vessels. He proposed that this authorisation would require seven to eight years to complete and would cost approximately $380 million. The House Naval Affairs Committee held hearings on 22/23 January and reported favourably by unanimous vote. In the floor debates, Vinson stressed that this bill would have the effect of stimulating the shipbuilding industry, so another naval shipbuilding programme was made politically palatable as a jobs programme. The bill was approved. On 5/6 March, the Senate debated the measure and passed it sixty-five to eighteen, with thirteen members abstaining. On 29 June 1936 President Roosevelt signed the bill into law. The Vinson–Trammel Act authorised sixty-five destroyers, thirty-two submarines, four cruisers, one aircraft carrier and 1,184 aeroplanes, at a projected cost of $580 million. FDR signed the bill into law and approved $40,661,000 for fiscal year 1935 to start construction on the first twenty-five ships and 225 aeroplanes. This was the first authorisation for the construction by the United States for new warships after the First World War.[18] The long drought was over and Vinson had turned on the tap for naval appropriations.

Among the destroyers built with this funding were the ten ships of the *Benham* class. They were laid down in 1936/37 and commissioned into naval service in 1939. Two more ships of the *Gridley* class were built. The *Gridley*s used a low-speed turbine but had higher temperature and pressure in the boilers. One of the class, USS *Maury*, achieved the highest speed of any US destroyer ever during her sea-trials when she attained 42.8 knots.[19]

Carl Vinson said during the debates on his bill that when the fleet was brought to treaty strength by 1942 it would consist of fifteen battleships, six aircraft carriers, eighteen heavy cruisers, seventeen light cruisers, thirteen heavy destroyers, eighty-four light destroyers, and thirty-eight submarines, as well as approximately 1,910 aeroplanes. This would result in a fleet of 191 warships. This would also fund 122 auxiliary vessels, such as minesweepers, repair ships, tugs, etc, to support the warships. He further estimated that the navy would require 7,941 officers and 110,000 enlisted personnel.[20] Vinson also championed a bill to modernise the battleships of the fleet. These were in reaction to the Japanese declaration to leave the 1922 Washington Treaty regime.

From the Washington to London naval treaties (1922–1930) there was a sense of stability and predictability in naval construction between the great sea powers. Once Japan withdrew, the 'treaty regime' was terminated and uncertainty again predominated. Each power was thereby unconstrained in pursuing a naval shipbuilding programme with regard to consideration of international diplomatic strictures. This lack of certainty exacerbated ambiguity for naval planners. The navy's budget was formulated in a process that usually began about eighteen months prior to the start of a fiscal year. The various offices (bureaus) which composed the Navy Department were: Yards and Docks; Supplies and Accounts; BuAer (aircraft) and BuOrd (ordinance); Construction and Repair; Engineering; Navigation (Personnel); and Medicine and Surgery. One of the department's priorities was to maintain employment at the shipyards. In order to facilitate this agenda, a priority was laid to have 'continual construction'. The 'continual construction' faction within the navy championed this approach to shipbuilding. This entailed a construction programme which would have the yards working on new ships without a break, as opposed to an immediate burst of construction, thus stable employment was maintained at the yards.[21]

The competing faction within the Navy Department was the 'acceleration' faction that felt that there was a pressing need for immediate construction, so as to bring the Fleet up to the maximum allowable by law as quickly as possible. The Secretary of the Navy, Claude Swanson, was the primary spokesperson. The tension between factions came to a head during the fiscal year 1936 negotiations. This tension was exacerbated by Swanson's chronically poor health: for nearly half the year he was debilitated. The Assistant Secretary, Henry Roosevelt, also had very poor health and he died on 22 February 1936. The absence of leadership in the navy's top civilian offices hampered the manoeuvring through Congress for the budget. Into this breach, Admiral Adolphus Andrews, head of the Bureau of Navigation, stepped in to lead the department. However, he did not prove to have a significant effect on shepherding a budget through Congress.

A compromise was attained between the 'acceleration' and 'constant' factions. The Director of Shore Establishments, Henry Lackey, recommended a basis for the navy's budget priority. He 'suggested that domestic considerations be given priority over naval defense needs for the sake of producing better labor conditions in the navy yards.' For Lackey, new construction would be a means of stabilising yard employment against the fluctuations of maintenance work. The staff at the Chief of Naval Operations rejected this paradigm. As an alternative, the War Plans Division was charged with making the estimates for 1938. Their assumption was that war was inevitable, but not necessarily to be initiated in the coming year. The division recommended that building be guided by the understanding that the navy be built up to a standard that would enable it to effectively implement War Plan Orange (the plan for the US–Japanese war in the Pacific). The head of the War Plans Division, Roy Ingersoll, recommended that a building programme should be formulated 'based on the number of vessels of the various categories required of our needs to attain and maintain the necessary relative strength as regards other powers'.[22] The CNO and his staff endorsed this recommendation. By consequence of the successful recommendation by the War Plans Division, the tradition of the various bureaus submitting estimates was broken and henceforth it would be the War Plans Division that would develop the recommendations for the navy's prospective budget. The transition from bureau-based budget formulation to formulation by the War Plans Division set the Navy Department on course to plan to build independent of treaty conventions, and instead to use the standard of capacity to implement plans: this required estimations of relative naval strengths.

By 1937 the Navy Department had weaned itself from using work-relief as a justification for its building programme. It argued that naval defence should be pursued independently of social and economic reforms. In part, this was actuated by the Navy Department's desire to be freed from strictures requiring adherence to labour wage standards. The Walsh–Healey government contracts bill, enacted on 20 June 1936, required all organs of the federal government to mandate a forty-hour work week and the payment of minimum prevailing wages for awarded contracts. This made navy contracts look undesirable to private shipyards. The navy argued, unsuccessfully, that requiring adherence to this law made naval shipyards uncompetitive in comparison to private yards, which were exempt from the act. This argument failed. The navy then appealed to the Department of Labor, asking for a blanket exemption; this was denied. By November 1936 there was a manifest trend among industrial associations (the coalitions representing the management of private shipyards) to refrain from bidding on a navy contract. On 30 December the navy notified the Labor Department that it could no longer secure bids for structural steel. The associations were not bidding on naval contracts, so as to pressure the navy to relax labour laws. In effect, the major shipyards were boycotting naval work, and thereby undermining gains in wages by the shipyard workers. Secretary Edison argued that the Walsh–Healey provisions placed one department of the executive, Navy, subordinate to another department, Labor. In February the American Federation of Labor (AFL) added their support to the navy's claim. The AFL president, William Green, said, 'the seriousness of potential layoffs in Navy Yards warranted the granting of an exemption.' This was accepted and on 2 March the navy readvertised its bids without the additional cost from the Walsh–Healey provision. By the 1939 budget, a clause had been inserted which permitted the Secretary of the Navy to let bids on the basis of the needs of the service on a competitive basis, save those requirements for the faithful execution of a contract.[23]

The United States was girding for war. By 1937 the annual naval budget had increased from $477 million to $556 million. This represented a nearly 17 per cent increase. However, the other major naval powers were also building their fleets.

- Great Britain increased funding for naval construction in her 1937 Estimates from £60 million to £105 million pounds, a 70 per cent increase.
- France's naval budget went from 2,903 million francs to 3,395 million francs, a 16.9 per cent increase.
- Italy's naval budget went from 1,265 million to 1,793 million lire, a 41.7 per cent increase.
- Germany's naval budget went from 695 million to 1,478 million Rentenmarks, a 112.6 per cent increase.
- Japan's budget went from 72,983 million to 206,342 million yen, a 182.7 per cent increase.[24]

By 1937 naval rearmament was starting to gain momentum in the world's major navies and the US Navy had begun to initiate their naval rearmament in accordance with a global wave of rearmament. Germany cast off the strictures of constraining treaties and marshalled resources, so that in 1938 the country was able to launch the Z-Plan for the development of a balanced fleet. The Royal Navy's construction was hobbled by a constricted economy and a civilian government frequently driven by austerity. However, by 1937 the Royal Navy was also committed to a naval construction programme. Carl Vinson now placed the third naval expansion authorisation into the legislative queue. The second naval expansion act was the Battleship Overhaul Act of July 1935. This bill provided for the modernisation of *Tennessee, California, Colorado, Maryland* and *West Virginia*.[25] On 4 November 1939 Vinson, with the backing of the president, the Navy Department and the majority of the Naval Affairs Committee, introduced his naval expansion legislation, HR8026 (the Naval Act of 1938 or, the second Vinson Bill). This bill appropriated $1,300 million for the next four years, which was to fund three aircraft carriers, eight cruisers, fifty-two destroyers, thirty-two submarines and twenty-two auxiliary ships.

Hearings for Vinson's bill began in January 1940. The initial proposal would have authorised a 25 per cent increase (400,000 tons) in the size of the combatant fleet. This was too much for the Republican opponents and Vinson scaled back the proposal to a mere 10 per cent increase. This would (by his own admission) glut all of the country's shipyards through to 1942. The revised cost would therefore be $654,902,270. He brought the bill to the floor of the house and after five hours of debate the bill was passed by a vote of 307 to thirty-seven. The Senate passed the bill without demur and the Vinson Expansion Act became law on 14 June 1940 (the day after Paris fell to the German army). The act authorised the construction of twenty-one combatant and twenty-two auxiliary vessels.[26]

Two weeks prior to the passage of the second Vinson Bill, another law quietly passed. On 28 May Carl Vinson had successfully had a law passed which permitted the navy to award contracts by negotiation and not through public bidding. The navy was also permitted to advance up to 30 per cent of the total price to a contractor. The bill further allowed labour safeguards to be relaxed – workers could now be required to work up to forty-eight hours per week, albeit at time-and-a-half for the eight hours above forty. This bill passed 401 to one in the House.[27] The days of labour safeguards as a paramount concern for the FDR administration were ebbing in the face of the waxing tide of war.

The sluice for naval appropriations was now opened without reservation. On 17 June 1940 another bill, the fourth, sponsored by Vinson, was introduced into Congress. This one was for the authorisation of a 23 per cent increase in the combatant strength of the Fleet, at a cost of $1,200 million. However, Vinson felt that this was not adequate and solicited FDR for yet another increase in naval appropriations. FDR demurred and said that it was asking too much too soon, but Vinson was not dissuaded. He dropped the text of the bill onto both houses of Congress, less than a day after seeing the president. Five days after speaking with FDR, on 22 June, HR10100 passed in the House of Representatives. This law authorised an additional $4,000 million for naval construction. This equated to a 70 per cent increase in the navy's warship strength: 250,000 tons of destroyers, 385,000 tons for new battleships and 420,000 tons for cruisers were authorised. On 11 July, with one negative vote, the bill passed in the Senate and FDR signed the bill into law a week later. HR10100 has since come down to be known colloquially as the 'Two–Ocean Navy Act'. At the time of the passage of this bill, a new navy, projected to be completed by late 1946, would have cost approximately $10,000 million. This was more than the total budget of the United States government for the 1940 fiscal year.[28]

To pay for these appropriations would require new taxes. In fiscal year 1940, the federal government had a budget of $9.5 billion; fiscal year 1942 was expected to have a budget of $19 billion (the actual outlay was $34 billion). On 17 April 1941 the Secretary of the Treasury, Robert Morgenthau, met with the leaders of both Democrats and Republicans. He bluntly explained that new defence expenditures would be paid for mostly by raising taxes. They would borrow about one-third of the $19 billion, 1942 expenditure, and raise $12.33 billion through new taxes. The Congressional leaders agreed. In September both Houses of Congress had approved the new taxation bills.[29]

As government-funded contracts were awarded, questions of the distribution of this wealth and the quality of working conditions came to the surface. The unions sought to expand their membership and political weight. Additionally, the Communist Party was a significant force in organised labour. By 1940 the Communist Party of the United States had a membership of nearly a hundred thousand. A strike at North American Aviation in Inglewood, California, lasting six weeks from 24 May to 2 July 1941, and led by the United Auto Workers and the Congress of Industrial Organizations, immobilised the plant. They demanded an 11-cent an hour pay rise, and an increase in the minimum wage at the plant from 50 to 75 cents per hour. A deadlock developed. During the weekend of 7/8 June, 2,000 army troops were brought into the plant. FDR signed an executive order, mandating the strikers' return to work on Monday, or US troops would remove the encamped and protesting strikers. The government had seized the plant and forced the cessation of a strike. On 2 July a deal was made between labour and management in which labour's platform was accepted. However, by 11 June the government was promulgating regulations to the effect that the military could fire Communists and Fascist sympathisers from defence plants, and that independent strikes at defence plants could result in the loss of draft deferments for the strikers.[30] President Roosevelt had thus made it clear that the preservation of labour interests could not impinge upon preparation for war.

Part of Carl Vinson's vision of how the nation and the navy should prepare for the coming war was to restrict the prerogatives of organised labour. On 15 April Vinson began hearings on HR4139 (the Smith–Vinson Act). This legislation called for compulsory mediation between labour and management at naval defence plants. The bill also debarred 'closed shops' for plants that had naval work. The bill required a three-month 'cooling-off' period after mediation had ended before a strike could be declared. Vinson placed into the record a list of seventy-one strikes or work stoppages that had been called since 1939 in defence plants. The Naval Affairs Committee unanimously approved the bill. However, once this legislation was made public, organised labour balked. Throughout the country there was controversy over the bill. Unions were riled, while Democrats in Congress permitted the bill to languish; FDR would not support the legislation and Democrats quailed at this. Vinson met defeat.[31] Despite this, he was able to insert into the *Congressional Record* testimony to the effect that as of 9 September 1940, nineteen shipyards were then employed building 201 naval vessels at a cost of $3,788 million.

In the United States, the tension between New Deal social and economic reforms was subordinated to the needs for industrial mobilisation for the war. Through the latter part of the 1930s a shift occurred both in the public's and in Congress's tolerance for war mobilisation. Internationally, the world's leading naval powers had concluded that the era of the treaty-constrained naval construction budgets was over. War was looming and the great navies of the world were preparing for another catastrophic conflict. The US Navy was now building a fleet suited to the demands of the coming catastrophe, free of the strictures of social and economic reform and the tenets of the now-defunct treaty regime.

By 1937 the US Navy had joined the other major maritime powers in re-arming for war. The Vinson–Trammel Act of 1936 opened the sluices for a cascade of funding. Among the ships that were authorised by the act were ninety-seven destroyers. These ships were part of the armada which replaced the navy in the Pacific that was devastated through the start of the war in that theatre. However, they were not available for the defence of the East Coast when the Germans struck. The relative nearness of these ships' availability may have hurt the defence of the coast. When Vice Admiral Andrews, the Commandant of the Eastern Sea Frontier, asked for reinforcements he was told by Admiral King to wait for new construction.

4

Submarine Warfare in the First World War

America's beleaguered entry into the First World War foreshadowed some of the same issues that would surface at the start of the Second – the country's agonised transition from neutral to belligerent occurred in both wars. During the process of the United States entering the First World War, the issue of neutrality rights became a central point of tension between the United States and Great Britain.

Once the US Navy deployed ships to Europe, it became, intentionally, a supplement to the Entente navies. Towards the end of the First World War, America had its first taste of a U-boat assault on the East Coast, but it was an anaemic attack. A total of six submarines were deployed to the coast, so the damage was contained.

American naval participation in the First World War foretold some of the challenges and tools that were expanded in the Second World War. From the start of first war, the British expected to be able to use their overwhelming sea power to impose a blockade of Germany. This was understood as the 'British way of war'. The blockade had been used with great success against another continental enemy of the preceding century – Napoleon's Revolutionary France. One of the sources of controversy in establishing this blockade was the tension between 'neutral rights' and 'belligerent rights'. If the blockade was pursued too aggressively, then neutrals (paramount among them, the United States) could become hostile over the curtailment of trade. However, the blockade was only as effective as it was tight. The British argued that the presence of contraband, cargoes that would be liable to be seized (generally munitions and goods that contributed to the enemy's war-making capacity), made the carrying vessel a legitimate target for seizure. The British Admiralty interpreted this liberally and ships coming into European waters were likely to be stopped, searched and possibly seized. The British practice violated the 1909 Declaration of London; this treaty, signed by Britain, excluded foodstuffs and raw materials from the list of contraband materials. By 1917 this practice of seizure brought tension between the British and a still-neutral America – arming of British merchants, their entry into American ports and the arresting of American merchant ships by British warships strained Anglo-American relations.[1]

On 5 November 1914 the British declared the approaches to Europe a 'military area'. This area extended from the Arctic Circle to the coast of Brittany and westward to the eastern coast of Ireland. Within this zone, the British declared they would search *all* merchant vessels. Neutral nations, paramount among them the United States, found this policy humiliating. The Royal Navy effectively controlled approach to the continent. In February 1915 Germany, in turn, declared a counter blockade, which extended from southern Norway, to Brittany and encompassing all of the British Isles. This represented the maximum effective operating distance for U-boats. On 11 March 1915 the British Admiralty promulgated a sweeping order: all trade to German ports would be interdicted. In addition, all trade to neutral ports adjacent to Germany would also be stopped. Since the preponderance of British naval mastery precluded any effective trade with Germany, the European neutrals acceded to the British quarantine. The British blockade was effective: trade to Germany was strangled. Between November 1914 and November 1917 the Royal Navy intercepted approximately 13,000 merchant vessels. Of these vessels stopped, 1,816 were brought to port under guard, 2,039 sailed to a British port voluntarily and 642 escaped.[2]

In 1915 the German submarine blockade was ineffective, however, and they were able to maintain no more than seven submarines in their blockade zone, around the British Isles. In addition to the marginal utility of the submarine zone, the German submarines had sunk three passenger liners, which resulted in American deaths. Public opinion in the United States condemned the Germans as barbarians. The Kaiser responded by calling off the submarine blockade of Great Britain in September 1915. However, the German naval staff prevailed upon the Kaiser and in February 1916 the blockade was reinstated, although this time there were strictures imposed on submarine captains. No passenger liners could be attacked anywhere and within the war zone only visibly armed merchant ships could be targeted, but the Kaiser again backed down and bound the U–boats to the prize rules. When, in March, a liner was attacked in the English Channel, eighty people were killed, including twenty-five Americans. A threat by the United States to sever diplomatic relations with Germany compelled the Kaiser again to order submarines near Great Britain to adhere to 'prize rules'.[3] This state of affairs persisted until it became clear that the Central Powers (Germany and the Austro–Hungarian empire) were becoming exhausted, and morale both in the military and at home was weakening. The final and most destructive iteration of the war against Great Britain was about to ensue. The First World War marked the debut of submarine warfare as a strategy, and the German Imperial Navy initiated submarine warfare in response to the impotence of their conventional surface fleet.

On 7 May 1915 RMS *Lusitania* was sunk by a German submarine in the war zone. Approximately 1,200 aboard were killed, and of these, 128 were Americans. The Allied nations and neutrals were aghast at this act. Although the United States did not immediately go to war, sympathies in the United States were irrevocably swayed towards France and Britain. President Wilson ordered the Secretaries of War and Navy to prepare for: 'the full deployment of the country's fighting forces, including "a consistent and progressive development of the Navy as the great defensive arm of the nation."' In Germany, the Kaiser ordered a day of thanksgiving and had a medal struck to commemorate this feat of German naval arms.[4]

On 22 December 1916 the Chief of the Naval Staff, Admiral von Holtzendorff, submitted a memorandum arguing for the assumption of unrestricted submarine warfare. He suggested 'an early opening of the unrestricted campaign on these grounds: "A decision must be reached in the war before the autumn of 1917, if it is not to end in the exhaustion of all the parties, and consequently, disastrously for us. Of our enemies, Italy and France are economically so hard hit that they are only upheld by England's energy and activity. If we break England's back the war will at once be decided in our favour."'[5]

On 1 February 1917 Germany finally and irrevocably declared unrestricted submarine warfare. The German general staff estimated that they should be able to force England to sue for peace within six months once unrestricted submarine warfare was instituted. They estimated that if they could maintain a sinking rate of 600,000 tons per month, the commercial shipping serving the United Kingdom could be reduced by 39 per cent. They also expected that approximately two-fifths of neutral traffic to Britain would cease. This reduction of imports would be unsustainable and the British war economy would collapse. The tempering consideration of antagonising the United States into belligerency was dismissed. If Britain could be brought to its knees by August, the United States would only be able to contribute an insignificant force to the war in Europe. In short, England would be forced to sue for peace before American entry into the war would matter. It was a bargain worth taking, and the only clear route to victory.[6] Now, German submarines were at liberty to sink on sight any vessel in the war zone without warning.

It seemed that the new strategy was effective. The losses from submarines rose from 328,391 tons sunk in January to 564,497 tons in March. In April the German submarine campaign attained its zenith for the war: 860,334 tons of merchant ships were sunk. During this time the Germans lost a total of nine submarines to all causes. The German warning led to a delay in neutral traffic to the United Kingdom that amounted up to a 30 or 40 per cent embargo in certain trades.[7]

The British, however, were far from idle in the face of this onslaught. A critical campaign was the construction of new merchant shipping. In 1917 the British Empire produced 1,163,000 tons of merchant shipping. However, there was a shortage of steel and men to work in the shipyards. The pace of shipbuilding was not sufficient to keep pace with losses from submarine depredations.[8]

In addition to building more merchant shipping, the British resorted to restrictions on neutral trading with Europe. Any neutral ship in a British port was only allowed to sail to another British port or promise to return from a neutral port with a cargo with an Entente (the British-French and Russian alliance) port as a terminus. Dutch and Scandinavian ships were particularly constrained. They were only allowed to sail home when another ship of their nation's registry arrived in a British port. Nevertheless, it was projected that if losses continued at this rate, the British would be forced out of the war.[9]

A significant element in the Royal Navy's defensive measures against the U-boats was the harnessing of technology. In order to direct the exploitation of new weapons the British instituted the Anti–Submarine Division (ASD) on 16 December 1916. This was composed of the Trade, Operations, and Intelligence divisions, in addition to the Submarine Committee. The task of this new administrative organ was to take 'overall charge of the A.S.D. ... to co-ordinate existing, and to devise new, measures and devices in the A/S campaign ... The A.S.D. relieved the Operations Division of control of all ships and aircraft engaged in A/S work.'[10] Here is the forefather of the United States Navy's 10th Fleet that did much the same in the next world war.

Among the technological innovations of the Royal Navy during the First World War, one of the greatest was the hydrophone, of which there were two types. One consisted of a microphone that was lowered into the water from a ship. Another was fixed to the sea floor and attached by cables to a shore-side listening station. A prototype of the latter type of hydrophone was developed and successfully tested in November 1914. By 1916 there were a number of listening stations operating. Towards the end of 1916, escort vessels were fitted with hydrophones and in 1917, submarines. Hunting groups of small escorts operated together. However, a hydrophone was only effective if the operating ship was stationary, as the ship's own noises would blanket the noise-detecting by the mechanism. Also a submarine that was lying on the seabed would not be detectable, and a very slowly moving U-boat would only be detected if very close to the listening vessel. A final inadequacy of the hydrophone was that it could not ascertain the direction of the submarine from the searching vessel. The last defect was corrected in 1917 when a directional hydrophone was deployed in spring of 1917. However, it also required the searching vessel to be stopped.[11]

A hugely significant anti-submarine weapon was the mine; however, at the start of the war the British were handicapped by a poorly designed weapon which was found to be unreliable. When the British had the good fortune to have some German mines wash ashore, they adapted its features and produced serviceable weapons, the H-2 (300lb warhead) and the H-4 (150lb warhead). By late 1917 there was a sufficient supply of these weapons to begin a mining campaign to impede the U-boats.

In November 1917 the H-2 mine was deployed to close the English Channel at the Dover strait. Mines were sown in parallel rows from England to France. An opening was left at the shoreward ends and patrolled by light ASW craft. The field was illuminated at night by searchlights on lighters, in the hopes that the illumination would force the U-boats to remain submerged, thereby inhibiting their ability to transit to the Channel due to exhaustion. When the minefield was completed in August 1918, a total of 10,000 mines had been sown. The second field (or barrage) was planned to close the North Sea.

The United States entered the war with a serviceable mine, the Mark 6. The Mark 6 had an advantage in that its antenna was floating and could detonate up to 100ft from the body of the mine. A plan was developed to lay a barrage from the Orkney Islands to Bergen, Norway, a space of 235 miles by 50 miles. This would close the northern egress from the North Sea. The US Navy took responsibility for the central 134-mile wide section and 100,000 mines were ordered. These were shipped in waves to depots in Scotland where they completed their assembly and were thence deployed. By the end of the war, nearly 73,000 mines had been sown, mostly of the Mark 6 type. Six submarines are estimated to have been destroyed in the Northern Barrage.[12] Between the two minefields, German submarines' freedom of action was impeded, and egress from the North Sea was a considerably more hazardous undertaking.

Another important ASW innovation was the cultivation of radio intelligence. When the war began, wireless telegraphy was less than fifteen years old. However, despite its newness, all of the major navies of the world had adopted this technology to better control their fleets – all of the combatant navies used wireless for submarines to communicate with headquarters. The U-boats did so while on patrol. Royal Navy and commercial radio stations had been detecting these German transmissions since the start of the war, and the Navy chose to intercept and decrypt these messages as opposed to jamming them. By the end of the war, fourteen radio-intercept stations had been established throughout Scotland and England. By triangulating the bearings of wireless messages received at these stations, a general idea of a transmitter's location could be surmised. The Royal Navy was able to fix a transmitting U-boat's location to within twenty to fifty miles.

Sir Alfred Ewing was the Royal Navy's Director of Naval Signals Intelligence. On the first day of the war he was approached by Rear Admiral Henry Oliver, Director of Naval Intelligence, to examine the intercepted German transmissions to see if they could be decoded. Ewing was granted space and he set up a small staff. This became the nucleus of

Room 40 in the old Admiralty building. Through both world wars, Room 40 provided the Royal Navy with a critical intelligence advantage.

Initially, work in Room 40 was laborious and only marginally successful. However, in October they received a gift from the Russians that would alter their operations. The cruiser *Magdelburg* grounded in the Baltic and the Russians seized the ship and scoured it for useful intelligence. Among the treasures gleaned from the cruiser were the codebooks and maps used by the German navy. The Russians sent this cache to the Admiralty, and it was deposited with Ewing and his staff. After a month of poring over this treasure, Room 40 was able to read the vast bulk of German naval transmissions for the remainder of the war. So as to maintain this advantage, in 1917 the British began to dispatch divers to the wrecks of German submarines in sufficiently shallow waters to dive into them and take what could be had. Room 40 was able to supply a daily estimate of all U-boats at sea. This information was sent to Dover and Queenstown (Cobh), the principal ASW commands. This information was used not only to route shipping away from suspected German submarine areas, but also to ambush the U-boats with their own submarines.

German efforts to break Royal Navy codes, in contrast, never advanced past a primitive stage. The Royal Navy's operations were never imperilled by German signals intelligence.[13]

A tactic used that proved to be of limited utility was the Q-ship. The Royal Navy organised the Special Vessel Service, known more popularly as Q-ships, in November 1914 at the prodding of the First Lord of the Admiralty, Winston Churchill. These were smaller merchant and fishing vessels operated by the Navy. Ultimately the Royal Navy deployed 180 of these vessels. They were heavily armed, but their weapons were concealed or camouflaged. Their armament consisted of guns, depth charges and torpedoes. The ships would sail in areas suspected of U-boat activity. Once a U-boat stopped them in accordance with prize rules, the ships would heave-to and a 'panic party' would abandon the ship. The submarine would then approach the stricken vessel to put aboard a prize crew. Once the German submarine had closed to a short range, the disguise would drop and the Q-ship would deliver a barrage sufficient to cripple or sink the submarine. Thus was the theory. The first submarine sunk was *U-36* on 23 July 1915 off the Hebrides (off the northwest coast of Scotland). A variant of the Q-ship was to use a trawler towing a submerged submarine, maintaining a telephone contact. When the surface ship spotted an enemy submarine, the trawler would telephone the details of the U-boat. The British submarine would then torpedo the enemy unawares. This Q-ship–submarine combination accounted for fourteen submarines throughout the war. The tactic was terminated in October 1915 after it became apparent that the Germans were aware of the ruse.

Q-ships were rendered ineffective once the Germans adopted unrestricted submarine warfare, as they were only useful as long as the U-boat was compelled to approach its quarry on the surface and was thus vulnerable. Once there was no necessity to search their quarry, the U-boats could torpedo their prey from underwater and thus not be vulnerable to a Q-ship on the surface.[14]

The United States deployed only one Q-ship. The Royal Navy transferred a Q-ship to the Americans in late 1917, commissioned as USS *Santee*. She operated from Queenstown and after a month of operations was torpedoed. Although she returned to port on her own power, the US returned her to Britain and declined to operate any other such ships.

However, the paramount innovation that defeated the U-boats was the introduction and universal application of convoy. This was a tactic that had been used to great effect in the Napoleonic wars. In Lloyd George's memoirs, he recounted that the convoys from 1793 to 1797 encompassed 5,827 ships: only 1.5 per cent were attacked by French raiders; thirty-five ships, 0.6 per cent, were lost. Admiral Mahan, the American 'philosopher of sea power', said that convoy was the only viable answer to commerce raiding.[15] Convoying in the past had certainly proven its worth.

At the beginning of the war, the Admiralty was concerned with attacks upon seaborne trade. However, the Navy deployed forces and instituted tactics to repel surface ships as commerce raiders. Little consideration was given to the prospect that submarines might be an effective weapon against commerce. The Admiralty used the blockade of Germany, patrols by warships, arming merchant ships and dispersing merchant shipping in waters suspected of enemy activity or mines. The policy of escorting non-warships was only for troop transports, ships with a high-value cargo, and ammunition ships. These ships were typically escorted one ship at a time or in small convoys. A cruiser or merchant cruiser would be used for oceanic voyages and in submarine danger zones; one or more destroyers would comprise the escort. Aside from these small concessions, the body of Royal Navy officers felt that deploying warships to escort merchant vessels was contrary to the offensive tradition of the Royal Navy. The Service, which counted Nelson as its forefather, would not be content to deploy its warships to wait for the enemy to strike at hapless merchants.[16] They, and the public, expected their navy (to paraphrase Nelson) 'to engage the enemy more closely'.

Despite the general antipathy for convoying, there were some officers who were convinced of its efficacy. Among them was David Beatty, commander of the 1st Battle Cruiser Squadron at the Battle of Jutland. However, when John Jellicoe, the admiral in charge of the Home Fleet, was asked in November 1916 if the adoption of convoys would be wise, he said that it would not. It was felt that merchant ships could not keep station. In January 1917 the Admiralty handbook on trade defence categorically refused to countenance convoys as a means of trade defence. It said: 'The system of several ships sailing in company, as a convoy, is not recommended in any area where submarine attack is a possibility ... The overwhelming objection of the decision-makers at the Admiralty to a system of regular ocean convoy was the alleged dearth of escorting ships.' An Admiralty study in 1917 recommended an effective trade escort force of sixty-two cruisers and 125 destroyers. At the time, there were fourteen destroyers and twelve sloops available. Although there were some four hundred such escorts in commission (350 destroyers and sixty sloops), they were devoted to escorting the battle fleets, small convoys or single-ship escorting, or fruitless patrolling for submarines.[17]

The objections by the Admiralty decision-makers had proved not to be true once convoys were begun. On the Gibraltar to England convoys, the ships were at sea for approximately ten days; the danger zone was in the immediate vicinity of the British Isles. The convoys spent at least an hour a day on station-keeping exercises, so by the time they reached the approaches to Britain, they were an efficient unit. Another objection was the notion that convoys concentrated targets for the U-boats and thus therefore made the hunting easier for German submarines. On occasions when a submarine was able to attack a convoy, they generally only sank one ship, and at no time did a convoy lose more than two ships. By mid-September 1917 a convoy system had been codified. They were organised by port of destination and speed (Slow: 8¼–10 knots, Medium: 10–12½ and Fast: above 12 knots).[18]

The final objection was that gathering a convoy together would create bottlenecks when unloading and therefore lead to delays, which would have the effect of diminishing the available shipping. Between 1914 and 1917 the United Kingdom imported 34 million tons. During the first quarter of 1918, at the peak of the U-boat campaign, shipping was reduced such, that over the year, the UK lost 5 million tons. The delays in port caused by convoy bottlenecks amounted to 4–5 million tons. This was dire, in the extreme. However, upon closer examination it was found that the primary cause of these delays was the unpredictability of the independently sailing merchant ships.[19] Once these sailings were put on a schedule, as in gathering convoys, the delays became manageable.

Admiral Scheer, the Chief of Staff for the High Seas Fleet, wrote to the emperor on 21 September 1918, singling out three areas that were contributing to the decline of the efficacy of the U-boat war. He attributed this to: '1. Improved and strengthened enemy defensive measures were the primary cause; 2. The loss of seasoned commanders; 3. The steady increase in enemy mercantile construction, which would in the foreseeable future exceed shipping losses ... As regards the second, which is a fact of 400 commanders a scant 20 or so were responsible for approximately 60 per cent of all Allied sinkings from submarine action.'[20]

Convoy was eventually understood to be the single most important factor in defeating the U-boats. The efficacy of the convoy was manifest in the volume of shipping that was safely making it to Britain by the end of the war. In December 1917 approximately half of all shipping was organised into a convoy. By the end of the war, 90 per cent of this traffic was organised into convoys. During 1918, 16,102 ships arrived into Great Britain in convoys. Of this great volume of ships, thirty-five were sunk (a loss rate of 0.2 per cent).[21]

The Germans failed in their efforts to defeat the convoys. Between 10 May and 25 May 1918 the Germans concentrated up to ten submarines in the Western Approaches to England. They sank two and damaged three merchant ships from 183 convoyed merchant vessels that had passed through this area homeward-bound, and 110 ships outbound during this time. For these 'successes', two U-boats were sunk.[22]

The convoys ran like clockwork, organised by the Admiralty. Due to the efforts of shipbuilding throughout the world, mostly American, new construction exceeded losses in March. By August 1917 over ten thousand merchant ships had been convoyed; losses amounted to 0.5 per cent, and none that had left North American ports had been sunk. By September the British shipbuilding industry had replaced the cumulative losses suffered for the duration of the war.[23]

The United States enters the war

Admiral Sims was dispatched to London with the title of Commander of the United States Naval Forces Operating in European Waters. Within a few weeks of his arrival, Sims was meeting daily with Admiral Jellicoe, the First Sea Lord, and Sims was given unfettered access to all levels of the Royal Navy and attended Board of Admiralty meetings. In November Sims received the 'weekly appreciations'. These were the summation of the war situation as prepared by the Admiralty for the War Cabinet.[24]

In contrast to the Second World War, the US Navy acted as a subordinate component of the Royal Navy. In the autumn of 1917 a series of staff talks in London between the French, British and American services led to integration of planning which culminated in the establishment of the Allied Naval Council in Paris at the end of the year. At the same time, a joint Anglo–American naval planning section was established.[25]

The initial American contribution to the sea war in Europe was a deployment of six destroyers. On 13 April 1917 Commander Joseph K Taussig, leader of the 8th Division, Destroyer Force, Atlantic Fleet, was ordered to make preparations for six destroyers to be made ready for 'Special Service'. These were the newest destroyers in the fleet. On the 24th these ships sailed from Boston for the war in Europe. Their orders were: 'to assist the Entente powers in every way possible.' This squadron was based in Queenstown, Ireland. By July 1917 there were fifty-two destroyers and twenty-seven escort yachts. These vessels were used for convoy escort duties in the waters of the German war zone.[26]

Ultimately, the Entente prevailed. This was caused not only by a preponderance of convoy-escort craft, but also the deployment of superior weapons and organisation. Chief among these weapons was the depth charge. When the United States entered the war, construction on battleships was diverted to build destroyers. Eventually, 200 were authorised. However, what was paramount was the organisation of convoys. At Queenstown the naval staff created sailing instructions for merchant ships in a convoy. In May 1917 the first weekly convoys left the United States. In London, the Admiralty established a Convoy Room. Here were tracked all convoys at sea and the best known position of U-boats, as determined by Room 40's wireless intercepts. The success of the convoys sailing from America led to the formalisation of these convoys. The American convoys bound for England were designated HH, since they embarked across the Atlantic from Hampton Roads, Virginia. By the beginning of July, a formal convoy system was extended from New York City for merchant ships from Canada and elsewhere on the American coast. In 1918 the convoys were extended to include those serving the American army in France, with ports in the Bay of Biscay as their terminal. By the end of the war, some 9,250 ships had arrived in British ports, in convoys. Of these, 104 were sunk, a loss rate of 1.11 per cent.[27]

Before America's entry into the war, the US Navy had designed a small anti-submarine vessel to be used in coastal waters. This was the 80ft or 110ft all-wooden sub-chaser. Initially, these were deployed as patrol boats off the US Atlantic coast, but it was soon determined that these vessels, if they were to have any utility, would need to cross the Atlantic and be added to the ASW forces in Europe, not least because they could not keep the sea adequately to be of use as convoy escorts. Although the crews were largely reservists, they all made it across. and Admiral Sims was effusive in his praise of the sailors:

> Ignorant of salt water as these men were, they really represented about the finest raw material in the nation for this service. Practically all, officers and men were civilians, a small minority were amateur yachtsmen, but the great mass were American college undergraduates ... That they knew nothing at first about navigation and naval technique was not important: the really important fact was that their minds were alert and their hearts filled with a tremendous enthusiasm for the cause, their souls clean, and their bodies ready for the most exhausting task.[28]

Two squadrons of sub-chasers, thirty-six vessels, were deployed for coastal escort in southwest England and no merchant ship was sunk while these doughty fighters were shepherding their charges.

Admiral Sims had warned that when the United States entered the war, they should expect submarine assaults on the East Coast. However, he also said that any such submarine assault would be insignificant and any significant diversion of ASW assets from the war zone would be a mistake. It was also the policy of the navy that maximum protection was to be afforded to troop transports going to Europe – the navy transported approximately two million troops to Europe without loss.[29] Regardless of U-boats off the coast, the focus of ASW efforts should remain the protection of the transports.

Nevertheless, American waters were not immune to the tincture of war. On 18 April 1918 *U-151* sailed from Kiel westward. She arrived off the American coast on 22 May, and laid minefields off the Chesapeake and Delaware bays. The Delaware field damaged a 5,300-ton tanker. *U-151* then proceeded northwards and on 2 June sank three small sailing vessels off the coast of New Jersey, before returning to Germany after a ninety-four-day cruise. The naval authorities claimed she had accounted for 51,336 tons of shipping, albeit in smaller, coastal vessels.

One of the most significant innovations to combat the German submarine was not a weapon or a tactic. Instead, it was a room at the Admiralty, where there was a comprehensive review of the submarine situation made daily. Vice Admiral Sir Alexander Duff led this effort; the American assigned was Captain Byron A Long. Captain Long would co-ordinate American convoys with those of the other Entente powers. The most significant feature of the room was a chart, from floor to ceiling, which displayed the Atlantic Ocean. The ports of embarkation and debarkation were identified and threads were strung from a convoy's port of debarkation to a point in the Atlantic, terminating in a small paper boat. This marked the location of convoys as they progressed towards the war in Europe. The paper boats were moved daily in accordance with situation reports. On the map, at the Western Approaches to England, little circles were drawn. These circles were estimations of a lurking submarine.[30] This room was reactivated by the Royal Navy and replicated by the United States Navy during the Second World War.

How were these submarines tracked? There was no more than an average of eight submarines in the 'prime hunting grounds' of the Western Approaches at a time. Fortunately, the Germans were garrulous with their use of the wireless. They ran a commentary with one another and with the German Admiralty. British radio direction-finding could then home in on a beam from a submarine. Merchant ships were under orders to report by wireless any sighting of a submarine. A surfaced submarine was estimated to travel at about 10 knots, so the little circles represented the distance a submarine might travel in a day's time.[31]

Due to wireless intercepts the Americans were aware that U-boats were headed to their coast. Coastal shipping was promptly organised into convoys under the jurisdiction of naval districts; air and sea patrols were also instituted. On 3 June 1918 the Chief of Naval Operations ordered convoys to be instituted between Rhode Island and Cape Hatteras. In addition to coastal convoys, a hunting squadron was formed composed of the destroyer USS *Jouett* and six sub-chasers. A message to all coastal shipping was sent by wireless for all traffic to retire to port unless in a convoy. The Secretary of the Navy reported to Congress that it was not necessary to withdraw ASW assets from Europe for coastal defence.[32]

A total of six U-boats were sent to American waters for the duration of the war. They were *U-151*, *U-156*, *U-140*, *U-117*, *U-155* and *U-152*. These submarines sailed from Germany between 16 June and 5 September 1918 and were ordered by the high command to operate under the pre-war 'prize rules', which impinged upon the U-boats' potency. They sank a total of ninety-three ships of 166,907 tons. Secretary of the Navy, Daniels, however, in his annual report for 1918 wrote that: 'German submarine operations against the American coast [were] "one of the minor incidents of the war".'[33] The German high command restricted these submarine attacks because, although the United States was now a 'co-belligerent', the Germans did not want to needlessly inflame American opinion. President Wilson was looked to as a potential intermediary for peace talks, and unrestricted warfare had proven to rouse American opinion against Germany.

As early as 4 May the US Navy did respond to an attack off the coast and circulated a letter indicating the steps to be taken in case of a submarine attack. This included arrangements for a coastal convoy system. On 3 June the Chief of Naval Operations ordered the naval districts from Rhode Island to Cape Hatteras to begin instating convoys and routing shipping, while at the same time a wireless warning was also sent to all shipping off the coast to immediately seek port until further notice. The coastal convoys were ad hoc affairs, escorted by the 110ft sub-chasers. Once sufficient numbers of merchant ships were collected, a convoy set sail under escort to its coastal destination.

In addition to the coastal convoys, a 'naval hunt squadron' was organised out of Norfolk, Virginia, which consisted of the destroyer USS *Jouett* and six sub-chasers.[34] Although this squadron never engaged a U-boat, the collective efforts off the coast and the desultory commitment by the Germans to a coastal campaign prevented significant harm befalling the American eastern seaboard. This was a great contrast to the later U-boat assault on the East Coast, which, for a time imperilled Allied efforts in the Second World War.

Assistant Secretary of the Navy, Franklin Roosevelt

Franklin Roosevelt, the Assistant Secretary of the Navy, strongly supported the British and French in the war. He knew that eventually the United States would have to pull for them. However, the president's adherence to an even-handed neutrality, between the Entente and the Central Powers, hampered support to the belligerents; a declaration of war would be premature as there was still considerable anti-war sentiment in the Senate. The United States was able to afford the Entente powers considerable capital through mostly private bank credit extensions, though there was no allocation of munitions from the United States.

Within a week of Germany's declaration of a war zone on 1 February 1917, President Wilson severed diplomatic relations with Germany. On 6 April, after more Americans were killed on torpedoed ships, the US Congress issued a declaration of war. In 1917 Roosevelt met with the leaders of the shipping industry to discuss the war situation. Once these meetings had been concluded, Roosevelt presented a memorandum to Secretary of the Navy Daniels, dated 10 February. He wrote that without Congressional permission, there is no authority to sell munitions to nations at war: 'however, guns may be *loaned* provided a suitable bond be given ... The matter could be taken care of by an executive order from the president.'[35] Here was the origin of the tactic that Roosevelt would use to such profound effect two and a half decades later.

Before the war, the US Navy had 3,094 officers and 47,515 enlisted men. By November 1918, navy personnel had expanded to 32,474 officers and 497,030 enlisted men. In six years personnel strength had grown tenfold.[36]

Roosevelt became disenchanted with Daniels, who seemed to be too slow in mobilising the navy for war. FDR was chafing at the bit to become more involved with the war and he pestered Daniels to be allowed to go to

Europe. Finally, the Secretary relented and FDR went to Europe on a two-month inspection tour. He arrived in Portsmouth on 21 July and proceeded to meet with all of the significant personnel in the English and French navies. At a dinner during this tour Roosevelt met Winston Churchill, who had been appointed Minster of Munitions. FDR did not get a good impression of his future ally and wrote that he found Churchill to be patronising and dismissive. In a 1939 letter to his ambassador to England, Joseph Kennedy, he would write: 'I have always disliked (Churchill) since the time I went to England in 1918. He acted like a stinker at a dinner I [was?] attending, lording it over all of us.'[37] While in France, in August 1918 FDR experienced modern war intimately for the only time in his life. He toured the front and was appalled by the high casualty rates, especially the toll of the fighting at Verdun on US Marines. In Italy, he became reacquainted with a New York City politician. The future president observed the future mayor of New York, who was then serving as a captain in the Army Air Corps, Fiorello La Guardia, giving propaganda speeches.

Franklin Delano Roosevelt was ambitious and not averse to scheming. In 1913 he had put this to use so as to promote his own career. He would deploy these same skills later, as president, to manoeuvre the country into a better state of preparedness for the Second World War. When Woodrow Wilson was inaugurated as president, Roosevelt took the train to Washington, DC, where he met up with Josephus Daniels, once of the *Raleigh News and Observer*. Daniels was now the designated Secretary of the Navy in the incoming Wilson administration and Roosevelt baldly asked if he had appointed anyone to be his Assistant Secretary. When Daniels said that he had not, young Roosevelt said: 'If you have no one for the position, I would like to make a recommendation. I told him I would like him to appoint Franklin D. Roosevelt, and the reason I was quick on the trigger was I knew that there would be a number of applicants and that by filling the position at once, we would not be under the necessity of rejecting any applicant.'[38] Roosevelt was sworn in as Assistant Secretary of the Navy on 17 March 1913. At the age of thirty-one, he was the youngest incumbent of that position and would serve as Assistant Secretary until August 1920, the longest tenure of any Assistant Secretary.[39] The primary function of the Assistant Secretary is to administer the Navy Department's budget. For FDR's first year this was $143,497,000 (20 per cent of the federal budget) and look after the welfare of the 65,000 personnel that comprised the navy. He also negotiated the department's contracts for coal, steel, oil, etc, and had primary responsibility for the service's shore-based assets. He was also expected to serve as the acting secretary if circumstances required. FDR's uncle, Theodore, had also served in this position – the admirals cheered the return of a Roosevelt to the office.

The cheering of the admirals was for Franklin alone: the senior admirals felt that Daniels was a country bumpkin. In private, they made fun of his southern accent; Roosevelt joined in the mockery. He both shared their opinion and was content to be accepted by the naval fraternity. However, through the course of the first year in office, Roosevelt grew to respect Daniels. The Secretary had ideas about making the ships 'floating universities'. He wanted the enlisted men to use their time afloat to better their education. Roosevelt respected reformers and appreciated attempts to 'better' the common man, and these attitudes were to prove crucial for facilitating those innovations vital for war mobilisation when the United States was preparing to enter the Second World War.

Surrender

By 1 November 1917 Sir Eric Geddes, First Lord of the Admiralty, reported to Parliament that the race against the U-boats was being won and that the threat in the area of the Atlantic immediately west of Great Britain, though still significant, was now manageable. He said: 'in September 90 per cent of the total ships sailing in all Atlantic trade were convoyed, and since the convoy system was started – and it has been criticized in some quarters – the total percentage of loss per convoyed vessel passes through the danger zone [the Western Approaches to the United Kingdom] is 0.5 per cent or 1 in 200.'[40]

The deteriorating morale in the German navy, and the German armed forces generally, compelled an overture towards Wilson for peace terms. The German military high command sent a note to the emperor advising him that terms for an armistice should be sought. On 20 October all German submarines were ordered to return from operations.[41] The German surface fleet had been rendered unreliable owing to plummeting morale and revolutionary fervour among the sailors. The arguably marginal effectiveness of the surface fleet and the potency of the U-boats led to an

SUBMARINE WARFARE IN THE FIRST WORLD WAR

unbalanced fleet during the Second World War, in which the German navy was designed to raid British sea lanes rather than challenge the Royal Navy for supremacy.

In the Royal Navy, there was also a sense of the impending end of the war. However, there was no sense of elation. Instead, the Service understood that the defence of trade and the blockade of the Central Powers were decisive in the imminent victory; there was no climactic battle, no Trafalgar. On 19 and 21 October the Royal Navy informed the War Cabinet of its terms for the German surrender. It wanted the surrender of the 3rd and 4th Battle Squadrons (which contained the ten newest ships), the fleet flagship *Baden*, all six battlecruisers, eight cruisers, fifty of the most modern destroyers and all of the operational submarines.[42] Eventually, the Allied Naval Council agreed that the German fleet should be interned for the duration of the Armistice and the final disposition of the fleet would be determined through the peace negotiations, which were to follow.

The terms of the surrender of the German navy were codified in three articles: XXII: surrender of 160 submarines; XXIII: internment in neutral ports, or failing them, in Allied ports, of ten battleships, six battlecruisers, and so on, the ships to be designated by the victors and with only (German) care and maintenance parties left on board; XXXI: No destruction of ships or of materials to be permitted before evacuation, delivery or restoration; XXVI: continuation of the Allied naval blockade for the duration of the Armistice; XXIX: provided for the return of Russian warships in the Black Sea seized by Germany. The Armistice was signed on 11 November 1918. There were no neutral ports that could accommodate the High Seas Fleet's surrendered ships and the Royal Navy base at Scapa Flow was designated to serve as the cage for the captured German surface warships. On 21 November the Grand Fleet met the High Seas Fleet, not in combat as the tars of the Royal Navy had earnestly thirsted for during the war, but instead to escort the defeated enemy to their jail. By noon, the flower of the German navy was anchored at the British naval base. The submarines, however, were interned at Harwich.[43] The Great War at sea had come to an end.

Admiral Sims concluded that the American contribution to the overall war effort was both relatively small and late in coming. However, it was vital. He wrote that it would have been an error to insist upon an independent American command in European waters. The Royal Navy:

... had developed its own methods of working and ... was a great 'going concern.' The crisis was so pressing that we simply did not have time to create a separate force of our own; the most cursory examination of conditions convinced me that we could only hope to accomplish something worth while only by playing the game as it was then being played, and that any attempt to lay down new rules would inevitably decrease the effectiveness of our cooperation, and perhaps result in losing the war. ... Therefore, I decided that our forces should become, for the purpose of this war, virtually a part of the Allied navies; to place at the disposal of the Allies our ships to reinforce the weak part of their lines; to ignore such secondary considerations as national pride, naval prestige and personal ambitions; and to subordinate every other consideration to that of defeating the Hun.[44]

The US Navy's involvement in the First World War as an active combatant was peripheral to the success of the Entente. The Chief of Naval Operations understood that the US contribution was best made as an auxiliary to the French and (more so) British navies. As regards the American experience with U–boats, it was mostly vicarious. The Royal Navy did the real work of combating the U–boat. However, all of the lessons that would eventually be put to good use in the Second World War were there to be learned in the First. Paramount of these lessons was the potency of convoys as the effective means of escorting merchant shipping. The British employed a crude (relative to Second World War experience) form of signals intelligence to locate U–boats. The Q–ship was attempted and was found to be a failure as a tactic. Finally, the experience by American naval officers of working closely with their British counterparts went a long way to lay the ground work for the amity between the two services that was to prove fundamental to success in the Second World War.

5

Diplomacy and Submarine Development Between the Wars

The termination of hostilities, and the subsequent diplomacy that resulted in the peace treaty at Versailles and the treaties following Versailles, set the international environment for the period preceding the Second World War. A further consideration was the relative decline of the Royal Navy vis-à-vis the US Navy. The strictures of the interwar treaties set the tone for the development of submarines in the United States and other interwar treaty signatories, and led to the trend for the development of the 'fleet submarine'. This move to the fleet submarine led to certain attitudes towards ASW doctrine and promoted a disastrous blindness to the effectiveness of submarines as commerce destroyers. These technological and doctrinal developments of submarine and anti-submarine systems were to have profound effects on the German assault on the East Coast of the United States.

An armistice among the warring powers went into effect on 11 November 1918, but forging peace was a protracted battle. The leaders of the formerly warring nations gathered in January 1919 in Paris to negotiate the permanent peace. In Britain and France there was a mood for revenge. However, a popular contradiction was emerging: a recognition of the urgency to rebuild devastated economies to be set against the desire for revenge upon the Germans as the instigators of the war.

The spectre that was wafting above these negotiations was the US President Woodrow Wilson and his 'world building' sentiments. Wilson sought to impose upon the world his aspiration for an international order based upon law and clear notions of conduct by national governments. He saw the American people as anointed to bring this new order to pass. As early as 1916 Wilson had proclaimed that: 'the object of war should be to make the world safe for democracy.' At the peace conference Wilson's influence pressured the victors to seek more than the restoration of Belgium and Serbia and the return of Alsace–Lorraine to France. At the end of the war the aims had shifted to also include: 'self-determination for Czechs, Poles and other subject peoples in Eastern Europe, opening the straits [Dardanelles, Turkey] to world shipping, and establishing the President's League of Nations.'[1]

There was friction among the victors at the peace conference in Paris in 1919. British Prime Minister Lloyd George was opposed to restrictions on naval blockades; French Prime Minister Georges Clemenceau insisted that Germany be made to make reparations for civilian damage and deaths. Wilson, however, was not brooking squabbles in Europe. He threatened that if Britain and France did not conform, the United States would make a separate peace. The French and British fell in line. A precondition for peace was the abdication of the Kaiser and on 9 November Kaiser Wilhelm II abdicated from the throne of Germany. Two days later in a railway carriage in a forest in Compiègne, France and Germany signed an instrument of surrender and the First World War ended. The German army was required to withdraw to the Rhine: a demilitarised zone ten miles deep was established, and Allied and American garrisons were established at the three main river crossings over the Rhine. The Germans were required to relinquish war material including their surface fleet, submarines, air force and transportation.[2] Germany was made prostrate. Until the surrender was signed, the Entente maintained their naval blockade, exacerbating the misery into which Germany had been plunged.

The disposition of the surrendered fleet was contentious. Although the winners were united in coveting the German navy and making sure that the High Seas Fleet would not rise again to contest the North Sea, there was disagreement over how to dispose of the fleet. As an interim solution the German navy was ordered into the ports of neutrals and Allies. Eventually, the ships were escorted into the Firth of Forth on Scotland's North Sea coast: the expectation was that the German ships would remain there until a final peace treaty codified the ultimate disposition of the navy. The British succeeded in convincing the United States that the surface navy should be sunk; the former felt that their numerical superiority would be threatened if other nations got the German ships. Instead, if the ships were sunk, British naval supremacy would not be undermined. The French and Italians wanted the ships distributed to the victors as prizes and the negotiations deadlocked.

Talks devolved to the naval advisory staffs. By March 1919 these talks among naval officers also ground to a halt, for the same reasons. Admiral Benson, the Chief of Naval Operations and the naval adviser to President Wilson in Paris, clashed with the First Sea Lord, Sir Rosslyn Wemyss. Benson insisted on parity with the Royal Navy. To cut this Gordian knot, on 27 March 1919 Daniels and Benson met with the First Lord of the Admiralty (the civilian head of the Royal Navy), Viscount Long, who told the Americans that Great Britain would not tolerate enduring the war to emerge as a second-rate naval and commercial power. Benson insisted that if Great Britain were to pursue this attitude, then war between the two nations would ensue. Daniels confirmed this attitude. Long, horrified, recommended that the president and the prime minister should be consulted, respectively. When Wilson was appraised of the debacle, he told Daniels to take up the matter, without naval officers, with Lloyd George.[3]

On 1 April Josephus Daniels and Long met with Lloyd George. This also resulted in a stalemate. The prime minister suggested that construction of American capital ships could be suspended until the signing of the treaty for the League of Nations. Daniels countered that these ships were needed to enforce the Monroe Doctrine in the western hemisphere; he explained that the United States needed a considerable fleet to enforce its hegemony and exclude foreign (especially European) intervention in the hemisphere. Wilson sought to break this new impasse by threatening to walk out of the Paris peace conference. Over the next few days, Lord Robert Cecil and Colonel House met. Both men understood that the higher priority was to try to make the League of Nations viable. Cecil argued: 'that to inaugurate the League of Nations by a competition in armaments between its two chief supporters would doom it to complete sterility or worse.' Cecil suggested that the United States abandon or modify the 1916 building programme until after the signatures for the League of Nations. House counter-offered that the 1916 building programme should remain intact, but the second authorisation in 1918 would be scrapped. These terms were accepted and the impasse was broken.[4]

To the chagrin of the Royal Navy guarding the German ships, the Germans determined the fate of their own warships. A rumour began to spread that the negotiations would be concluded on 21 June. Once the peace treaty was signed, the British commander at the Firth of Forth, Rear Admiral Sydney Fremantle, would be empowered to board and seize the German ships. The sailors would not abide this ignominy and on the 17th an order to prepare for their own fleet's destruction was circulated clandestinely throughout the High Seas Fleet. Unbeknownst to the German sailors, the treaty signing was postponed for two days and in light of this postponement, Fremantle thought it safe to exercise the fleet. The 1st Battle Squadron steamed out of Pentland Firth at dawn for battle exercises with only two destroyers remaining as sheepdogs over the seemingly pacific flock.[5] At 10:00 on 21 June 1919 the High Seas Fleet began their synchronised scuttling. A prearranged signal, 'confirm paragraph eleven', from the fleet commander, Rear Admiral Ludwig von Reuter, was sent to all the ships at anchor: this was the signal to scuttle the fleet and their self-destruction commenced. Thus ended the surface fleet that had challenged the British Empire.

At the negotiations the Germans were prohibited from possessing submarines and naval aircraft. The entire navy was to have no more than 1,500 officers and warrant officers, the fortifications at Heligoland were to be demolished and the Kiel Canal was to be internationalised.[6] The permitted German navy remaining was thus reduced to a coastal defence force.

Reparations by Germany to France and England were of great moment for the two victorious European powers. Claims of £300 million were advanced against Germany. However, Germany's economy was also in tatters and a rift developed between the United States, Britain and France. The United States sought to limit Germany's exposure to payments. The Americans understood that the repayment by Britain and France to the US of war debts would rest on Germany's payment of reparations to them. America wanted any German payments to be tied to the German economy's capacity, the French wanted restitution for their devastated lands and infrastructure, and in Britain there was popular pressure on the government to make the Germans pay for Britain's war effort.

A compromise was reached by establishing an inter-Allied Reparations Commission. This was empowered to settle the figure for Germany's reparations. On the commission were representatives of the leading Allied and associated powers and Belgium. In 1921 the commission codified Germany's war debt at £600 million. In December of the following year the commission had certified that Germany was in default of her reparations payments of timber. The British were prone to overlook this default as trivial, but the French were less forgiving and the French and Belgian army occupied the Ruhr industrial area in January 1923.[7]

The occupation of the Ruhr reverberated throughout Germany: the Weimar government was seen as impotent and feckless, and extremist parties of the Left and Right made much of this 'humiliation'. In Britain the French action was viewed as precipitous and provocative, and the former wartime allies drifted apart. The distancing of Britain from France undermined the French efforts to extract reparations from Germany. This rift led to French efforts to contain Germany shifting to defensive means – the Maginot line was started.

The United States reacted to this newest crisis by dispatching General Dawes to Europe. Dawes worked with the Reparations Commission and in 1924 the Dawes Agreement was presented. A two-year moratorium was enacted for German war payments and a withdrawal of French and Belgian troops from the Ruhr. America pledged a $40 million loan to Germany and a cycle was created whereby American loans would be made to Germany. Germany would pay reparations to Britain and France, who would then repay their debts to the American treasury. Despite this American help for Germany, the Germans continued to complain of the onerous economic conditions these reparation payments made.

In 1929 new loans, the equivalent of £40 million, were made by America to Germany and a new fifty-year spread of German reparation payments were made. The British and French were also induced to end their occupation of the Rhineland early. However, the onset of the global economic depression produced a truncation of German payments in 1932 to a token amount.[8]

A significant consequence of the First World War was the loss of British and French economic, military and diplomatic prominence. The assertions of the United States' power and Germany's (questionable) weakness produced a constriction on British and French capabilities. The populations and economies of France and Britain were exhausted and confrontations with the United States over Germany would be unviable both politically and economically. The appearance of a supine Germany oppressed by the British and French would be unsupportable. 'It was their inability to reconcile conflicting interests, and the United States' reluctance to help rehabilitate Europe, and particularly the new successor states of the East which it is now argued, facilitated a renewed German challenge for the mastery of Europe, a challenge which the peace settlement of 1919 was too weak to contain.' Britain sold approximately 24 per cent of her overseas assets and France about 50 per cent of hers to finance the war. In addition, both European powers saw their domination of overseas markets contract. By contrast, the United States emerged from the war as the world's primary source of credit: world finance was now headquartered in New York, not London.[9]

The treaties era

Tension was growing between the two English-speaking powers. The General Board of the US Navy considered British policy was to 'strive to maintain naval supremacy for the defense of the empire' and for 'the domination of world markets.' The relative decline of the Royal Navy vis-à-vis the US Navy was a considerable motivator for the series of naval arms limitation treaties that developed between the wars. In December 1920 the Royal Navy's leadership acknowledged that they could no longer maintain a two-power standard: 'The utmost we can hope for in the near future is to possess a fleet as large as that of any other single power. This "One-Power Standard" was accepted by the Imperial Conference of 1921 as "the Basis of Imperial Defence", and remained so until the expiry of the Washington and London treaties for the limitation of naval armaments at the end of 1936.'[10]

The British had a considerable wish to enter into negotiations, especially with the United States. The British navy was in decline. A Fleet Committee report dated 7 December 1931 argued that none of the available battleships should be retained in service due to obsolescence. They recommended that battleships should be replaced at the rate of not less than one per year. 'But this would entail an increase in the [annual naval] Estimates of (say) four or five million pounds a year.'[11] Given the weakness of the British economy, this amount would have been unsupportable.

On 29 August 1916 President Wilson had signed into law, 'An Increase in the Navy'. This authorised the construction of ten battleships:

carrying as heavy armor and as powerful armament as any vessels of their class, to have the highest practicable speed and greatest radius of action...

four of these to be begun as soon as practicable. The law authorized him to undertake other construction prior to July 1, 1919. ... 50 torpedo boat destroyers: 20 to be started immediately; nine fleet submarines, 27 to be built soonest; three fuel ships, a repair ship, a transport, a hospital ship, two destroyer tenders, a submarine tender, two ammunition ships and two gunboats. The appropriation was $139,345,287.[12]

Once the United States entered the war, construction of capital ships had been suspended. In October 1918 battleship construction resumed. In addition, more battleships were authorised and an additional twenty battleships and twelve battlecruisers were added. The resumption of capital ship construction was a cause of consternation for the British. The end result of the American building programme would be the termination of British naval supremacy. The English and French had mortgaged their respective empires to fight the war. A resumption of American naval construction on the scale of the 1916 programme was beyond any capacity of the British. This recognition of British economic inferiority to America precipitated a schism in the Royal Navy's planning. By 1924/25 the Royal Navy would be inferior to the United States in post-Jutland battleships. One faction held that in the event of an Anglo-American war, the US Navy would not be able to deliver a catastrophic defeat. Neither side would be able to impose itself and a stalemate would emerge. The opposing faction, which included Winston Churchill, argued that such a conflict as between the US and Great Britain would sufficiently damage the United Kingdom as to render it subordinate. Churchill maintained that the right course was for Britain to 'establish a great unity of interests with the United States'.[13] The two-hundred-year-old tradition of British naval hegemony was teetering on the brink of dissolution but Lloyd George protested that any agreement that left the 1916 programme intact was not tenable. Added to this was the conflict over the fate of the German High Seas Fleet. The French and Italians firmly opposed the destruction of the fleet; the Americans and British were equally set on sinking the German ships. When Admiral von Reuter ordered the scuttling of the conquered warships, this source of friction between the wartime allies also sank.

In the United States, a shift in the political preponderance in Congress from Democrat to Republican in the elections of 1918 aborted the naval bill. Eventually, a rump version of the 1916 bill authorised sixteen battleships.[14] The British, however, were feeling the competition from American building. The Royal Navy hosted the largest assembly of dreadnoughts. In the hopes that they could set an example for the rest of the world, in 1919 they declared a 'naval holiday' and refrained from laying down any new keels for capital ships. Only HMS *Hood* would be completed. However, by 1921 the pressure from international capital-shipbuilding was too worrisome for the British and Lloyd George announced that four new 'super-*Hood*s' would be laid down, which would displace over 52,000 tons and mount twelve 16in guns and have a maximum speed of 32 knots.[15] A new naval arms race was in the making and in this race it was the Royal Navy that was hobbled by a weak economy.

Political pressure was mounting to dam the tide of spending on capital ship construction. United States Senator William Borah of Idaho introduced a resolution in the Senate on 14 December 1920 enjoining the president to 'establish immediate consultations with Great Britain and Japan aimed at mutual reductions of 50 per cent in naval armaments over the next five years. Five days later, on 25 January, the senator submitted a motion calling for a six-month suspension of all naval building and a full investigation of what "constitutes a modern fighting navy."' Senator New and Representative Anthony then introduced legislation directing the Secretary of the Navy to place some German warships that had escaped the scuttling at Scapa Flow at the disposal of the Army Air Service for experimental purposes.[16] Here was the birth of the army–navy quarrel over the future of military air power, which would have a significant effect during the early part of the US defence of the East Coast in the coming Second World War.

Beginning on 21 June 1921 Billy Mitchell and his Army Air Corps flyers set out to prove that whatever a navy did was obsolete in the face of air power. To prove his point he wanted to demonstrate that aircraft could destroy battleships. Throughout the month, bombers attacked moored and undefended former German ships. Three U–boats were bombed and sunk, then the destroyer *G-102* and the penultimate ship, the cruiser *Frankfort*. Ultimately, the show came to the main attraction, the bombing of the German dreadnought *Ostfriesland*. After a full day of being bombarded, the ship remained afloat. Observers boarded her and determined that the ship had suffered no considerable damage. At dawn, armed with 2,000lb bombs the aircraft returned to pummel the ship. Through the course of the day the ship suffered three near-misses. *Ostfriesland* listed heavily and went down by the stern. She had been mortally wounded. 'Former secretary of war Benedict Crowell, standing near (Admiral) Fullam, saw numerous captains and admirals sobbing, while others hid behind handkerchiefs.'[17] The reign of the battleship as the yardstick of naval power was nearing its end.

Invitations for the Washington conference had gone out on 11 July. On the 17th, Assistant Secretary of the Navy, Theodore Roosevelt, Jr, asked for an analysis by the Navy General Board on the relative strength of the navies represented at Washington and the implication for naval building. He asked that a common measure of naval power be established. The General Board recommended that the United States should complete its naval building programme. This would give the US Navy parity with the Royal Navy by 1927 and increase the tonnage of capital ships to approximately one million tons. The expectation was that the participants would assemble at Washington, DC, on 12 November. However, the conference was purposefully postponed until the bombing trials against the former German warships were concluded. One month later, Secretary of State Charles Evans Hughes had received a formidable pile of papers from the General Board. Instead of wading into this pool of papers, he asked the Navy Department to cut to the chase. In a letter dated 1 September, he wrote to the Navy and asked for 'a yardstick by which to measure existing armaments and which can also be applied as a standard of measurement in any general plan of reduction.'[18]

The General Board responded on 8 October with a paradigm which afforded the United States the rationale to retain the fifteen battleships then building. Britain could complete the four super-*Hood*s. Japan could finish seven battleships, of the sixteen that had been planned. Hughes reacted with approbation. He wanted to use the new measure to reduce naval building, not as a justification to continue (he felt) this profligate and wasteful spending.

Under pressure from Evans, the Naval Board returned a modified plan on 14 October. Under this revised plan, eleven battleships were to be completed. The Royal Navy was still to complete her four battlecruisers. The Japanese felt slighted: they were afforded two new battleships. The Secretary protested these as being too extravagant and the board insisted that the eleven capital ships were the absolute minimum they could find acceptable. Hughes was stuck with this platform and it was these eleven ships he was compelled to present as the American bottom line at the conference which opened on 12 November.

Charles Evans Hughes was not above showmanship. He was the appointed chair of the conference and made the opening remarks. His speech initiated the Washington Conference on the Limitation of Armaments. Hughes said that armament building was an evil for the world's nations. He said: 'There is only one adequate way out and that is to end it now.' He said that at the core of the position of the United States government were certain principles:

> first, that all capital ship construction either actual or projected be suspended for no less than ten years, second that further reduction be made through scrapping of older ships; third, that all reduction be based on the existing naval strength of the powers involved; and last, that capital ships be used as the yardstick of that naval strength.[19]

In one speech, the United States had set the tone for the conference and claimed the political high ground. It was a masterful political and diplomatic manoeuvre. From a naval viewpoint, it may not have been so stellar.

So as to codify this munificence, Hughes applied these principles to the US Navy. The US would scrap all fifteen building battleships as well as all the navy's pre-dreadnoughts. This American altruism would eliminate 845,740 tons of capital warships. The Royal Navy was invited to scrap 583,375 tons of ships, including the four super-*Hood*s being built. The Japanese were asked to abandon building all of their capital ships, 448,928 tons. In less than an hour Charles Hughes had sought to sink 1,878,043 tons of warships.[20] Since it was mostly politicians that were in attendance, the proposal was met favourably.

The technical advisers to the mission, however, were naval officers, and they were not so happy with the Secretary's suggestions. Negotiations over the details by the naval officers from the represented nations deadlocked. By 30 November, Hughes suspended indefinitely talks among the naval advisers. The Japanese delegation insisted that they would complete their battleship *Mutsu* and that the Americans should pledge to abstain from fortifying their possessions in the Philippines. Hughes consulted with Assistant Secretary of the Navy Theodore Roosevelt, Jr, and crafted a compromise. The price for Japan to retain her building battleship would entail the United States' completion of *Colorado* and *Washington* (later replaced by USS *West Virginia*).[21]

The question of battleship construction was not the only area of friction. The United States suggested that it and Great Britain should both be afforded 90,000 tons of submarines. The French, however, nearly torpedoed the deal, demanding parity. An impasse was looming and it was the British who put forward a radical solution: they recommended the *complete* abolition of the submarine. However, this recommendation only succeeded in isolating the British delegation. The French negotiated from the brink, threatening the collapse of the negotiations. Their position was that their acceptance of the 175,000 tons for capital ships was contingent upon the refusal to consider the abolition of the submarine. This statement effectively killed any chance to abolish the submarine and thus a chance to spare the world a vehicle for immense destruction was lost.

A codicil to the treaty was a supplemental agreement negotiated subsequent to the Washington treaty. This was the Treaty Relating to the Use of Submarines and Noxious Gases in Warfare, Washington, 6 February 1922. The British-led attempt to abolish the submarine failed. In its stead, the use of submarines as commerce raiders was banned. This agreement mandated that submarines were not exempt from safeguarding the crews of merchant ships and were also not exempt from the rules covering warship attacks on merchants. Furthermore, there was no exemption for officers on submarines that put merchant crews in danger from these strictures. It stipulated: 'any person in the service of any Power who shall violate any of those rules ... shall be deemed to have violated the laws of war and shall be liable to trial and punishment as if for an act of piracy and may be brought to trial before the civil or military authorities of any Power within the jurisdiction of which he may be found.'[22] Not only were submarines effectively prohibited from acting as commerce raiders, but also crews who did so, if caught, were liable to be hanged as pirates.

The US Navy Board scrutinised the treaty and issued recommendations. They took exception to the submarine clauses, which threatened to try submariners as pirates. They conceded that according to international law, the prize rules required submarines to conform to hitherto-agreed norms regarding search and seizures. What they argued for was that there should be a clear line between warships and merchants. This entailed a prohibition on the arming of merchant ships. Furthermore, they recommended that if a government declared unrestricted submarine warfare, then the subordinate commanders should be exonerated and, instead, the commanders who ordered the abridgement of international law should be the ones tried. Nevertheless, Congress ratified the treaty.

Since submarines were now ensconced securely in the world's naval order of battle, the delegation turned to forging rules for its conduct in war. 'Of course, the idea of postponing an attack until a victim refused visit and search was nothing less than ridiculous, given what had happened during the Great War'. Despite the delegates' unanimous adherence to prize rules for submarines, one wonders at their professed credulity. Within weeks, Japan, Britain, France and Italy had signed off on the treaty and their publics hailed the treaty as a major foreign policy accomplishment. However, in the United States the ratification of the treaty demoralised the naval officer corps. In the Royal Navy it was recognised that the Washington Naval Treaty signified:

> the passing of the Royal Navy's long period of world dominance; while American naval opinion deplored the postponement of the long-standing aim to build 'a navy second to none'. Yet the truth was that economic considerations alone made it impossible to prolong her period of naval dominance; while the attempt to do so might well have had long-lasting, and possibly fatal results on Anglo–American relations.

The decline of the Royal Navy was precipitous. Between 1919 and 1923 the Naval Estimates went from £157 million in 1919 to £64 million in 1923, a drop of approximately 58 per cent.[23]

The United States, like the other navies, struggled to develop a submarine that could operate with the battle fleet. The result was the 'V'-class submarine. She took between three and four years to build, had poor trim control and dived slowly. By the later 1920s naval planners had concluded that the 'fleet submarine' concept was dead. In trying to develop a submarine that could operate with the fleet, an unwieldy and inadequate craft was made. The General Board thereby recommended that submarines as a warship type be abolished. They could not conceive of a role for submarines independent from the battle line.

The next round of arms control talks were held in Geneva, Switzerland, in 1927. The League of Nations held preparatory meetings for disarmament in May and September 1926. These were discussions by various technical committees. Between 21 March and 26 April 1927 the British and French delegations submitted proposals for a general convention for disarmament. So far as concerns warships, the French proposed limitation on the aggregate tonnage of all ships employed for home defence and defence of overseas territories. They also proposed new maximums for each ship and the calibre of their main guns. The British proposal, presented by Lord Cecil, encompassed the French recommendations and added maximum tonnages permitted for each ship class (and there were a total of nine classes codified). The French counter-proposal was to recommend four classes of ships. These were: capital ships, aircraft carriers, surface ships under 10,000 tons and submarines. However, they added a caveat that there was to be no limitation to transfer tonnage between the classes. The French and British were at loggerheads and the preparatory conversations were terminated.[24]

The US Navy's General Board issued an analysis of the most significant five naval powers, with the expectation of another naval arms limitation treaty conference. The board looked at the Royal Navy's policy for the continuing maintenance of naval supremacy, domination of global maritime trade, the defence of her empire, and the impediment of a hegemonic power in Europe. The priorities for the United States were to have no 'entangling alliances', the preservation of the Monroe Doctrine, and the Open Door in China. They recommended maintaining the aspiration of having a 'navy second to none', parity with Britain. There was also a section measuring the relative strengths of the varied nations' merchant marines. The American proposal was to divide the remaining unrestricted warships into three classes: cruisers, destroyers and submarines.[25]

The expectation was that the ratio system of the Washington treaty would be extended to auxiliaries. The US delegation had no figure of political consequence. It was staffed largely by naval officers, including Adolphus Andrews, who would play a significant role when the U-boats visited desolation upon the US East Coast in the next world war. The talks became deadlocked and the head of the US delegation, Hugh Gibson, terminated them.

President Coolidge, seeing that negotiations were not going to yield progress, changed course. In 1927 the president reversed his formerly parsimonious attitude and asked Congress to approve a seventy-one-ship building programme, including twenty-five heavy cruisers. (It was upon a question of the number of cruisers that the United States and Britain had their principal friction at Geneva).[26]

When Herbert Hoover took office as president in 1929 he reflected the popular notion that arms races contribute to war. To add credence to this notion was the revelation that one of the guiding spirits at the recently failed Geneva talks was a lobbyist, William Shearer, hired by arms manufacturers to sabotage the talks. Hoover manipulated and exacerbated public outrage to build support for an arms conference.

The London Naval Conference of 1930 had one element of controversy, the submarine. The British position was for its complete abolition and the Americans adhered to this position as well. The rest of the naval powers, however, did not. The French would not countenance any limitations on submarine numbers. The only stricture was a prohibition on submarines over 2,000 tons, which was wanted by none.

A second naval arms control conference was convened in London, in 1935. Roosevelt authorised the American delegation to offer up to a 20 per cent reduction in total tonnage, some reduction in battleship quality and the abolition of submarines. The second London conference opened in December 1935 on a fractious note. France categorically rejected parity with Italy. The Japanese however, sent a torpedo into the hull of the talks:

Admiral Nagano detailed the Japanese position, which included fleet parity among the three major naval powers, great reductions in overall tonnage, no qualitative limitation before quantitative agreement, and, as a last nail in the arms control coffin, the abolition of battleships and carriers. There was something in this proposal for all the other participants to hate, and the Japanese delegation simply withdrew from the conference.[27]

The arms control regime withered. When the Japanese left the conference, on 15 January 1936, they took with them hopes for substantial naval arms control. The era of naval arms limitation was nearly finished.

A final European-only attempt at naval arms limitation was attempted. After preliminary talks between the British and French, a conference of Mediterranean powers (plus Germany and the Soviet Union) was called to address the issue of submarines on 10 September 1937 in Nyon, Switzerland. By 14 September an agreement had been reached. It was reaffirmed that submarine attacks on merchant vessels would be considered acts of piracy. Regarding the civil war in Spain, any such attacks would be deterred by lethal force. Britain and France were empowered to patrol the Dardanelle Straits and any other territorial waters, at the request of the local government. Initially, Italy had refused to participate in the negotiations, as they were involved in the war in Spain, but by the end of September Italy had joined the pact and she dutifully patrolled the Adriatic.[28]

Submarines between the wars

The role and place of submarines between the wars was contentious. The usefulness of international covenants was suspect within the officer corps. Then Lieutenant Hyman Rickover wrote in the September 1935 issue of the *United States Naval Institute Proceedings* (the professional magazine of the navy's officer corps) that new rules were needed for 'new weapons whose significance had not yet been fully understood prior to the World War. Obviously naval weapons which are capable of attacking from under water and in the air can hardly be regulated in a satisfactory manner by rules evolved at a time when naval operations were limited to the surface of the sea.' He further argued that since the termination of the Washington treaty system was imminent, due to Japan's announcement of its intention to withdraw from the treaty regime, submarines could not be regulated out of existence as Britain had hoped. The matter at hand for Rickover was how submarines could be expected to be employed in any future conflict. He cited the London Naval Treaty of 1909. It stated that: 'In case a merchant vessel was destroyed, international law, as it stood before the World War, imposed a clear duty on the warship to first place all persons on board in safety and to take on board all the ships papers and documents … The only exception was to this rule was the case of a vessel which, after having been summoned, took to flight or resisted visit and search.'

Here was the rule from the past as applied to commerce raiding. There was a clear duty of any raiding ship to ensure the safety of merchant crews, passengers, and to take aboard the ship's papers. This responsibility could only be breached if the merchant ship resisted the order to stop and be searched. At the turn of the century this was perfectly reasonable. Surface ships could stop and search a ship at their leisure; there was no wireless, or aerial observation. Under the conditions of the First World War, when both were present and used extensively, conforming to these rules could place a raider at risk. During the war, the position of the Entente and neutral nations was that there was no exemption to the prize rules for submarines. Submarines were to be treated as any other man-of-war. The Central Powers did not contest this interpretation and asked for no such exemption: 'Germany defended her practices as measures of retaliation against alleged allied violations of international law'. A diplomatic note sent to the US government by Germany on 8 March 1916 argued:

> Germany was compelled to resort, in February 1915, to reprisals in order to fight her opponents' measures, which were absolutely contrary to international law. She chose for this purpose a new weapon, the use of which had not yet been regulated by international law and, in doing so, could and did not violate any existing rules but only took into account the peculiarity of this new weapon, the submarine boat.[29]

In 1926 the Naval War College examined the nature of the submarine as an instrument of warfare and concluded that there was no special consideration to be afforded it. The submarine was indistinguishable from any other warship so far as the rules of commerce raiding were concerned. However, Rickover argued that the submarine, due to its nature, could not conform to the extant prize rules. He argued that submarine crews were too small to afford a prize crew to man a merchant ship. The prize rules required that a crew be placed aboard the captured vessel and brought to a prize court which would be in either the capturing vessel's country or a neutral with an Admiralty court that could condemn (validate the capture of) a prize.

Furthermore, a submarine might only operate effectively in areas that the enemy had a preponderance of strength:

> The very fact that a belligerent must resort to the use of the submarine in commerce warfare indicates that the enemy is in control of the area of operations. The conclusion is inevitable that, except in rare circumstances, it is impossible for the submarine to carry on commerce warfare in accordance with international law as it stands today.[30]

For Rickover, it was manifest that submarines, in fact, were a different sort of warship and the rules that had hitherto regulated commerce warfare were anachronistic vis-à-vis the submarine.

Compounding the divergence between international law and coherent tactics for submarines had been the experience during the First World War. Britain routinely armed her merchant ships. To require a submarine to adhere to the rules for search and seizure would expose a submarine to the guns of the merchantman. A submarine would necessarily have to close to a relatively short range in order to put a boarding party aboard. She would thereby be placed in the gravest danger if a merchant was armed. Rickover went on to write that the Advisory Committee to the American delegation to the Washington Conference had taken up the matter of the arming of merchant ships and its effect on submarine warfare. It concluded that the 'defensive armament was almost sure to be used offensively in an attempt to strike a first blow ... It proposed that laws should be made prohibiting the arming of merchant vessels as well as the use of false flags by them.' This advice was not heeded and the matter of arming merchantmen was not discussed, nor curtailed. Although Rickover offered no solution to the problem of commerce warfare in these changed conditions, he did assert that 'the submarine problem cannot be treated as an isolated question, but must be considered as part of the larger problem of the effect of "changed conditions of modern warfare" on the laws of war in general.'[31] The Royal and US navies did not address the particularity of submarines as commerce raiders. Submarines were manifestly a different sort of warship. Because submarines were qualitatively more vulnerable on the surface and had smaller crews, they were not capable of conforming to the then extant rules of commerce warfare. As Rickover pointed out, changed conditions would need to change the rules of warfare. This is not what happened during the interwar period. One consequence of this lack of modification to war rules was the return to unrestricted submarine warfare once the Second World War erupted, both by Germany and the United States.

If the US Navy was unimaginative in its approach to the countering and use of submarines, the Royal Navy was no better. Up until 1939 the British Atlantic Fleet conducted exercises which remained coloured by the experience of Jutland. It was still the expectation that command of sea would be secured by battle fleets. The 1920s were a period of tactical sterility. The strictures of a contracting economy precluded the extensive use of ammunition for practice and manoeuvres at high speeds were deemed profligate. In 1928 a committee was formed to make recommendations to revise the venerable Fighting Instructions (guide for tactics). 'But not one exercise in the protection of a slow mercantile convoy against submarine or air attack took place between 1919 and 1939.' There was no coherent British naval submarine and anti-submarine/convoy escort tactics until the Western Approaches Convoy Instructions were issued in 1941.[32]

The German navy, though prohibited by the Treaty of Versailles to have submarines, planned for their construction. In 1922, with the tacit permission of Admiral Behncke, commander-in-chief of the German navy, a secret submarine construction business located in The Hague under the cover as a Dutch company, was formed – Ingenieur Kantoor voor Scheepsbouw (IvS, Ltd). The firm was under the directorship of a former head construction official of a German shipbuilding company, Germania-werft of Kiel. This was a shipyard that produced seventy-eight U-boats during the First World War. The purpose of this 'Dutch' firm was to train a design staff for the eventual return of overt German submarine production, and keep an eye on the international state of the art regarding submarine construction. The German Admiralty incorporated a naval design business, Hector Bilanz, in Berlin in 1927 to provide a clandestine link between the German navy and IvS, Ltd.[33] In 1928 Hector Bilanz was liquidated (this was the same year that Admiral Erich Raeder became commander-in chief of the German navy). A new company was formed, Ingenieurburo fur Wirtschaft und Technik (Igewit, Ltd). The purpose of this company was to prepare for the rapid reconstruction of the U-boat fleet in such a way that the German government was not implicated.

The first open violation of the Versailles Treaty occurred in November 1932. The chancellor of the increasingly moribund Weimar Republic, General Kurt von Schliecher, approved the disbursement of funds for the construction of sixteen small U-boats. In March 1934 Raeder proposed a shipbuilding programme 'of eight battleships, three aircraft carriers, eighteen cruisers, forty-eight destroyers and seventy-two submarines to be completed in fifteen years, that is, by 1949 ... Germany simply did not possess the financial and material resources to build a modern fleet in addition to a large modern army and air force.'[34] On 21 May 1935 Hitler approached the British with an offer they apparently could not refuse. He offered that the German navy would not exceed 35 per cent of the tonnage of the entire Royal Navy. The British snapped the bait and the Anglo-German Naval Treaty was ratified. The agreement maintained the Royal Navy's superiority over the Germans. The Germans now planned to build five battleships, twenty-one cruisers and sixty-four destroyers. The terms of the agreement allowed the Germans to build submarines and, moreover, to build up to 60 per cent of the Royal Navy's submarine fleet, without regard to the combat qualities of the U-boat. Again, the economic weakness of the British undermined their security.

The consequences of the Anglo-German treaty had significant adverse effects for the (future) Allies. The Germans could build a navy as fast as their industry could afford. The accord permitted the Germans to build up to 35 per cent of the entire Royal Navy, not just the Home Fleet. What this meant is that the Germans could build up to 400,000 tons for their navy as compared to 351,000 for the Royal Navy's Home Fleet. Furthermore, the Germans, of course, would have a much newer fleet, and therefore superior to the Home Fleet in quality. The zenith of German naval aspirations came in the form of Plan Z. This was the nine-year naval construction programme that assumed Great Britain as the target. The plan's vision was for a navy that prioritised commerce warfare, and aspired to build a fleet with battleships and submarines as the mainstays. The navy would be composed of the following warships: five battleships (the existing *Scharnhorst* and *Gneisenau*, *Deutschland*, *Admiral Scheer* and *Graf Spee*) and four more 56,000-ton battleships, two 42,000-ton battleships (the building *Bismarck* and *Tirpitz*), eight heavy cruisers, seventeen light cruisers, four aircraft carriers and 221 submarines of both coastal and sea-going types. Commander Heye estimated that the 'Z' fleet would be able to remain at sea for approximately three months before problems of logistics rendered it incapable of further operations. It was assumed that the Royal Navy would impose a blockade, which would preclude any return to Germany, and since there was no substantial fleet train, there was no possibility for considerable at-sea replenishment that would be required. Dönitz's pleading for an accelerated submarine-building programme continued to be ignored.[35] Raeder pushed for a more balanced fleet; Dönitz wanted naval construction to focus on U-boats.

In the Royal Navy, experiments perfecting ASDIC continued. In July 1920 a sea trial for a set was made and deemed successful. As ASDIC proved to be a capable technology to detect submarines, the Royal Navy initiated an anti-submarine warfare specialist enlisted rating; by 1928 the British had a corps of competent ASW personnel. Manoeuvres of the British fleet included the development of techniques to perfect screening capital ships from submarines. However, there was little attention paid to the protection of commerce.[36]

In the US Navy sonar development work was begun belatedly. They had started development of an underwater detection device in 1919; however, a sea-going set was not deployed as an experiment until 1927 and a dependable set was not deployed until 1932.[37]

Meanwhile, the concept of a fleet boat was discarded and the banning of the submarine was recognised as untenable. If the submarine had any use, it was to be used against enemy warships. In May 1941 the General Board remained adamant that the United States would not use submarines as commerce raiders:

> During the 1930s, a group known as the Submarine Officers' Conference began making recommendations for a general-purpose boat of something over 1,000 tons mounting a large number of torpedo tubes, and having a range on the order of 12,000 miles ... These culminated in the ten–tube 1,475-ton *Tautog*. At the time of the attack on Pearl Harbor *Tautog* constituted the most advanced long-range submarine in the world and was the basis for the American construction programme during World War II.[38]

In the US Navy the permutations in diplomacy and the consequent development in submarine doctrine and technology influenced thinking about anti-submarine warfare. Submarines were regarded as long-range scouts and the defence against submarines was oriented towards defence of the battle line and capital ships from submarines. The notion of trade defence was not considered. When the U-boats attacked commerce along the East Coast, there was no cadre of trained crews or escort groups ready to engage them with a coherent doctrine for ASW.

6
New York City Enters the War

New York City was at the centre of America's war in the Atlantic and Europe. The bulk of supplies and troops flowed from the city, and in addition, the city was an indispensable transportation and industrial hub. New York City was also the economic centre of the country and the headquarters of the defence of the East Coast. Any disruption of the city's transportation and economic infrastructure would impair the country's war effort. When Operation Drumbeat was unleashed along the East Coast, the Germans initially targeted the city. The naval leaders both in the city and in Washington were extremely anxious about how New York would be affected and they engaged the criminal underground to damp down potential espionage and labour disruption.

On the eve of the Second World War, New York City was the nation's largest and most important city with a population of 7,454,995 people, which represented nearly 18 per cent of the nation's' population. By contrast, the city now contains just below 3 per cent of the country's population, although it remains the largest city in the nation.

Since the country's independence, New York had been an important port. However, there had been periods of contraction in the port's development. Its relative volume of the United States' trade was 68 per cent (of imports) and 46 per cent (of exports) in 1880, but by 1890 it had changed to 40 per cent and 65 per cent respectively. The American merchant marine had also suffered and by 1910 British-flagged merchant ships carried the greatest part of the port's trade; American-flagged ships carried a mere 10.7 per cent. However, the First World War ultimately proved to be a boon for the port. By the end of the war, trade with the

Central Powers had evaporated, but trade with the Entente had blossomed. In 1913 the value of exports from the port was $913 million, but by 1916 it had grown to $2,790 million, which represented 50 per cent of US exports by value.[1] The port was also the primary point of embarkation for the American Expeditionary Force. Three-quarters of the two million American troops bound for France left from New York. No transports were lost throughout the course of US involvement taking troops to Europe and only three were sunk when returning. On 19 July 1918 a mine laid by a U-boat ten miles southeast of the city sank USS *San Diego*. New York emerged from the war largely unscathed, save for one incident.

On Saturday, 29 July 1916 there was a massive explosion at Black Tom, a mile-long strip of land extending from New Jersey towards the Statue of Liberty. This was the largest ammunition-handling facility in the country. During the evening there were thirty-four trainloads of ammunition on sidings, as well as ten loaded barges of munitions. Shortly after midnight the night watchman sounded the alarm: flames were seen from one of the ammunition train cars. At about 02:30 a blast, followed by a more massive explosion, was felt. Black Tom terminal was completely destroyed and fragments of the terminal, trains and barges descended as far away as Governor's Island, across the harbour. There was speculation that this explosion was caused by sabotage and a number of potential culprits were identified. Eventually, the explosion was confirmed to be the result of sabotage, and the German government accepted liability for war damage to the United States and paid them an indemnity of $95 million in 1953, which included the claim for the Black Tom explosion.[2] This one, considerable act of sabotage would engender a sense of vulnerability for the port of New York, which would lead the navy to make a bargain with criminals in an effort to have tight surveillance on the waterfront. When the sinkings from U-boats off the East Coast began in earnest in January 1942, there was a fear that spies were again active in the New York City area and that damage was imminent.

After the First World War, the city retained its importance in the nation's trade, and so that this trade could be better rationalised, the Port of New York Authority was created in April 1921. The authority was charged with planning and administering transport through the port and the maintenance of the transport infrastructure. It could issue bonds, though its activities were mainly funded by receipts from tolls. All terminals and other assets were held in trust for the states of New York and New Jersey, as the port had assets in both states.

As the new war approached, American trade suffered. In 1937 US-flagged merchant ships carried nearly $3 billion of goods to the war zone, which amounted to nearly 40 per cent of total US exports. Ninety ships were employed in European trade. After the declaration of war by England and France, this fell to thirty ships. Of the remaining trade to Europe, New York was the dominant port for embarkation. By 1940 the port accounted for nearly 48 per cent of US exports by volume and the port's share by value was $1,944 million of a national total of $4,025 million. New York's share of imports was about 48 per cent of the total in 1940, which was $92 million above the volume in 1939.[3] Although American trade had constricted as war erupted, the port of New York remained the nation's shipping hub. This concentration of trade value in the port of New York made the nation and the nation's war effort particularly vulnerable to any disruption of New York as the nation's premier port.

New York was also the most important port in the nation for the repair of commercial ships. At the start of the war there were 'fifty floating docks, two commercial graving docks and four navy graving docks, which could be used by merchant vessels when no commercial dry dock was vacant. These dry docks were suitable for ships ranging in size from 200 to 27,000 tons.' One of the most important shipyards in the country was the New York Navy Yard (still known locally today as the Brooklyn Navy Yard). Through the course of the war, the yard launched approximately five thousand vessels, and there were an additional thirty-nine yards throughout the city. At Staten Island's Bethlehem Steel yard, forty-seven destroyers, seventy-five landing craft, five cargo ships and three ocean-going tugs were built. The Brooklyn Navy Yard had been the nation's oldest and most important public shipyard for 165 years and the yard built and repaired ships from the 1790s through to the 1980s. Some of the most iconic warships in US naval history were built here: USS *Monitor*, *Maine*, *Arizona*, *North Carolina* and *Missouri* were launched here. In short, New York City and its environs contained the nation's greatest concentration of shipyards.[4]

As a war asset, such a concentration of ship repair and cargo handling facilities made New York among the most vital hubs in the effort to keep the Allies supplied. So as to protect this concentration of vital elements, the New York City Police Department operated a squadron of eleven patrol launches, which guarded the city's 585 square miles of docks and waterfront. The New York City Fire Department (NYFD) operated a fleet of ten fireboats. The Marine Division of the NYFD had been operational since 1800 and this flotilla was crewed by nearly four hundred firemen, most ex-naval personnel. The army maintained the military defences of the port. The primary installations were at Forts Tilden and Wadsworth (at Rockaway and Staten Island) in New York City and Fort Hancock at Sandy Hook, New Jersey. There was also a minefield lain at the approaches to New York harbour. The US Navy erected and maintained an anti-submarine net across the narrows.[5]

The workforce at the port of New York was vast, and approximately four hundred thousand people were employed in tending to shipping in some fashion. There were 25,000 longshoremen directly involved in the loading and unloading of ships. At the peak of the port's war effort, there were 400 ships present every day. One ship departed from the port of New York every fifteen minutes, and approximately 575 tugs were stationed in the harbour. Between 1938 and 1941 the volume of goods that flowed through the port of New York rose by more than 15 million tons, a 100 per cent increase. By the end of the war, the magazine *Popular Mechanics* wrote that the port of New York 'was big enough to hold every ship afloat on the globe.'[6]

Once war came to the United States, the city responded immediately. Mary Read, who had been singing impromptu to travellers passing through Grand Central Station since 1928, was enrolled into the Manhattan Concert Band (a New Deal work programme) and became a staple for the commuters passing through the terminal. During the evening rush hour of 8 December, she sang 'The Star-Spangled Banner' and the station was brought to a halt. The day after the bombing of Pearl Harbor, 2,500 had signed up to be inducted into the military throughout New York City.[7]

East Coast oil shortages

New York City and the East Coast (from New England to Florida, West Virginia and Pennsylvania) represented only 14 per cent of the country's land area, but 49 per cent of the population, 39 per cent of the motor vehicles and 32 per cent of all oil-burning appliances and machinery. It accommodated the world's greatest concentration of industrial power.

The area, however, produced virtually no oil and 95 per cent of the region received its oil from the Gulf of Mexico or South America, all imported by tanker.[8]

Once war erupted in Europe the demand for tankers spiked. The Atlantic and European ports were closed to American commerce due to Germany's conquest of Norway, France and the Low Countries, and there was a glut of US-flagged tankers; Standard Oil even retired some from service. The Maritime Commission, a government organ created to regulate the American merchant marine, withdrew tankers from the East Coast delivery of fuel and allocated some for British use. However, this created an oil shortage on the East Coast as American industry prepared for war. By April 1941 a petroleum shortage was looming, but regardless of the dislocations in the local, New York and American economies, a decision to maintain the flow of oil to the United Kingdom was deemed to be a more important priority

A conference was convened on 19 June to discuss the oil shortage and more than five hundred representatives of the oil industry attended. Chaired by FDR's appointed Oil Co-ordinator, Harold Ickes, a plan to rationalise oil consumption was agreed upon. The nation was divided into five districts, the East Coast being named District One. An arrangement was reached whereby the railroads were to reduce shipping rates on oil and by August 1941 Standard Oil was using 770 rail tankers to bring 21,000 barrels of oil a day to the New York City region from the Gulf of Mexico primarily and South America to a smaller extent.[9] By the end of 1941, the situation had been substantially restored but it was about to face the onslaught of Operation Drumbeat.

Between 7 December 1941 and 20 April 1942 thirty-nine US-flagged tankers had been sunk in the Gulf or along the East Coast. However, through to August there were an additional four tankers sunk off the East Coast and the destruction of the tankers expanded from Canadian and US East Coast waters to encompass the Caribbean and Gulf of Mexico. From January to August 1942 a total of 143 tankers were sunk in these regions. Shipments by tanker to the East Coast had declined from 1,418,000 barrels per day to 477,323 by April 1942. By May 1943 oil imports by tankers had fallen to 73,843 barrels per day. The combination of tanker losses and the transfer of tonnage to Britain was impinging upon the northeast's economy. Rationing for civilians was instituted on 19 March 1942.

Gasoline deliveries to dealers were reduced to 80 per cent relative to the previous year. On 16 April, this was reduced further to 66 per cent. On 15 May the nadir of gasoline consumption was reached, 50 per cent relative to the preceding year. As of 22 July 1942 rationing by percentage was suspended by order L70 and gasoline was distributed by coupon. All families received coupon books: 'A' coupons, the basic ones for families, were allocated 4 gallons per week; this was later reduced to 3 gallons in November 1942. Consumption boards in the districts would determine the value of coupons in relation to supplies. No rationing was introduced for the armed forces. From 18 to 21 December all gasoline sales, except for essential purposes, were banned. By January 1943 the East Coast had a one-day operating supply of oil. Disaster was averted only because the US Navy released 25,000 gallons to the civilian market.[10] Ultimately, the stress on oil stocks was only ameliorated by the war ending.

Counter-intelligence

The U-boat menace was not the only threat: espionage was another. The FBI was handed a major break when William G Siebold, an American citizen who had emigrated from Germany, turned himself in as a spy. He had returned to Germany in February 1936 to visit his mother in Hamburg. While there, the Gestapo visited him. He had a police record in Germany, and was threatened with prosecution unless he spied for Germany when back in America. Siebold, afraid that harm might be visited on his family, consented. However, when he visited Cologne he went into the American consulate and told them of his plight and agreed to co-operate with the FBI.[11] In February 1940 he returned to the US; he had been told by his Abwehr (the German military intelligence unit) handlers to send photographs of sensitive installations, but instead he assisted the FBI to arrest thirty-two alleged spies. They were tried and were collectively sentenced in excess of two hundred years.

Concern over espionage was exacerbated by the memory of events of the First World War, and by the conspicuous presence of supporters of the Axis governments. This was of particular concern to the navy given the events of the previous world war and the central role that the city played as a port of embarkation for European supplies and (eventually) troops. Lieutenant Commander Charles Radcliff Haffenden, who had been in the navy in the First World War, was appointed to head the Third

Naval District's investigations section, located at the district's headquarters at 90 Church Street, in Manhattan.[12] The intelligence staff included pre-war FBI agents, detectives, federal and district attorneys and their investigators, Treasury Department operatives and lawyers. They all now wore a naval uniform.

This concern over espionage was certainly warranted. As it turned out, Hitler had ordered that an attempt be made to use agents to commit acts of sabotage in America. In April 1942 agents who had been recruited for the operation were sent to train in a small town outside Berlin. In May 1942 two teams of four saboteurs each (composed of agents who had lived in America prior to the war) were stowed aboard U-boats sailing from France to America's East Coast. They were ordered to strike vital industrial centres and the operation was named Pastorius, after Franz Daniel Pastorius, the leader of the first group of German immigrants to America in the sixteenth century. The head of the Nazi secret service, Admiral Canaris, felt that a mission of sabotage to the United States was a mistake and a waste of resources and spies, reckoning that efforts would be better directed at espionage, rather than sabotage – nevertheless, Hitler insisted. The officer placed in charge of the mission was Colonel Erwin von Lahoussen. The aim was to damage one of the pillars of the American war economy, the aluminium industry, although this was later expanded to factories, railways and the Hell's Gate Bridge at New York's harbour.[13]

On 13 June *U-202*, the first U-boat carrying a sabotage team, arrived at Amagansett, Long Island, New York. The second team was landed at Jacksonville, Florida, four days later. The Amagansett team split up to meet later in New York City. The leader was George Dasch but when he arrived in New York City he had a change of heart and on 18 June he contacted FBI headquarters in Washington. After considerable effort to get someone to believe that he was a Nazi spy trying to turn himself in, he was able to get an agent to hear him. All the would-be saboteurs, who had brought enough explosives for a two-year campaign of destruction, were rounded up and captured, having accomplished nothing.[14] There were no further attempts at sabotage and Canaris asserted that his reservations had been justified by the failure of Operation Pastorius.

Not all of the espionage efforts in the city were by 'enemy' powers. In June 1940 the British prime minister sent William Stephenson, a Canadian millionaire, to New York City. His public mission was to see that the armament and supply orders placed for Britain were completed. Covertly, Stephenson was the head of all espionage efforts by the British in the western hemisphere and one of his most significant charges was to try to influence American public opinion towards a more active association with the Allied powers. He persuaded columnists that the cause of the English was vital for the United States.[15]

Training Naval and Coast Guard Reserves

The city's contribution to the naval war extended to more than the equipping and launching of ships; schools were fertile ground for the production of naval reserves and by the end of the war, 23,000 college students had received a commission into the Naval Reserves. On 1 September 1940 three training schools were opened across the nation to expand the ranks of ensigns. Unmarried men between the ages of nineteen and twenty-seven with two years of college were eligible to enrol into officer training programmes. The schools were at Northwestern University at Chicago, the United States Naval Academy at Annapolis, Maryland, and Columbia University in New York City. Throughout the course of the war, New York City produced 6 per cent of naval officers. The navy's female contingent was also put to the wheel and approximately 81,000 WAVES (Women Accepted for Volunteer Emergency Service) graduated for naval service. The first campus for WAVES was opened in the Bronx, New York, campus of Hunter College (now part of the public university system in New York City). Here, in addition to the WAVES, the Coast Guard also graduated 1,800 SPARS (from the Coast Guard motto: Semper Paratus – always ready).[16]

In February 1942 the federal government paid $2.5 million for a property in Manhattan Beach, Brooklyn, to be developed as a Coast Guard training centre. The Coast Guard had a tradition of desegregation that dated back to the nineteenth century, unlike the navy, which did not accept blacks outside of the galley service until the end of the war. At Manhattan Beach there were both white and black recruits. Although classes and duty stations were integrated, berths and mess remained segregated. The recruits endured a four-week training class, at the end of which they were rated as coxswains, radiomen and pharmacists. The Manhattan Beach facility trained both men and women (for SPARS).[17]

New York helps Britain

Despite the federal government's official position as neutral regarding the war, there was considerable sympathy for the Allies in New York City. In January 1940 a Manhattan socialite, Mrs Natalie Wales Latham, sought to aid the British. She convinced the owner of a vacant retail property to use the storefront rent-free. She and a group of her society friends bought some wool and they set to knitting socks, mittens and scarves for British sailors and soldiers. While thus engaged, one of the women taped a silhouette of a sailor on a trawler to the window. This attracted the attention of passers-by and by the evening the store was packed with knitters: thus was born Bundles for Britain. By the end of the year, there were 270 chapters throughout the country sending knitted goods to the beleaguered British. The relief efforts burgeoned: college campuses throughout the city held fundraisers to help buy ambulances for Britain; Wall Street bankers joined the student efforts, and the city's medical professionals donated surgical and medical equipment; schoolchildren collected money and donated clothing. Benefit concerts were held and the city's major department stores ran 'Buy something British Week', where products from Britain were given choice spots in displays.[18] The head of the federal government may have professed neutrality, but the heart of the city was pro-British.

Mayor Fiorello La Guardia

Presiding over the city of New York throughout the war years was the remarkable mayor, Fiorello La Guardia (1882–1947), known popularly as the 'Little Flower'. He had been the first Italian-American member of the House of Representatives in 1910, before serving in the US Army Air Service in the First World War. As mayor, La Guardia controlled a government apparatus of 140,000 employees and a budget of $600 million. The only government larger in the United States was the national one.[19]

Mayor La Guardia was now the head of state for New York City. He adopted a 'foreign policy' which was decidedly anti-Nazi: he was repelled by what was happening in Fascist Europe and found Hitler loathsome. What made this revulsion most pressing for the mayor was that there were appeals by European Fascists and Communists to New York's expatriate populations, who were susceptible to appeals to their ethnic loyalties. La Guardia was not without humour, though. When the German consulate in

New York requested police protection, La Guardia ordered Police Commissioner Valentine to organise an all-Jewish division of officers to guard the consulate.

La Guardia's war preparations were more than rhetorical barbs against the Nazis. He named Police Commissioner Valentine as head of the newly reactivated Disaster Control Board, and as president of the US Conference of Mayors exhorted other mayors to make preparations for coping with mass panic air raids. In New York City, 115,000 enrolled to be air-raid wardens, albeit that the city had no sirens. On 9 December 1941, two days after the attack on Pearl Harbor, an air raid was sounded. Enemy planes were erroneously reported to be two hundred miles at sea and approaching New York City, and all of the city's police cars and fire engines sounded their sirens simultaneously. However, this was not heard above the typical New York din and no one took notice of the 'raid'.[20]

La Guardia advocated for the city to receive military contracts. Manufacturing in New York City was predominantly light manufacturing: these were small factories which made New York unattractive for military contracting so it seemed that the largesse of military contracts would not flow to New York. But by 1942 there were 50,000 more people unemployed in New York City than in 1939 and La Guardia repeatedly petitioned FDR for contracts for his city. The president ordered federal authorities to consult with the mayor on how New York City's labour force and industrial plant could be best used in the war mobilisation. There was an immediate opening of the war-contracting sluice. Between July and October 1942, 12 per cent of all naval contracts went to New York City. By November, 200,000 were employed in war production in New York City and by 1943 the city had an effective unemployment rate of zero per cent.[21]

The SS Normandie *fire*

As the war in Europe escalated and the fortunes of the Allies seemed to lurch from one defeat to another, New York City was riven with anxiety over possible Axis and Nazi subterfuge. Before the war, it had been the port of embarkation for those who sailed to Europe aboard ocean liners. Among these symbols of national pride was that exemplar of opulence and technical prowess, the pride of France, the ocean liner SS *Normandie*. At 79,280 tons and capable of 30.58 knots, she had won the coveted Blue Riband in June 1935 for the fastest Atlantic passage. She had been stranded in New York since August 1939: as long as she was berthed there was an anxiety that she would be the focus of sabotage. When France surrendered, *Normandie*'s parent company ordered her to remain for fear that she would be sunk if she tried to return to Europe. The company paid the crew's wages and established a telephone link to the New York Police and Fire Departments and maintained a fire and security watch aboard the ship.[22]

However, on 5 May 1941 the Coast Guard Captain of the Port of New York, John Baylis, together with two other officers, boarded the ship and announced that following orders from Washington, the Coast Guard was assuming responsibility for the ship's safety. On 2 November 1941 the US Navy took over from the Coast Guard and the following month all French ships still in the United States were seized by the navy. As of 27 December *Normandie* was officially renamed USS *Lafayette* and preparations were made to convert her to a troopship. This was her death sentence. She was divided into 128 fire sections, had 504 outlets for fire hoses and an alarm switch from the bridge connected directly to the New York Fire Department, although this was ultimately all for naught. The navy was committed to converting the ship into a troop transport and this entailed substantial interior alterations. At this point in the war there was a dearth of dry-dock space and so the work was to be conducted pier side as no alterations were required on the hull's exterior. By 9 February 1942 the end of the arduous conversion was nearing and all that remained to be done was to remove some of the columns in the grand salon; 1,200 workmen, Coast Guard and naval personnel were aboard the ship. By 14:30 workmen were ready to cut the columns using an acetylene torch and shortly afterwards a spark from the torch ignited a pile of lifejackets. The workmen sought to extinguish the flames with a fire extinguisher on hand, but it was empty, and the ship's fire suppression system had been disconnected the previous week. Reports of the fire reached the bridge, where the fire alarm switch was located, but a workman had deactivated this switch at some point and no one had noticed.

A Coast Guard officer heard the shouts of fire rebounding through the ship. He grabbed a fire hose and ran into the now burning main salon. To his dismay he discovered that the American fire hoses did not fit the French fire mains. Another officer ran off the ship and onto the wharf to raise the alarm and found a policeman on patrol. The New York City Fire Department was now alerted to the impending catastrophe. At 15:00 Admiral Adolphus

Andrews, Commandant of the Eastern Sea Frontier and therefore the highest ranking naval officer stationed in New York City, Captain Baylis and other officials arrived at the scene of the mounting tragedy.

Someone who might have had the greatest stake in the ship's survival, however, the ship's designer, Vladimir Yourkevitch, was barred from arriving. As his ship was burning he pushed his way through the crowds at Pier 88, where the ship was moored and when he reached a policeman holding the gawking crowds away from the liner, he was told that all was well in hand. Rebuffed from playing a role in saving his creation, he returned to his Manhattan apartment and watched in sorrow as the ship burned.[23]

When the alarm was raised, the fireboats *John J Harvey* and *Fire Fighter* were deployed to assist. By 18:00 the ship's interior had been gutted by fire and, due to the water that had been pumped aboard to fight the fire, the ship had developed a list of 10 degrees to port. At 18:30 the fire was declared under control, but the list was not and this was now the paramount concern. Initially, there was some hope that counter-flooding could settle her on an even keel in the shallow waters near the pier. However, the dense smoke suffusing the interior thwarted these efforts. An attempt was made to cut holes in the hull on the starboard side so that hoses could be inserted to counter-flood, and water from the Hudson River was pumped into the ship. The list was reduced by a few degrees. By 21:30 the list increased to 17 degrees, and at midnight it was estimated at 35 degrees. At 00:30 Admiral Andrews ordered the ship to be abandoned. The fireboats alone had pumped 839,420 gallons of water into the ship. Fifteen minutes later, the pride of pre-war France rolled onto her beam-ends, nearly crushing an attending fireboat.

The effort to fight the *Normandie* fire entailed the greatest concentration of fire department equipment in the department's history: twenty-four pumper trucks, six ladder trucks and three fireboats had been deployed by the time the fifth alarm was sounded at 16:08. Of the total $53 million insurance claim, $24 million was paid by the United States government to France in compensation for the ship's loss. Sabotage was immediately suspected. Less than seven months before, the FBI had made the largest spy arrest in history: thirty-three spies had been arrested and tried in Brooklyn and all were found guilty. The Attorney General of New York City, the FBI, both houses of Congress, and the US Navy conducted investigations, but the attorney general's summation was apt: 'There is no evidence of sabotage. Carelessness has served the enemy with equal effectiveness.' Ultimately, the hulk of the ocean liner was sold for scrap in 1946 for $106,000.[24]

The Mafia and the war

The destruction of *Normandie* brought the Mafia to the attention of US Naval Intelligence and the suspicion of sabotage afforded imprisoned Mafiosi the opportunity to cut a deal with the government. They saw this as a chance to play upon naval leaders' fears that New York City was vulnerable to sabotage and, indeed, Naval Intelligence was afraid of Axis agents' penetration of the waterfront. If Axis spies were working the quays through sympathetic Italian stevedores and fishing crews, then convoy movements might be disrupted and disclosed. The memories of the destruction of *Normandie* were recent enough to cause concern for the port's integrity.

By the time the war began, support for Italian Fascism was twenty years old. In 1924 the Fascist League of North America was established, but support for Mussolini was apparent in New York as early as 1921, when in May of that year Italian war veterans formed a group supporting Fascism. The government in Rome was wary of this group and the Italian ambassador to the US, Gelasio Caetani, wanted to limit their activities to charitable efforts. In New York, the Fascio Centrale was inaugurated, in 1920 with headquarters at 220 East 14th Street in Manhattan, with 800 members. There were violent confrontations between New York Fascists and Socialists. In 1926 they tried unsuccessfully to assassinate the editor of the premier anti-fascist newspaper *Il Martello* (The Hammer) with a bomb during an anti-fascist rally. In December 1929 Mussolini ordered the Fascio Centrale disbanded.[25]

Following Mussolini's crackdown on the Mafia in Sicily after he came to power, some members of the organisation were able to escape to the US. Charlie 'Lucky' Luciano was one of these and by 1931 controlled prostitution, narcotics, loan-sharking, gambling and labour racketeering throughout New York, but in 1936 Luciano was sentenced to thirty years for prostitution. Although he was now in jail, this did not mean that Luciano's nefarious empire had been suppressed, and he had regular meetings with his lieutenants. Luciano had read in the newspapers that the navy was nervous about sabotage on the waterfront and, as head of

New York's underworld, he had a plan to exploit his position. If there were strikes or disturbances among the workers loading ships, or if the workers on the docks were susceptible to being infiltrated by pro-Axis spies, then the Allied war effort would be damaged. Since the Mafia had control over the waterfront, Luciano could guarantee the stability of the docks. In essence it was a protection scheme and it was the navy that would be the victim.[26]

To put the plan into operation, Luciano reasoned, they would need some front-page news that highlighted shipping's vulnerability. The heads of the Mafia's control on the waterfront were Albert and Tony Anastasia, the former being prominent in the Longshoremen's Association, the union that organised the East Coast docks. The Anastasia brothers were aware of Naval Intelligence agents snooping around the docks and the Mafiosi saw this interest as an opportunity to exploit. The destruction of *Normandie* provided the opportunity they sought.

The destruction of the French ocean liner had alarmed naval officials, but the officer charged with naval intelligence in New York and New Jersey, Captain Roscoe C MacFall, Chief Intelligence Officer of the Third Naval District, had a plan to assuage this fear. He met Frank Hagan, the New York District Attorney, and Murray Gurfein, the head of the District Attorney's Rackets Bureau, on 7 March 1942, a month after *Normandie*'s sinking. They agreed to develop a scheme to further Naval Intelligence's penetration of the docks. Lieutenant Commander Haffenden, the lead officer of the Third Naval District's investigation unit, suggested that the underworld leaders might be useful to the navy in gathering intelligence and Gurfein recommended that they contact Joseph 'Socks' Lanza, who ran the Fulton Fish Market for the Mafia, and was currently under indictment for conspiracy and extortion: 'Not one fishing boat landed in New York without paying him a $10 tribute, not one truck left without paying him $50. He got his name from "socking" anyone that got in his way.'[27] Gurfein suggested that they use his lawyer, Joseph K Guerin. Lanza had told Guerin that he was afraid to be seen with government officials as his underworld contacts would think that he was selling out to them and was an informer, but he was nonetheless interested. Lanza and Gurfein then met at the Hotel Astor with Commander Haffenden, in naval uniform. Lanza made it clear that he was motivated solely out of patriotism and wanted no quid pro quo, and he offered to help the government with information about any aid being given to offshore submarines, and to identify any fishing smacks that were being used to help the U-boats.

Haffenden wanted to get Naval Intelligence operatives out on some fishing smacks to see whether there was collusion between the fishermen and Nazi submarines, and Lanza agreed to get the undercover agents fishermen union cards. The latter was able to get agents onto fishing boats from Maine to North Carolina, and in two weeks a network of naval intelligence was in place along the northeast Atlantic coast of the United States. Agents were on fishing smacks off Long Island; they were posing as truckers who brought the catch from the boats to the Fulton Street Market in Lower Manhattan; there were agents on trucks taking fish as far as Ohio. Ship-to-ship and ship-to-shore radios were installed on the fishing boats to report any untoward activity and secret codes were assigned for these transmissions.[28] In his turn, Lyons, New York State's chief of prisons, was happy to accommodate the navy, and a plan was formed to arrange contact between Naval Intelligence officers and Luciano.

Everything seemed to be going well, but Luciano anticipated trouble. On 16 April he told his attorney that he felt that he was not receiving whole-hearted co-operation from other Mafiosi. He suspected that the indictment over him was creating suspicion about the questions he was asking of other mobsters, and that they were suspicious that he had turned informer. Lanza told Guerin that if Luciano were not involved, the arrangement would collapse.

Haffenden told Howard Nugent, the Police Inspector, that it was a matter of national importance that he be able to talk to Luciano, and Nugent authorised Haffenden to get in touch with Lyons. In April 1942 Gurfein contacted Polakoff, Luciano's lawyer, and asked to talk to Luciano, telling him that: 'We want to set up a network of informants among the Italian element concerning any information about sabotage ... We want the help of Italian fishermen who operate fishing fleets, concerning any possible enemy submarines off our shores.' Polakoff needed no more persuasion and he promised to take the request to Luciano, but then telephoned him to advise that a better person to negotiate with Luciano was Meyer Lansky, the gangster of the Luciano 'hit squad' days, who had already offered to intercede on the behalf of the United States Navy with Luciano. Lansky then agreed to see Luciano with Polakoff there to monitor the conversation.[29]

Lansky and Polakoff were introduced to Commander Haffenden, who attested to the navy's concerns following the fire and destruction of *Normandie*, explaining that they were anxious about the security of the waterfront. After the meeting, Lansky instructed Frank Costello and Anastasia to co-operate with the navy, while Haffenden hired Felix and Domenic Saco to act as liaison between the Office of Naval Intelligence and Lanza.

The process to transfer Luciano was initiated by Haffenden. He had a subordinate write a letter to Commissioner Lyons requesting that Luciano be transferred to a more convenient facility for the visiting naval intelligence officers and he was moved from Dannemora to Great Meadow Prison at Comstock, New York, on 12 May 1942. Lyons made a further accommodation for the navy, instructing the warden at Great Meadows, Vernon Morhous, to waive the fingerprinting requirements for all visitors for Luciano, and that they be allowed to have conferences with him in private.

Sometime between 15 May and 4 June Lansky and Polakoff had their first interview with Luciano at his new prison. Lansky sold the proposition of co-operation to Luciano. He told him that by co-operating with Naval Intelligence he might get a reduction in his sentence. Luciano was happy to help the government and emphasised that through his extensive contacts among significant people on the waterfront he could provide whatever the government might want, as long as the asking had his sanction.

Luciano's assistance was not completely without recompense, and he asked that consideration be given to the terms of his eventual deportation. Since he was not an American citizen and was under an order of deportation back to Italy, he wanted all his dealings with Naval Intelligence to be kept private. 'When I get out – nobody knows how this war will turn out – whatever I do, he said I want it kept quiet, private, so that when I get back to Italy I'm not a marked man.' The navy agreed and so were given his consent to talk to any mobster in New York.[30] Post-war records confirm at least twenty meetings between Luciano, Lansky and Polakoff between 15 May 1942 and 21 August 1945. The meetings typically lasted from ten o'clock in the morning to one o'clock.

Lansky would report the gist of the conversations to Haffenden. The gangster and the naval officer then discussed how the navy could use the Mafia more efficiently. The two negotiated plans to make the docks more

Right: Chief of Naval Operations, Harold Stark. He was CNO from 1939 to 1942, and author of the 'War Plan Dog' memorandum.

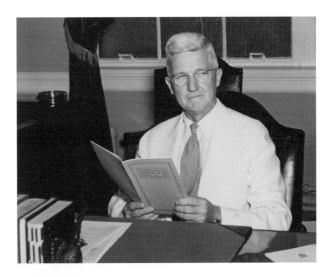

Left: Carl Vinson, Chairman of the House (of Representatives) Naval Affairs Committee from 1931 to 1947, and Secretary of the Navy Charles Edison (son of the famous inventor). (US Library of Congress)

Below: Carl Vinson and Secretary of the Navy Charles Edison conferring in January 1940 over the Vinson Expansion Act which authorised a 25 per cent increase in the tonnage of the US combat fleet. (US Library of Congress)

Above: Signing of the Two-Ocean Navy
Act: President Franklin Roosevelt and
Carl Vinson, 27 March 1934.

Left: Fleet Admiral Ernest King, CNO
successor to Admiral Stark.

Below: First World War-era destroyers in
'mothballs' in Philadelphia, 1919.

Above: The meeting at Placentia Bay, Newfoundland, between President Roosevelt and Prime Minister Churchill, 10–12 August 1941. Roosevelt was transferred from USS *McDougal* to HMS *Prince of Wales*.

Above: The departure of President Roosevelt and British Prime Minister Winston Churchill from Placentia Bay, aboard USS *August*. This meeting resulted in the Atlantic Charter.

Top: Naval station, Argentia, Newfoundland.

Above: Hvalfjörður, Iceland.

Right: United States relieving British troops in Iceland.

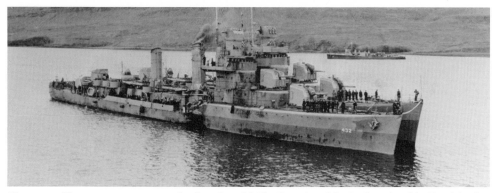

Top: USS *Kearny* crew at mess in October 1941 after the ship had arrived in Reykjavik, Iceland.

Centre: USS *Kearny* with torpedo damage after arrival at Reykjavik, Iceland, 19 October 1941.

Bottom: USS *Kearny* alongside USS *Monssen* in Iceland.

Top: USS *Reuben James* at anchor in 1939. Note the peacetime pennant number.

Above: Main navy building, Washington, DC, headquarters for the Navy Department during the war. The building was constructed in 1918 and was torn down in 1970.

Left: Admiral Adolphus Andrews, Commandant of the Eastern Sea Frontier. He was assigned as Commandant of the Third Naval District on 7 January 1941. The Eastern Sea Frontier was established on 1 March 1941 with Andrews as commandant.

Below: Admiral Andrews and Mayor of New York City, Fiorello La Guardia. (From the bequest of Mrs Berenice Andrews to the Denison, Texas)

Top: Commissioning oath for WAVES and SPARs in New York City.

Above: Salvage of uss *Lafayette* (ss *Normandie*) at 48th Street, Manhattan, in 1942.

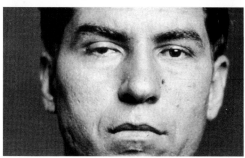

Top left: Meyer Lansky, instrumental in arranging the Mafia–Naval Intelligence collaboration. (US Library of Congress)

Top right: Thomas Dewey, District Attorney for New York. He successfully prosecuted Charles 'Lucky' Luciano. (Dictionary of American Fighting Ships)

Centre: Lucky Luciano.

Bottom: German-American Bund march on 86th Street in Manhattan. Their headquarters was at 175 85th Street. The Bund was the most prominent pro–Nazi American group prior to the war. (US Library of Congress)

Left: Fritz Kuhn, leader of the Bund, who was prosecuted later for fraud. (US Library of Congress)

Below: New York Navy Yard, popularly known as the Brooklyn Navy Yard, was the nation's first shipyard, founded in 1801 and closed in 1966. (US Library of Congress)

Below left: USS *North Carolina* commissioning at the New York Navy Yard, 9 April 1941. (From the bequest of Mrs Berenice Andrews to the Denison, Texas)

Below right: Secretary of the Navy Frank Knox and Admiral Andrews at the USS *North Carolina* commissioning. (From the bequest of Mrs Berenice Andrews to the Denison, Texas)

Top: USS *Akron*. Within the navy there was a debate as to whether the airship or the aeroplane would be the navy's main aircraft. The airship's primary advocate, Admiral William Moffett, was killed in the crash of the *Akron* off the coast of New Jersey on 4 April 1933.

Above: PBM 3 (Martin Marine patrol bomber) on ASW patrol off the coast of Florida, 1943.

Top: Admiral Andrews conferring with the captain of a Norwegian freighter prior to sailing in 1942.

Centre: U-123 returning from patrol. Under Kapitänleutnant Reinhard Hardegen she was the most successful of the 'Drumbeat' boats, sinking a total of nine ships for 53,173 tons. (Jak Showell)

Bottom: USS *Roper,* which sank *U-85* off Cape Hatteras in April 1942.

efficient, how to prevent strikes, to better secure the waterfront against sabotage and maintain the secrecy of ship movements. To better enforce this Mafia–navy accommodation, Johnny 'Cockeye' Dunn was brought from prison and anointed as the waterfront enforcer; no one was to 'blab' about troopship movements or other sensitive information. The password on the docks, fishing fleet, restaurants and nightclubs was 'working for the Commander'. It was assumed that 'the Commander' was a Mafioso nickname, not a genuine military officer.[31]

Lansky claimed that the net was so tight over the waterfront that it was he who first found out about Operation Pastorius. He claimed that the brother of an Italian fisherman told him that his brother had seen four spies exit from a submarine and row ashore. Lansky passed this on to Haffenden, who then alerted the FBI. The Mafia–navy alliance grew so intimate that on some occasions, navy men would service Mafia-run club vending machines.

The association with the Mafia helped to keep the dock labour force docile. When Harry Bridges, a West Coast labour organiser arrived in Brooklyn to clean up the Longshoremen's Union, he was persuaded to desist. Rumours began to circulate that he was going to organise a strike – such a labour action could impede the functions of the war effort. Haffenden contacted Lanza and conveyed his concerns about Bridges. Bridges was going to hold a meeting with Longshoremen. Before this could start, Lanza got to him first. Bridges was on a plane back to the West Coast, replete with East-Coast bruises. He never returned east and the docks stayed quiet.

The navy–Mafia connection transcended the New York waterfront and East Coast. During the American and British invasion of Sicily, a decision was made to exploit the navy's Mafia connections. Haffenden reported his contacts to Captain Wallace, the head of naval counter-intelligence. Again, Meyer Lansky acted as an agent for Luciano, who recommended people to talk to Naval Intelligence. Drug smugglers were prominent among those who spoke to the navy, one being Vincent Mangano, who had run an import–export business between Italy and the United States as a cover for drug smuggling, set up by Luciano. The intention was to use these contacts to have first-hand information about the geography, culture and economic situation in Sicily for the coming invasion. A plan was approved by the joint chiefs, the Special Military Plan for Psychological

Warfare in Sicily on 9 April 1943. The plan called for the use of dissident organisations to foment revolts and sabotage in Sicily, paramount among these groups being the Mafia, who had a thirst for vengeance following Mussolini's purges. When the Allies came ashore on Sicily on 9 July 1943, among the troops were four members of Naval Intelligence. They made contacts with local Mafia leaders and those who had been deported from the United States. Among the results from this contact was a raid on local Italian and German naval headquarters which yielded code books and maps of minefields.

Luciano asked for a price for his assistance: he wanted to be freed from jail and given liberty to operate behind the lines in Sicily. This was denied, but in 1946 New York State Governor Thomas Dewey commuted Luciano's remaining sentence. After nine years, nine months, Luciano was freed on condition that he depart the United States. He was transferred to Ellis Island, where his family had immigrated to the United States thirty-nine years previously. His Mafia associates provided him with $2,500 in traveller's cheques. After some parting, and in the company of three Broadway showgirls, 'Lucky' Luciano was returned to his native Sicily, with the provision that if he ever set foot on American soil he would be treated as a fleeing convict and compelled to serve the maximum of his sentence.

Charles Haffenden went on to serve in the Pacific and returned to New York wounded from the fighting on Iwo Jima. While recuperating in hospital, he wrote a letter advocating for Luciano, but after the war this came back to haunt the commander. A post-war investigation by the FBI confirmed that Haffenden had been seen playing golf with Mafia figures. He was appointed the New York City Commissioner of Marine and Aviation, and in this position he was able to hand out concession licences at the city's ports and airports. As a result of the FBI investigation, Haffenden was forced to resign in May 1946.[32]

Nazis in New York

In Manhattan, the Yorkville neighbourhood had a considerable ethnic German population and it contained both the most virulent pro-Nazi organisation in the city and the strongest anti-Nazi groups. The pro-Nazi German-American Bund, which had a considerable membership there, was founded in Buffalo, New York, in 1936. As pro-Nazi displays, such as the flying of Nazi flag, increased, so La Guardia's rhetoric against Hitler increased in vitriol and reached a head in March 1937 during a speech he gave to the American Jewish Congress. He said that he hoped that the upcoming World's Fair should 'have a Chamber of Horrors' for 'that brown-shirted fanatic'. The epicentre of New York Nazism was 178 East 85th Street, in Manhattan, the offices of the pro-Nazi newspaper, *Deutscher Weckruf und Beobachter* and the residence of the German-born leader of the American Bund, Fritz Kuhn. Kuhn was born in Munich and, after serving in the German army in the First World War, had emigrated to the United States, being granted American citizenship in 1934. Here also was the German American Business League, a business leadership group that published a list of companies exhibiting sympathy towards the regime in Germany. In the same Yorkville neighbourhood was also a concentration of anti-Nazi organisations which included the German Workers' Club, the German General Book Store (which made a point of stocking books banned in Germany), the New York Labour Temple and the anti-Nazi newspaper, *Deutsches Volksecho.*[33] Agitation and violence spread through Yorkville.

Indeed, there had been considerable anti-Nazi sentiment throughout the whole city. On 10 May 1933 a protest march wended its way through Manhattan with 100,000 people marching from Madison Square to the German consulate at the Battery (at Manhattan's southernmost point) to protest against the Nazi decree that all Germany's Jewish civil servants be ordered to retire and quotas set on Jewish enrolment in high schools and universities. The Nazi government also exhorted its citizens to boycott Jewish-owned businesses. Not only were the city's two million Jews enraged by this affront from Hitler, but Mayor John O'Brien presided over the march, watching from City Hall, and the city's clergy and Christian politicians added their numbers to the ranks of the protesters. Among the groups represented in this protest was the Jewish Undertakers' Union, marching behind a banner that read: 'We Want Hitler'. In July 1935 a sailor, Billy Bailey, with some other sailors boarded the German ocean liner SS *Bremen* as it was about to sail from New York. Billy made his way to the ship's bow and tore down the Nazi flag, letting it fall into the Hudson River – his escapade made national news in the *New York Times.*[34]

There had been rumours that there were 200,000 Bund followers ready to rise in insurrection to establish a Nazi-style government. At its height there were estimated to be 8,500 members and another 5,000 'sympathisers'. The organisation operated summer camps where they tried to indoctrinate youth in Nazi propaganda, modelled after the Hitler Youth in Germany. They aped the anti-Semitism from Germany and distributed Aryan pamphlets outside Jewish-owned businesses, and held rallies replete with swastikas and other Nazi paraphernalia. In 1936 the group campaigned against the re-election of Franklin Roosevelt. There were acts of violence against Jews and Jewish-owned businesses. By the mid-1930s Kuhn had won the moniker of the nation's most virulent anti-Semite.

The government in Germany grew perturbed over this group. The German ambassador to the United States, Hans Heinrich Dieckehoff, wrote to Berlin: 'that the Bund would never succeed in America because no German "minority" existed in the U.S. in the European sense ... the organization was only creating anti-German feelings among Americans.'[35] There was no greater sympathy for the Nazis among German-Americans than there was in the country generally. On 1 March 1938 the German government promulgated a prohibition on German nationals joining the German-American Bund and Nazi symbols being displayed at Bund events. Kuhn travelled to Berlin to try to have these decrees overturned. He met with Hitler's aide, Captain Wiedemann, who told him that the decision was irrevocable. Kuhn returned to New York and lied that he had met with Goebbels and Goering.

The activities of the Bund spread from the confines of its Manhattan neighbourhood. In February 1939 Fritz Kuhn led a rally in New York's Madison Square Garden. In front of a portrait of George Washington stories high, with 22,000 in attendance, he railed against Franklin Roosevelt, calling him Frank D Rosenfeld, and the New Deal he called the 'Jew' Deal. He also called Mayor La Guardia as 'the Jew *lumpen* La Guardia'. A fight in the crowd ensued between protesters and some of the 3,000 *Ordnungesdienst* (the militant arm of the German-American Bund).[36] Rabbi Stephen Wise contacted Meyer Lansky, Luciano's Mafioso lieutenant, and asked that something be done about the Bund. A winking relationship between the leaders of the Jewish community and the Mafia was born. 'In return for breaking up Bund rallies, but not actually killing Bund members – a disappointing constraint for the gangster – Lansky received the names of leading Bund activists and the locations of their meetings.'[37] Tension built between the Jewish community and the mobsters: although Lansky and his gang were happy to rough up Bund members and break up their meetings, they were also receiving bad press, and some in the Jewish community felt it to be morally compromising to use violence against the Nazis. Lansky was asked by Rabbi Wise to cease activities against the Bund, to which he grudgingly acquiesced.

The Mafia also helped curtail Nazi activities in Manhattan. Meyer Lansky, the Jewish Mafioso, persuaded restaurant owners in Yorkville to hire German-speaking agents from Naval Intelligence to act as waiters, who would then overhear conversations at the tables. Any matters that were suspect were then reported back to Commander Haffenden at Third Naval District headquarters.

The Bund was becoming an embarrassment for La Guardia and he asked that they be investigated. On 2 May 1939 the District Attorney's office dispatched investigators with subpoenas to their headquarters. They seized newspapers and the group's English-language magazine, *The Free American*. Two weeks later, on 18 May Fritz Kuhn appeared before a grand jury. He was indicted for larceny and forgery. The hopeful Führer of a conquered America also confessed to additional charges of drunkenness, carrying on extra-marital affairs and stealing $15,000 from the Madison Square Garden rally. He subsequently fled and was picked up in Pennsylvania, trying to head to the West Coast.[38] On 9 November 1939 Kuhn was brought to trial, found guilty and sentenced to two to five years in prison. After the war, he was deported to Germany, where he died in 1951.

Once Kuhn was arrested, the Bund collapsed and on 8 December 1941 it was officially disbanded. The leaders were hunted by the FBI. The successor to Kuhn, Gerhard Kunze, was arrested in Mexico, extradited to the United States, tried and sentenced to fifteen years' imprisonment for subversive activities. Twenty-four other Bund leaders were convicted of conspiracy. Other leaders committed suicide to evade arrest. Once the leaders were disposed of, the rank and file was left unmolested by the authorities.[39]

The Bund was not the only anti-Semitic group active. The Christian Front, founded in New York City in 1938 by Father Coughlin, a Catholic priest who had a syndicated national radio programme, was a national organisation with its roots in the city. Coughlin envisaged an organisation dedicated to battling what he perceived as the encroaching and pervasive, though covert, influence of Communism and Jewish influence in America. The group used 'sporting clubs' to arm and drill clandestinely. A more militant offshoot of the Christian Front, the Christian Mobilizers, came to the attention of the police. They espoused an overt anti-Semitism and were not above using violence. In January 1940 eighteen men from the Christian Mobilizers were arrested in Brooklyn and were charged with conspiring to overthrow the US government. FBI agents confiscated twelve rifles, eighteen cans of explosives and 3,500 rounds of ammunition. Trials were held in April and the government contended that the Front intended to destroy bridges, bomb Jewish newspapers and ultimately install a Nazi-style government and eradicate all the Jews in the United States. Nine of the thirteen who went to trial were acquitted and the remainder were freed when the jury could not reach a verdict. There was also evidence uncovered of police sympathy for the group. Mayor La Guardia ordered a questionnaire circulated throughout the police department. The officers were asked if they belonged to the Christian Front or any other subversive organisation: 17,000 questionnaires were distributed, 407 were returned acknowledging current or past membership in the Christian Front.[40] Ultimately, nothing came of a mayoral investigation and although two policemen were cashiered from the force later in the war, they were reinstated. La Guardia was forced to invite one of the discredited officers to his radio show and have the officer announce that he was not an anti-Semite.

Conclusion

New York City was the epicentre of the American war effort in the Atlantic. Since the time of the American Revolution the port of New York has been central to the country's economy. The mayor of New York City, Fiorello La Guardia, was a potent politician and a stalwart anti-Nazi and he shepherded the city through the crisis of war and solicited the federal government for the city's share of war-related contracts. Central to the war economy was oil and the destruction of oil tankers and the decision to transfer oil tankers to Britain over deliveries to the northeast created shortages, which imperilled the war effort.

The navy was anxious to secure the port against sabotage, and the fire which destroyed SS *Normandie* only compounded their fears that the city had been infiltrated, to the extent that led to an alliance between naval intelligence and the Mafia. Through this alliance the navy was able to infiltrate the waterfront surreptitiously with naval intelligence operatives being placed among stevedores, in the fishing fleet and into the seafood distribution network throughout the nation. Although there were no Axis operatives who were able to operate against the city, this alliance offered the added benefit of suppressing any nascent labour unrest among workers, which may have disrupted the war effort. The cost of this alliance was a co-option by the Mafia of the navy's efforts for their own ends. The depredations off the coast caused by the U-boats exacerbated fears of the city's penetration by Axis spies, but as it turned out, the actual attempts to place Nazi spies into the city were merely comical and the fear proved to be overblown. However, there was a very real division within the city, especially just prior to the US's formal entry into the war. Northern Manhattan was shaken by street battles between Socialists and Jews against Nazi sympathisers and pro-Italian Fascists. Once the United States entered the war, such divisive and subversive activities became politically isolated and were suppressed judicially.

7

Replacing the Losses to the Merchant Marine

The fulcrum around which the Battle of the Atlantic turned was the destruction of the Allied merchant marine. Prior to the declaration of war against the United States, Germany's submarines had played havoc with British merchant shipping. A dearth of merchant shipping had created bottlenecks for the British as they had to choose between supporting operations around the globe, or bringing in a greater volume of supplies to Great Britain. By the time of the assault on the East Coast, the war on the Allied merchant marine was not going in Germany's favour. However, when the U-boats struck the Atlantic coast, a second 'Happy Time' emerged. As the German submarines destroyed commerce off the coast, the US government marshalled its resources and perfected its organisation to produce more merchant shipping than was being sunk. Dönitz was correct insofar as he understood that the U-boat war would be won or lost on the volume of the merchant tonnage sunk. As seen in the preceding chapter, the destruction of tankers off the coast imperilled the war effort.

The destruction of merchant shipping had been a critical factor in the First World War, and in the Second, one of America's most significant contributions was the production of merchant tonnage, but at a profoundly increased intensity: factories and labour were marshalled and subordinated to the national war mobilisation. This harnessing of industry was a critical factor in the volume of merchant ship production, which ultimately turned the tide against Dönitz's raiders.

The Maritime Commission

In order to rationalise and expand the American merchant marine as part of America's war mobilisation, the 1936 Merchant Marine Act created the US Maritime Commission, which was empowered to build merchant shipping. The commission was composed of five members, appointed by the president and confirmed by the Senate. The duty of the commission was to survey the condition of the American merchant marine fleet and report any required additions and/or replacements for the fleet. The vessels proposed would have to be readily convertible to 'transport and supply' vessels in the event of a national emergency, and designs for the vessels would be developed by working closely with the navy. In addition to making an assessment of the condition of the American merchant fleet, working with the navy to design vessels convertible for public uses, and surveying the condition of shipyards and making recommendations for their expansion, the commission was to investigate and make rules governing the working conditions of US merchant mariners in ocean-going merchant ships. This included minimum manning and wage scales for all officers and crew. The legislation also required that all officers and not less than 80 per cent of the crew were required to be US citizens. Any non-citizen crewman would be required to have an affidavit attesting to their intention to become a citizen (or other documentation of their legal entry to the country); anyone lacking this could only be employed as a steward. Any violation of these citizenship strictures would result in a $50 fine per person. Furthermore, any officer, if not ineligible, was required to be in the Naval Reserve.[1]

The first chairman of the commission was Joseph P Kennedy. His charge was to clean up the scandalous administration of mail contracts. Once this was completed, he resigned in February 1938 to become the ambassador to the United Kingdom. The next and final chairman of the Maritime Commission was Emory Scott Land. Land was a former rear admiral, and had been an original member of the commission before being promoted by FDR to the chairmanship. FDR and Land had known each other for over twenty-five years: when Roosevelt was Assistant Secretary of the navy from 1913 to 1920, Lieutenant 'Jerry' Land was attached to the Bureau of Construction and Repair so they knew each other through working on budget-related matters. In 1937 the Maritime Commission started a programme expecting to build fifty ships a year for ten years, for $1.25

billion. However, once the war began in Europe the construction programme was accelerated. The commission's employees numbered 1,754 by 1940. On 27 August 1940 the commission's executive board voted for 200 ships to be built by July 1941; by October 1940 forty-seven ships had been launched. This schedule was increased thereafter up to 400 per year in 1941.[2]

Subsidies

An important boon for the construction of merchant shipping came from subsidies through the Maritime Commission. The subsidised shipping companies were required to return 25 per cent of the construction cost back to the commission, and the full subsidy within twenty years from the date of the company's acceptance of a vessel. The construction of such subsidised ships was required to be in domestic shipyards, which were required to return to the commission any profit in excess of 10 per cent of the cost to build the ship; any loss on a contract would be allowed as a credit against any future excess profits.[3] The operating companies had to make ships built with such construction subsidies available for government use whenever an emergency arose, without compensation.

The commission was also authorised to subsidise shipping routes. If the commission determined that a route was considered of vital importance, but a shipping company operating such a route claimed it was unprofitable, the commission was authorised to subsidise the operation of such a route. The subsidy could pay for 'fair and reasonable cost of insurance, maintenance, repairs not compensated by insurance, wages and subsistence of officers and crews, and any other items of expense in which the Commission shall find and determine that the applicant is at a substantial disadvantage in competition with vessels of the foreign country'. Such a subsidy had to be applied for annually for each route. Accepting a subsidy from the commission was not a scheme whereby private interests could glut themselves at the public expense, as any charter that resulted in profits in excess of 10 per cent per annum had to be returned to the commission. Also, every charterer could be required to provide a deposit and a security with the commission; the charterers were responsible for maintenance of the ships under contract. Furthermore, since the commission had the power to subpoena, they could audit a shipping company's books at will, and refusal to comply with a demand to inspect their records would result in the rescinding of contracts. The act also specified what conduct and conflicts of interest would constitute a criminal misdemeanour. If a violation warranted as a misdemeanour was found, the guilty party would also face a fine of up to $10,000 and up to five years' imprisonment.[4]

Prior to the Merchant Marine Act, American shipyards had struggled to weather the Great Depression. By 1938 there were five big shipyards: Newport News, Federal, New York, Sun and Bethlehem. Two other yards were important as specialised shipyards: Electric Boat produced submarines in New London, Connecticut, and Bath Iron Works at Bath, Maine, produced destroyers. In 1940 Admiral Land determined that these shipyards were insufficient to meet the developing needs for the United States in the approaching war. Seven new yards were built to produce the famous 'Liberty ships', divided into three types, C-1 to 3 – the number designation related to the relative sizes of the ships. The new yards were: Tampa Shipbuilding and Engineering Company of Tampa, Florida, which built C-2s; the Ingalls Shipbuilding Corporation at Pascagoula, Mississippi, C-3s; Pennsylvania Shipyards Inc, at Beaumont, Texas, C-1s; Consolidated Steel Corporation Ltd, at Long Beach, California, C-1s; Western Pipe and Steel Company at San Francisco, C-1s; Noore Dry Dock Company of Oakland, California, C-1s; Seattle-Tacoma Shipbuilding Corporation of Tacoma, Washington, C-1s. By November 1940, 177 ships had been launched at a cost of $101,100,000 (as compared to $5,000 million for naval construction). Significant expansions for merchant-shipping construction were made into law prior to the declaration of war by the United States. In 1941, 260 merchant ships were funded, sixty of which were for British service.[5]

All of this construction was bound to create bottlenecks. A conference was held on 14 March 1941 and merchant-shipping construction was afforded a priority comparable to naval construction. A division of the shipyards between naval and maritime construction was also delineated. The Sun yard at Chester, Pennsylvania (which made tankers) was relegated to produce only merchant ships. Newport News, New York, Bethlehem at San Francisco and Staten Island, New York, would have only naval contracts.[6]

Once the hostilities started in Europe, the commission went full-bore building ships. Since FDR's 'Arsenal of Democracy' speech, contracts had been awarded to the West-Coast industrialist, Henry Kaiser, and his partnering factories at Todd Shipyards for the construction of Liberty ships, named after Patrick Henry's famous 'Give me liberty, or give me death' speech. Kaiser had never built a ship before. However, he thought that mass-manufacturing techniques from the automotive industry could be applied to shipbuilding. Additional contracts were given to Bethlehem and Newport News shipyards. From the enactment of the emergency cargo-shipbuilding order in 1941 through to the end of the war, 2,700 Liberty ships were produced.[7]

The merchant ships

The Liberty ships were 441ft and had a deadweight tonnage (dwt) of 10,428; a full cargo load would be 9,000 tons. In their five holds they could carry 2,840 jeeps, 440 light tanks, plus ammunition, food and other supporting materials. They were rated to have speeds of 15.2 knots and had fuel consumption comparable to older 11-knot ships. The commission's designs included diesel power plants that had previously not been the norm. As of 1939 the commission also mandated high-pressure, high-temperature steam turbine power plants to be installed in C-3 ships. One of the first C-3 ships was *Sea Fox*, which attained a speed of 19.5 knots in trials.[8] The Maritime Commission also designed tankers with similar designations as dry-cargo ships: the T-1, -2 and -3 types.

Kaiser was dubbed 'Hurry up Harry'. He soon severed his partnership with Todd and struck out on his own, unfettered by the assumptions of the more traditional shipbuilders. He attained formerly unheard-of speeds in the production of the 442ft Liberty ships. One of these, SS *Robert E Peary*, he completed in four days, fifteen hours and twenty-two minutes. They used welding as opposed to riveting, which made the ships quicker to build. However, welding seemed to have made the hulls more rigid, some breaking and foundering in mid-ocean. A board of inquiry found that it was not welding per se, but poor welding practices that were at fault. The naval board of inquiry recommended that welding be continued, but all welds were to be reinforced, and some straps were added to strengthen important stress points. Shipyards under contract to the Maritime Commission produced a total of 50 million tons of merchant shipping between 1939 and 1945.[9]

The 1941 act provided not only for cargo ships, but also for tankers. Arguably, no commodity was so central to the making and maintaining of modern war than oil. Though America might produce vast fleets of ships and the Royal Navy could exploit its centuries-old traditions and training, without oil the Allied war machine would grind to a halt.

On 5 January 1938 contracts were let to four shipyards for T-2-type tankers. These ships were specified as having fast twin-screw turbines capable of 16½ knots loaded and 18 knots empty. The yards selected were Bethlehem, Federal, Newport News and Sun. Each was contracted to build three ships. Once launched and passed trials, the navy bought them after a short operational period in commercial service. By the end of the war, ninety-five tankers were built for private shipping companies.[10]

Shipyard labour

As the shipyards were expanded, the work force employed therein had to be expanded commensurately. As of June 1940 the total labour force employed in all naval and commercial shipbuilding and repair amounted to 168,000. At the peak of the wartime production this labour force amounted to 1,500,000.[11]

Among skilled labour, shipyard workers were relatively highly paid. In 1940 shipyard labour earned an average of $34.81 for a forty-hour week. Workers in durable goods manufacturing, earned an average of $28.44 for an average of thirty-nine hours worked per week. These higher wages were in part caused by a labour shortage, a consequence of the draft. One way that this was redressed was by expanding the employment of African-Americans, who before the mobilisation for war had filled positions for unskilled labour. There was no formal segregation at most of the shipyards – instead, African-Americans were relegated to the less skilled and therefore lower paid areas of employment. The federal government acted to bar racial discrimination in shipyard employment, reinforced by executive order and contracts signed with the Maritime Commission. To enforce these non-discrimination clauses the Fair Employment Practice Committee was formed. Some shipyards embraced this: at the Sun shipyards in Chester, Pennsylvania, for example, there was a deliberate effort made to recruit African-Americans, who by 1943 made up 18,000 of a total workforce at the shipyard of 34,000.[12]

There was relatively little opposition to the employment of African-Americans at shipyards. However, employing women was a more traumatic undertaking. By the end of the war, women comprised 20 per cent of the national shipyard workforce. However, only one woman made it to the level of a forewoman. Half of the women who came to work in war industries were minorities and poor. They were generally already employed, and working in a war industry represented moving to a better job. However, the demand was so great that war-related companies recruited women as they graduated from high schools. By the end of the war, women constituted one-third of the labour force (20 million) up from approximately a quarter (12 million) at the war's start.[13]

In managing labour relations, the federal government staked itself as an arbiter between labour and the owners with the Shipbuilding Stabilization Committee acting as a mediator between shipyard management and organised labour. Sidney Hillman was a leader in the CIO (Congress of Industrial Organizations); he consented to act as the champion of organised labour within the Roosevelt administration. He felt that the interests of organised labour could best be served by working in co-operation with the administration and sought to preserve the gains labour had made under the New Deal, like the forty-hour work week, by suppressing strikes and slow-downs. However, Admiral Land and procurement officials in the navy and Maritime Commission had the view that they were mandated to keep costs down, including labour costs, and to curtail the expansion of unionisation. In 1933 and 1936 Admiral Land took public positions opposing pro-labour bills in Congress. The point of agreement of all parties was to keep inflation down as there was a concern in the administration and among organised labour that inflation would mount due to war contracting. They sought to prevent workers moving between yards in search of better wages, and thereby fostering escalating wages and competition between yards leading to inflation. The solution determined was to standardise wages throughout the shipbuilding industry.

So on 27 November 1940 Hillman announced the formation of the Shipbuilding Stabilization Committee, the forum to guide collective bargaining throughout the shipbuilding industry. However, the first public act of the committee was to promulgate an interdiction on strikes. They then got down to the committee's real business, setting wage standards. The industry was divided into four geographic zones, which were administered under a collective bargaining conference. Each zone was subordinate to Washington and the Stabilization Committee and administered from regional headquarters. The zonal conferences would set prevailing wages and the first round of talks opened on 3 February 1941. The first point of agreement was to decouple closed-shop status (compulsory union membership) and wages. On 3 March 1941 the committee set an agenda for the zonal conferences. These were to set basic wage rates for skilled mechanics; overtime provisions; shift premiums; a no-strike and no-lockout clause; a provision against limitation on production; a clause outlining grievance and arbitration machinery; a two-year duration clause with provisions for periodic wage adjustments. On 1 April 1941 the Pacific Coast Conference agreed that $1.12 would be the prevailing hourly wage. The Atlantic Coast Conference convened on 28 April 1941, but here was the bastion of the old-guard shipyards and a more conservative union, the American Federation of Labor. An impasse developed over wages, and Washington intervened. The Federal Office of Production Management mandated that the scale of shipbuilders' wages should use the base of $1.12 per hour for mechanics. This became the prevailing wage throughout the nation, save in the Gulf zone, which was set at $1.07.[14]

The first test of the new labour and wage arrangement came shortly after the compact was made. On 10 May a strike erupted in the San Francisco Bay area against Bethlehem shipyard. Local 68 of the American Federation of Labor demanded $1.15 per hour as the base rate. Although the local represented 1,700 workers, 9,000 workers throughout the Bay area honoured the picket lines. Future president Harry Truman chaired a committee to oversee war contracting. Admiral Land testified before the committee about the gravity of the strike. He stated that the strike in the Bay area immobilised five shipyards and had effectively suspended half a billion dollars in contracts. The matter was referred to the National Defense Mediation Board on 1 June, which recommended that the company sign off on the increase. The following day the Bay Cities Metal Trades Council ordered its members back to work. By 28 June both the union and the company had returned to work with a new agreement. For nearly a month shipbuilding in the San Francisco area had been paralysed and the strike unbalanced the national shipbuilding schedule.[15]

By March 1942 the breadth of anti-labour action alarmed the Roosevelt administration. On 17 March, in his radio address to the nation, FDR said that he was opposed to anti-strike legislation; he asserted 'there is no strike problem'. However, Admiral Land was supporting an anti-labour agenda.

In a radio address on 24 March he said, 'It is pleasant to report that the strike problem – formal strikes – is not a serious one at this time. Last year strikes cost us 8 to 12 ships. But what is serious right now is loafing.' This allegation by Admiral Land resulted in an investigation by the Maritime Commission in March 1942. They found eight yards which had no incidents of loafing that slowed production significantly; seven were rated as 'fair'; eleven yards were found to be 'unsatisfactory' or 'disgraceful'. Most of these were the new yards. The report found that work slow-downs had a significant effect on production: 'Men sit around in the holds of vessels, around the ships in the yard and all over.' However, Roosevelt, although sympathetic to Admiral Land's statement, felt that the greatest bottleneck in ship production was not labour actions, but a dearth of steel plates. However, the bogey of Land's union-led slowdowns evaporated. By July, when new techniques in production and the increased number of shipways became operational, the productivity of the industry increased past the required 12.5 per cent increase to meet FDR's production goals. Furthermore, once the nation was plunged into war, strikes and union actions accounted for less than one-tenth of one per cent of work time from 1942–44.[16]

A number of means were employed to maintain labour and management amity. The main ones were labour–management committees at the yards, appeals to patriotism, honours to yards which exceeded production quotas, and awards in the form of war bonds to individual workers who made viable recommendations to increase efficiency.[17] A mix of exhortation and incentives kept the peace.

The day after FDR declared an unlimited national emergency on 27 May 1941, Admiral Land sent the president a note asking that merchant-ship production be expanded by an additional 50 per cent. In order to accomplish this he proposed adding forty-eight new shipways. He also offered an expanded production schedule. The quota for Liberty ships to be delivered in 1941 was raised from one to nineteen, and the total for 1942 from 234 to 267. On 25 August 1941 Congress voted an additional $1 billion for the added shipways and the total workforce employed in the shipyards was raised 600 per cent. By the end of 1942 US yards had a shipbuilding capacity of nearly 5 million tons per annum and by 1943 this was projected to expand to a 7 million-ton capacity. This compares with 341,219 tons of merchant shipping delivered before the war.[18]

The ships could be built as the yards were expanded. How were these new ships to be manned, however? The Maritime Commission took over the recruitment, manning and training of all merchant sailors. By the end of the war approximately two hundred merchant marine training centres had been established nationwide. The national United States Merchant Marine Academy was opened in Kings Point, New York (on Long Island, just outside New York City in Nassau County).

Merchant sailors

In order to better rationalise shipping, in the spring of 1942 the US Navy attempted to subsume the merchant marine. Their argument was that 'there has been a failure by cargo-laden crews and officers to obey the Navy orders and ... the discipline of the crews, afloat and ashore, is inadequate.' However, the shipping companies thwarted this attempt with the assistance of the seamen's unions. They feared the loss of contracts from government chartering would be considerable and that this takeover would hit the seamen's and the companies' wallets. This successful derailing of the nationalisation of the American merchant marine ultimately damaged the seamen. Since these mariners were never incorporated into the military, they were not afforded the benefits or prestige accorded veterans. Merchant mariners were denied the benefits of the GI Bill, and after the war they could not access educational, housing and medical benefits on a par with the military veterans of the US Army and Navy. Ultimately, these mariners, who had a higher casualty rate than any branch of the US military during the war, were afforded veteran status only in 1988 as a result of a federal court ruling, though 250,000 were made government employees with the creation of the War Shipping Adminstration. These mariners were federal employees, but they were not inducted into the military. This was a massive increase in merchant marine personnel, since before the Second World War there were only 5,500 sailors in the American Merchant Marine.[19]

Service in merchant ships excused sailors from being drafted. In order to maintain this exemption, a sailor needed to be on a merchant ship without a break of more than thirty days. Also, sailors were able to decline offers to serve on two ships, but had to accept a third berth. Moderate medical conditions would not disqualify a man from entering the merchant services, even though they would from military service. Although discipline was not of a military standard, no spirits were permitted aboard ships. However, despite the relative laxity of discipline, the merchant mariners returned to dangerous waters. In early 1942 over a thousand died from the German submarine onslaught along the eastern seaboard.[20] Although the merchant marine's morale was strained, it never broke.

A harsh test came on 2 April 1942. The freighter SS *David Atwater* was shelled by a U-boat, sinking her off the coast of Virginia. As the crew tumbled out and started to get their lifeboats away, the submarine machine-gunned the lifeboats. Of the crew of twenty-eight, only three survived. Another blow to the mariners fell on 26 May 1942. The tanker SS *Carrabulle* was in the Gulf of Mexico. A U-boat shelled her into a sinking condition: this time the crew was allowed to enter the lifeboats. The submarine approached the lifeboats and asked if all had got away. When they were told that there were still some crew aboard the ship, the submarine pulled off and sent a torpedo into the hulk. The ship exploded, blowing up the remaining crew and a lifeboat. Twenty-two of the twenty-four crew were killed.[21]

Entertainer Bob Hope paid homage to these unarmed sailors. In a 1944 radio broadcast he said:

> Listen, it takes nerves to go down to work in a hot engine room, never knowing when a torpedo might smash the hull above you and send thousands of tons of seawater in to snuff out your life. It takes courage to sail into waters of an enemy barbaric enough to tie your hands and feet and submerge you so you can drown like a rat, without a fight. It takes courage to man an ammunition ship after you heard how Nazi bombers blew up seventeen shiploads of ammunition at Bari and not a man was ever found of the crews.[22]

Merchant ships' armed guards

Merchant ships were not entirely 'sitting ducks': since the First World War, they had been armed. By the time the US Navy entered the First World War, conditions in England were dire. Admiral Sims, the navy's liaison with the Royal Navy, was told by the First Sea Lord, Sir John Jellicoe, that England had food supplies for only six weeks. He said: 'it is quite impossible for us to go on with the war if losses like this continue.[23] As we saw in Chapter 4, under pressure and reluctantly, the Admiralty adopted convoying in May 1917. In response to both convoying and the

British use of Q-ships, the Germans resorted to unrestricted submarine warfare and this did much to bring the United States into the war.

The United States severed diplomatic relations with Germany on 3 February 1917. On the 26th President Wilson asked Congress for the authority to arm merchant ships. He told Congress that since diplomacy had failed, it was necessary to resort to an 'armed neutrality'. Wilson then ordered the navy to begin furnishing guns, ammunition and gunners to American merchant ships that were sailing to Europe. The navy objected, arguing that this order would deprive it of needed munitions and personnel. But however distasteful, they did as they had been ordered and began to implement the president's directive.

Captain W Pitt Scott submitted a report detailing the arming of merchant shipping on 1 March 1917. He recommended which vessels should be armed, how to arm and man them, rules of conduct for the merchant ships' crew and rules of conduct for the naval armed guard (he recommended that the armed guard should be crewed without officers). Two guns per ship were specified. The gun crews were specified as being composed of between fifteen and thirty-two men, commanded by a petty officer.[24]

The manning of this allocation entailed the transfer of 668 enlisted and 149 petty officers at the outset. During the United States' involvement in the First World War, 30,000 men were assigned to the Armed Guard. Ships with armed guards made 1,832 Atlantic crossings. On these voyages they reported 347 sightings of U-boats, suffered 227 attacks by submarines and repulsed 197 of these reported attacks. The Armed Guard served aboard 384 ships. Of these ships, forty-two were lost, thirty-six to enemy action and six to other causes. Fifty-eight members of the Armed Guard lost their lives in the course of their service.[25] Once the war ended, the Armed Guard was disbanded and the men either returned to the Fleet for duty or retired from the service.

As the clouds of war again darkened the skies of Europe, the Armed Guard was revived. The passage of the Lend–Lease Act eventually led to the transport of $49,000 million worth of goods to the European Allies. The United States, in return, received $7.7 billion in goods transported from the British Empire. On 17 September 1941 the initial training centre, at Little Rock, Arkansas, for the Armed Guard for the Second World War, received orders to train 200 officers and 1,000 enlisted men. Its initial class of twenty-three officers and 184 enlisted men were expected to graduate by 6 January 1942.[26]

The task of activating the naval Armed Guard for this new war soon outstripped the capacity of the Little Rock faculty and a new training facility was opened at Camp Shelton, Virginia. The mandate of arming merchant ships also entailed an expanded mandate to modify selected merchant ships. In addition to providing guns and the crews to operate them, the navy also had to facilitate the protection of the ship's bridges and radio cabins. The navy had to install the guns, ammunition and the spaces for the additional gun crews to berth and mess; the navy also had to train merchant crews in darkening ships. The naval Armed Guard (AG) personnel consisted of more than the gun crews on merchant ships. The AG also provided the radio operators, signalmen and pharmacist's mates (on larger ships). Throughout the course of the war, 140,000 men (and some WAVES) were employed through the AG and served aboard 6,000 ships. They served in every theatre of war, from the Artic to the Pacific.[27]

The naval Armed Guard personnel, not surprisingly, felt isolated from the 'regular' navy and the merchant sailors. Unlike their civilian shipmates, they could not refuse an assignment to a ship. Regardless of the voyage's destination and the condition of the ship, they had to sail. The instructions in the Armed Guard manual were none too encouraging: 'You will engage the enemy until your guns can no longer be fired – until the decks are awash and the guns are going under'. After the war, Lieutenant Commander Beverly Britton (United States Naval Reserve) wrote in *Naval Proceedings* magazine that the naval AG was the 'navy's Stepchildren. It is not surprising that the AG quickly became known as the least-desired duty in the navy.' For any who wanted to make the navy a career, assignment to the AG was considered a 'career killer'. They were out of touch with the 'real' navy. Promotions were slow, and experience aboard a civilian ship would not help to qualify one for duty aboard a more desirable billet.[28]

Personnel of the AG also had a hard time with the civilian crew of the merchant ships. The civilian merchant mariners would scoff when the AG crew tried to impose their authority. The captain of a merchant ship was particularly sensitive to the imposition of authority by the AG crew. Although the naval personnel were officially responsible for the defence of the ship, this entailed the allocation of seamen to assist with the operation of the guns as needed (and therefore come under the authority of the AG crew). This diminished the authority of the merchant ship captain: crewmen resented being placed under naval discipline and occasionally the captain had to order his crew to take orders from the naval crew, which further reinforced the captain's diminution of authority.

The system of organising merchant sailors in Britain and the United States differed considerably. In Britain, all merchant sailors were required to register in pools in accordance with the Universal Conscription Act of 1940. The Ministry of Shipping controlled the employment of merchant sailors. They could be ordered onto ships and the sailors were required to go, without protest. The English merchant sailors had to undertake gunnery training, and it was the merchant sailors who fought the merchant ships, under the command of the merchant ship captain. The British seamen were paid the same rate whether ashore or at sea. In contrast to the British sailors, the American seamen were paid off at the end of each voyage.[29]

The Armed Guard did have merit during the U-boat assault on the East Coast. On 26 May 1942 *U-106* sought to attack SS *Atenas*. Once the lookouts reported the submarine, the ship's captain manoeuvred to bring the stern gun to bear and the accurate fire forced the submarine to dive. *U-106* resurfaced and engaged the merchant with gunfire, scoring seven hits. The AG crew fought with such tenacity that they again forced the submarine to dive and it did not resume the fight.[30]

Despite the difficulties the Armed Guard encountered, the men of the Guard earned accolades during the course of the Second World War: five Navy Crosses, two Legions of Merit, seventy-five Silver Stars, fifty-four Bronze Stars, twenty-four Navy and Marine Corps Medals and over eight thousand individual citations and more than thirty-six thousand combat and engagement stars. Seven members of the Armed Guard had navy ships named after them for their conduct during the war.[31]

The race between sinkings and erosion of merchant marine sailors' morale and the production of new ships and crews was the central battle in the Atlantic. The organisation of merchant-ship production entailed the expansion of the American industrial base and the labour force involved. In order to economically rationalise this industry a decision was made by the Roosevelt administration that the gains by labour from the New Deal were to be subordinated and sacrificed so that the ships could be rapidly produced. It was this organisation and the stresses in the labour force that led to the concern over worker morale as shown in Chapter 6.

8

The Kriegsmarine at War

The Versailles Treaty eviscerated the Kriegsmarine. However, as was described earlier, the submarine arm of the navy was secretly developed under corporations that were either extra-national or nominally unrelated to submarine construction. The circumvention of the Versailles Treaty and the revivification of the U-boat fleet were completed through the development of covert corporations. The Krupp Company, the premier German armaments firm, sent forty engineers to the Netherlands in 1922. A counterfeit company was established, Ingenieurskantoor voor Scheepsbouw. They developed plans for submarines, which were sold internationally. Two submarines were built, one, a 250-ton vessel for the Finnish navy and another, a 500-ton craft for Turkey. Clandestinely, German engineers, shipyard officials and naval officers went to inspect this construction. They posed as businessmen or students and observed the building of the submarines, the naval officers also relearning the handling of the boats. The submarines built provided the prototypes for the Type II coastal submarine and the Type VII, which became the workhorse of the Atlantic war. The smaller boat, the Type II, was launched in May 1933.[1] When the strictures of the Versailles Treaty were removed by the Anglo-German Naval Treaty of 1935, the Kriegsmarine and the Befehlshaber der U-Boote (U-boat Command), began openly to re-arm.

In the naval chain of command, Dönitz reported to Rear Admiral Otto Schniewind, the Seekriegsleitung (SKL, or Maritime Warfare Command) chief of staff. This was part of the naval high command; Erich Raeder, the commander-in-chief, had been the leader of the German navy since 1928. Raeder, in turn, reported directly to Hitler. Dönitz was promoted to rear admiral and made commander-in-chief for submarines in 1939. The relatively benign conditions for submarine warfare in the Mediterranean, where Dönitz had spent all his time as a submariner in the First World War, shaped his strategic vision in the next war. This experience was not a good model for the tonnage war he would lead in the Atlantic in the Second World War. His experience may also have exaggerated the effectiveness of U-boats. In the Mediterranean he had sunk (either as a watch officer or captain) forty merchant ships. The ASW doctrine in the Mediterranean in the First World War was not as robust as in the Atlantic in the Second, nor were there the same ASW resources. Another issue was his conception of how to measure success, which was to simply take the tonnage of ships sunk and to divide this by the total number of days U-boats were at sea. While this would yield the average of tons of shipping sunk per day per U-boat at sea, it did not take into account the varied danger and effort required to sink them, nor the different theatres of operation. A further flaw in the manner he conducted his command was to be found in his staff organisation. He used a small, dedicated coterie, which encouraged a unity of command that benefited the Germans at the start of the war. The operations staff amounted to five or six veteran U-boat captains, some specialists, aides and secretaries, and between one and four engineering officers. There were also between fifteen and twenty radiomen on duty. This small staff became overwhelmed, however, as the war wore on. They did not have the capacity to analyse and incorporate intelligence into operations, nor did they have the resources to analyse military operations, search procedures or weapons efficiencies.[2]

The officer responsible for the development of the Ubootwaffe, the U-boat arm of the Kriegsmarine, and its training and organisation, was Hans-Georg von Friedeburg, who maintained much the same position throughout the war, until he was promoted to commander-in-chief of the Kriegsmarine on 1 May 1945 and helped prepare for the surrender of the German armed forces.[3] Either because of sympathy or political astuteness, he approved of Hitler's early dictates to remove Jews from the military, which created goodwill between the Ubootwaffe and the SS; von Friedeburg used this modus vivendi to smooth out difficulties between submariners and military police.

The leader of the Kriegsmarine, Erich Raeder, took pains to keep the navy free of political influences. Once he was ensconced as commander-in-chief of the navy in 1928, he introduced a policy of discipline, which relied upon 'humane and intelligent treatment of all subordinates, and a respect for the dignity of the individual.' This was motivated by his, and other senior officers', intention that the mutinies of 1918 would never happen again.[4] Raeder preferred to postpone any conflict with Great Britain, as he recognised the vast inferiority of the German to the English navy, but after 1936 as Hitler accelerated rearmament, Raeder was reconciled to the notion that war was imminent. Ultimately, Great Britain was seen as the principal opponent at sea. He also sought to flex German naval muscle on the eve of the war. During the spring of 1939 German smaller warships and submarines cruised and showed the flag in the western Mediterranean and made port calls at Lisbon. Although Raeder strove to keep Nazi influences at a minimum, he did welcome Hitler's ascent to power and saw it as an opportunity to expand the fleet.

Recruitment, training and equipment of the Ubootwaffe

On the eve of the war, the Kriegsmarine's personnel strength was 50,000. By May 1941 conscription had raised this number to 404,000. By contrast, at the time of the attack on Pearl Harbor, the US Navy's authorised strength was 290,000. Within the Kriegsmarine the Ubootwaffe amounted to 4 per cent in 1940 and 6 per cent the following year.[5]

The Ubootwaffe constituted an elite and at the start of the war was composed of selected crews. The economic nadir of the 1920s and '30s and the restrictions of the Versailles Treaty afforded the Kriegsmarine an opportunity to be selective in their recruitment, and in the U-boat service to an even greater extent. A prospective recruit, between the ages of seventeen and twenty-three, would apply by letter to either the Admiral of the North Sea or the Baltic stating his desire to serve, and all applicants underwent a thorough examination. Once passed, the paperwork admitting him to the Kriegsmarine would be completed and at this point he was a naval recruit and would receive an assignment to a Sailor Reserve Pool for training. A recruit could choose to enter the technical, engineering or the seaman branch. In the latter branch one would be able to climb to Oberbootsmaat (senior bosun). However, there was a minimum required term of commitment of twelve years. The rejection rate of applicants was high, even on the eve of the war, and in September 1939 between only 8 and 10 per cent of those that applied for U-boat service were accepted.

Although the submarine service was populated by volunteers, the needs of the service became so pressing that by the middle of 1941 additional personnel were assigned.[6]

Training for the Ubootwaffe began in 1933 with the establishment of the Unterseebootsabwehrschule at Kiel, a school to train for anti-submarine warfare. Trainees learned aspects of submarine operations, design, weapon systems, propulsion systems and escape training. In 1935 the first U-boat training flotilla was formed, Unterseebootflotille Weddigen, composed of *U-7* through to *U-12*. In 1937 the Ubootwaffe established a school for submariners in Neustadt and three years later the school was redesignated the Number 1 Unterseebootslehrdivision and moved to Pillau. In November 1940 another school was opened at Gotenhafen (Gdynia). At the war's start, men underwent six months of training among the submarine training flotillas in the Baltic, in addition to the basic training which consisted of elementary infantry operations and weapon use. As the war progressed, the length of time trainees spent at the school became increasingly constricted as the demand for new crews expanded.[7]

The enlisted members of U-boat crews were not representative of the Reich's population and the former occupational composition of the crews diverged from that of the nation as a whole. Throughout Germany, agriculture represented 28 per cent of the workforce, but for the Ubootwaffe, only 3 per cent of the enlisted personnel came from an agricultural background. The dominant vocational background for U-boat sailors was in metalworking, contributing 56 per cent of submarine crews. There was a national glut of such workers by the time of the war, a consequence of a national policy requiring all high-school graduates to enter into industrial education programmes. Paramount among these industrial trades was metallurgy: the demand for this field grew with the nation's rearmament programme after 1933. Between 1933 and 1937 metal-working trades increased by 250 per cent. Unlike the army, the German navy relied upon volunteers. Unemployed metalworkers would be welcomed into the navy, as there was a demand for men with such skills for maintaining weapons and hulls.[8]

Naval officers underwent training for three years: five months were spent in infantry drill, then the next four months were spent at sea on a training sailing bark, followed by eight and a half months aboard a man-of-war, upon completion of which they were promoted to midshipman.

As a midshipman they spent seven months at the naval academy at Flensburg-Mürwik for academic studies. Then they had five months of weapons training. The final seven months were again spent at sea. Once these assignments were successfully completed, a midshipman was promoted to Leutnant zur See (equivalent to an ensign in the US Navy or a midshipman in the Royal Navy). As of 1941 midshipmen were included as crew members. They acted as understudies for watch or engineering officers. They would mark charts, stand watches as lookouts, and for uneventful watches, they would relieve watch and petty officers.[9]

Once an officer was commissioned, he was then assigned to the fleet. For the U-boats, a new officer was assigned to one of the seven training flotillas, all based in the Baltic Sea. These flotillas were the 21st and 22nd, based at Pillau (Baltiysk) and Gotenhafen; the 23rd and 24th, based at Danzig (Gdańsk) and Memel (Klaipėda); and the 25th and 26th, based at Libau (Liepāja) and Pillau. The final step was a ten-day mock convoy battle with the 27th Flotilla, also at Gotenhafen.

Most of the officers were career naval officers. They absorbed the received wisdom concerning the 1918 mutinies in the German navy – one of the deepest lessons ingrained from that experience was the failure of the officers to lead the lower decks. The first aim was to inculcate leadership qualities in officers. During the latter 1930s cadets were exposed to literature sympathetic to National Socialism and pacifism. Although reserve officers were admitted to the Kriegsmarine from 1935, they remained a minority of officers aboard submarines throughout the war. Those reserve officers who distinguished themselves in command of minesweepers or patrol craft could ascend to the command of a U-boat. Eventually, 179 such officers were rewarded with a U-boat command, mostly from 1943 onwards. The preference for regular, career officers was present throughout the war. In July 1942 reserve officers constituted approximately a quarter of the officers afloat in U-boats. The final pool for officers in U-boats was NCOs who had been promoted. From 1942 the practice of promoting NCOs to officers became increasingly prevalent throughout the German military, but this form of promotion never produced more than a trickle of candidates: 1943 saw the largest promotion of NCOs to officers and this amounted to only ten. Throughout the war, the Ubootwaffe's officers were composed overwhelmingly of career naval officers.[10]

Despite this careful planning, the U-boat captains were not well prepared for the reality of war. Like their American counterparts, they were not well-equipped by their pre-war training for the conflict when it did come. Although the officers of the Ubootwaffe were trained to high standards, the rigours of wartime operations and the need for sufficient nerve and aggressiveness proved too much. Dönitz was required to replace twenty commanding officers during the first five months of the war.[11]

Aboard a U-boat

What were the conditions aboard the U-boats at war? A war cruise typically lasted twelve weeks and at the start of a cruise they had 14 tons of supplies, plus munitions and fuel loaded aboard. Submarines were essentially surface vessels that submerged for short periods and when on the surface they were subject to the same vagaries of weather and sea conditions as any surface ship. As they had little freeboard, bad weather could result in water cascading through the conning-tower hatch, and they rolled abominably, as any other small vessel might. Once submerged, the U-boat's internal temperature would soar, and in the engine rooms, for example, it could climb to over 50°C (120°F). The ship's interiors were clammy and humid, and the high temperatures and dampness contributed to the ubiquity of mould. As compensation, and as was the case in American submarine service, submarine crews were given an extra stipend for submarine duty. There was recognition among the U-boat crews of belonging to an elite force, and here was a sense of kinship that was expressed through relaxed discipline and a more informal dress code.[12]

Dönitz strove to provide amenities to help his crews relax when they returned from their arduous patrols. Once the U-boat docked, half of the crew would be released for twelve days' leave. Dönitz had arranged for a dedicated train to take crews back to Germany. On average a sailor would be granted leave twice a year and he could expect to spend approximately one-third of his time in service either on leave or in port. An attitude of permissiveness amongst the crews while ashore was typical of military elites, and they were indulged with French wine and women. They disdained the military police and they expected to be left alone when 'letting off steam' while ashore.[13]

During patrols U-boat crews were divided into departmental watches. The engine room was split into six-hour port and starboard watches;

radiomen also stood six-hour watches, four during times of crisis. Seamen were organised into three four-hour watches. Off-duty time was spent by crewmen in playing chess and the popular German card game called *Skat*. Singing and limerick competitions took place and birthdays were celebrated. Whether on watch or off, music played an important part in the life of a U-boat crewman and amongst the cargo a submarine might stow for a cruise there could be up to a hundred records aboard, each with one or two songs. Jazz might be listened to when they could tune in to American radio stations, despite the regime's condemnation of the art, and the prohibition against listening to enemy radio broadcasts. The development of the crew was the responsibility of the officers and non-commissioned officers (NCOs) and watch officers held classes on navigation and seamanship. U-boats also practised traditional ceremonies that are celebrated in many navies, such as 'crossing the line' and Christmas.[14]

Successful U-boat commanders were celebrated throughout the Reich as celebrities. Dönitz went to great pains to maintain the high morale of the U-boat crews. He referred to them as his 'Grey Wolves', and he strove to imbue the Ubootwaffe with a sense of his appreciation for the men's efforts in order to bolster the *esprit de corps*; when crews returned from patrol, Dönitz would meet each boat and discuss with the crew members both military and personal matters. In return, the crews came to regard Dönitz as 'the lion' (*der Löwe*). He also broke with military tradition and greeted each man with the familiar *du* instead of the formal *Sie*, and he greeted each officer when they returned from a patrol with a handshake. He would even allow officers to borrow his own car on occasion. This familiarity did not extend, however, to his own sons, only embracing them after the rest of the assembly was dismissed. Both of his sons joined the Kriegsmarine and were killed during the war. Upon the return of a U-boat he would present awards and decorations, always supporting the recommendations of his captains. He wrote: 'I regard this practice of immediate awards to those engaged upon operations as psychologically important.'[15]

In addition to the efforts made by Dönitz, there were social and demographic factors that contributed to crew cohesion. Paramount among these was the similarity of social background of the crews. For the officers, most came from northern Germany, mainly Prussia. For enlisted personnel there was a more representative distribution from the country: 23 per cent of crews were from the north, 55 per cent from central Germany, 18 per cent from the south, and 4 per cent were from outside the Reich. Concerning religion, Protestant officers outnumbered Catholic ones by a ratio of 7:1. The U-boat officers were overwhelmingly well-educated. Prior to the war, all officer cadets were required to have attained the *Abitur*, the examination for university, which 10 per cent of students attained. During the war, this standard was dropped. However, a high level of education was still required: 15 per cent admitted as officer-cadets completed the *Mittlere Reife*, the level below the *Abitur*; overall, 20 per cent of students attained this level and in the period before the war this would have led to a career in business or the civil service. The officers also had a similar class background: 56 per cent came from the upper-middle class. The background of their fathers was that of respectable businessmen and civil servants, academics or career military officers. Enlisted men, by contrast, were substantially from the middle class – this socioeconomic grouping accounted for 45 per cent and the upper class 1 per cent. According to Timothy Mulligan, the author of *Neither Sharks nor Wolves*:

> The social character of the German navy had changed little from World War I, officered mostly by men from the upper and upper-middle classes who commanded lower middle- and working-class crewmen ... A small part of this cement could be attributed to the entrance of *Mittelstand* sons into the officer corps during the war, the first mingling of common backgrounds for officers and men.

Cohesion was also attributable to the similarity of geography, and a sense of elan. The crews were officered by commanders who had absorbed the lesson from the First World War never to repeat the estrangement between officers and crew that led to the mutinies of 1918.[16]

The navy was less political than the other military services. Hitler was alleged to have said: 'I have a reactionary Army, a National Socialist Air Force, and a Christian Navy.' This was echoed by Raeder who said that the service was aloof from politics and adhered to its tradition of 'patriotism and disinterested service to the State.' However, this claim to be aloof from politics and untainted by Nazi ideology is not tenable. At the time of the near civil war at the end of the First World War, it was naval personnel who comprised the membership of a few of the more virulent anti-Communist *Freikorps* in the Ruhr, Berlin, Munich and Upper Silesia.

U-boat crews were prominent in these organisations. When the Reichsmarine was established as the navy of the Weimar Republic, former members of the naval *Freikorps* constituted nearly 17 per cent of the service's personnel. For the Ubootwaffe, the influence was pervasive. The U-boat arm was known popularly as the *Freikorps Dönitz*.[17]

Despite this reactionary legacy, the navy was relegated to a lesser prominence within the Wehrmacht. The army, both within Nazi Germany and historically, held pride of place as the most important arm of the German military apparatus. The army was the focus of Nazi domination and its autonomy was undermined. The navy, aware of its relative inferiority, negotiated accommodations with the Nazi leadership. In June 1934 Jews were ordered purged from all of the armed forces and the navy complied, though Raeder personally intervened to reinstate officers he knew into the reserves once war broke out. However, the policy was not challenged. Nor did he confront Hitler when it became clear that the Führer intended a global war that the Kriegsmarine was woefully unprepared to wage. In 1940 the chief of the army general staff, Generaloberst Ludwig Beck, resigned in protest over his opposition to Hitler's confrontation with Russia, Britain and France over Czechoslovakia's Sudetenland. Although this policy brought the potential of war with the vastly superior Allied nations, Raeder remained silent while the army chief of staff resigned.

The relative isolation of ship's crews from events on land is exacerbated in submarines. This is in contrast to the experience of the army, which fought the greater part of the war in eastern Europe where they witnessed the regime's greatest horrors. However, Dönitz's affinity with the Nazi regime led to increased prominence of Nazi ideology and mores once he was appointed C-in-C of the Kriegsmarine in 1943.

Tactics at sea

Through the 1930s there was no coherent tactical doctrine for the employment of the U-boats. Kapitänleutnant Werner Furbringer, a First World War U-boat veteran, developed the notion of group tactics, but trained the U-boat forces to attack warships submerged during daylight. This was an approach that was also used by the contemporary American submarine force. Officers felt that ASW gave an overwhelming advantage to escorting forces, so submariners needed to be wary in their attacks. When Dönitz was installed as the commander of U-boats in 1935 he brought a sense of direction for the U-boat force. He found a sentiment among the training command that ASW was overwhelming and made close-in attacks untenable. Trainers were teaching that attacks should be made at long range against warships, at 3,000m (3,280yds). Dönitz reversed this and instilled new tactics and a new training regime. The main points were that optimum firing range was reduced to 600m (650yds); night surface attacks were to be undertaken on convoys; and that U-boats would be concentrated against convoys. In November 1939 Dönitz codified his notions for the development of the U-boat arm. He established a training schedule, which entailed the deployment of sixty-four newly-commissioned U-boats every six months and anticipated 800 U-boats in commission by autumn 1943. This would entail a personnel establishment of 3,336 officers and 33,120 NCOs and sailors. These elements were crystallised in the 1939 simulated attack on a convoy as an exercise in the Bay of Biscay. Although this exercise was considered a success, one failure that dogged Dönitz throughout the Second World War was lack of co-operation with the Luftwaffe. He considered aerial reconnaissance as vital in locating British convoys and thereby assisting the U-boats in their efforts against shipping, but the increasing demand for U-boat officers led to the transfer of trained naval aviators into the Ubootwaffe, which exacerbated tensions with the Luftwaffe.[18]

Signals intelligence was fundamental to the conflict in the Atlantic. The Kriegsmarine's unit was the *Funkaufklärung* (radio intelligence) and it was composed of two elements: the radio interception and interpretation office, B-Dienst, and the decryption unit that deciphered intercepted signals, xB-Dienst. By February 1942 the Germans were able to read Allied convoy codes and this was maintained until March 1943 when the codes were changed. During March 1942 several US naval codes were also compromised. In addition to breaking Allied codes, B-Dienst was also responsible for safeguarding the Kriegsmarine's own codes. In 1934 Enigma, the Schlüssel C coding device, was the navy's coding machine. In February 1942 a new code machine, the Enigma M4, was introduced after the loss of *Bismarck* and the Atlantic supply ships.[19]

B-Dienst was hard at work prior to the eruption of hostilities. By February 1940 the Germans were reading 80 per cent of the Allies' convoying radio traffic. This ability enabled Dönitz to place U–boats in paths of convoys up to twenty hours in advance.[20]

In contrast to the other principal belligerent navies of the Second World War, the Germans did plan to use their submarines for commerce raiding. Dönitz's conception of how to fight the war was simple: sink the maximum merchant tonnage for the least effort. At heart, the goal of the submarine campaign was to sink merchant shipping bound for Great Britain, wherever that ship might be found. How this notion of a 'tonnage war' was translated operationally can be surmised from an entry into the U–boat command's war diary. The entry for 15 April 1942 reads:

> The enemy's shipping constitutes one single, great entity. It is therefore immaterial where a ship is sunk. Once it has been destroyed, it has to be replaced by a new ship; and that's that. In the long run, the result of the war will depend on the result of the race between sinkings and new construction.[21]

However, there was a dearth of reliable statistics on the viability of the British economy. Dönitz expected the English to introduce convoys from the onset of the war since their effectiveness was clearly demonstrated towards the end of the First World War. To address this tactic, Dönitz perfected the wolf-pack attack in 1935. Originally conceived during the First World War, the intention was to locate the convoy and overwhelm the concentration of escorts. The interwar advances in radio enabled one boat to locate a convoy, relay its position, course and speed to headquarters, which would then vector in the other U–boats of the pack.[22] This preparation for wolf-pack attacks was perfected in the war game of September–October 1939 in the Bay of Biscay.

Type VII

The workhorse of the Atlantic commerce war, and the most numerous submarine class sent to America, was the Type VII ('C' variant). This class was also the most numerous submarine built for the Kriegsmarine. The Type VII U–boat was distinguished by having the fuel tanks inside the pressure hull, which gave added protection to these tanks. As was typical in all the major navies' submarines, the space between the outer hull and the pressure hull was free flooding. The pressure hull provided the streamlining to the submarine. Between the pressure hull and the main deck of the outer hull was considerable ducting. The main gun mount was situated forward of the conning tower. Ammunition, a dinghy and spare torpedoes were lashed in the space above the pressure hull, under the deck. These could be accessed through hatches or the removal of some of the deck plates.

The 'C' variant was developed as a platform for the newly deployed sonar search equipment, the *Such-Gerät*. This variant had an extended control room and conning tower to accommodate the new gear. The saddle buoyancy tanks had an added, smaller buoyancy tank fitted within them, providing finer buoyancy control. The electrical switching system was modernised and a new filtration system for the diesel engines was fitted. The compressors for the air tanks were converted to diesel power. Previously, this had been electrically powered and the modification reduced the strain on the electrical systems. These new submarines were of 67m (220ft) length overall (LOA), with a draught of 4.8m (15.6ft) and a displacement of 761 tons (surfaced) and had an endurance of 6,500 nautical miles (nmi) surfaced and 80nmi submerged. There were four torpedo tubes forward and one aft; the complement was forty enlisted men and four officers.[23] The Type VIIC U-boats proved to be a very successful design throughout the early part of the war.

The other submarine class that was sent against the American coast was the Type IX. These ships were designed as a longer-ranged vessel than the Type VII submarines. They were larger vessels and therefore more comfortable for the crew. The variants that were found off America were the 'B' and 'C' versions. They were 76.5m LOA and displaced 1,061 tons surfaced and 1,178 submerged. As armament, they carried a forward deck gun, a smaller one aft of the conning tower and an anti-aircraft gun on the conning tower, as well as four forward and two aft torpedo tubes. The Type C variants were a foot (0.3m) longer, 59 tons heavier surfaced and 54 tons heavier submerged. They both had crews of forty-eight.[24]

The primary weapon of the U-boats was the 533mm torpedo. This was the same model used for both submarine and surface warships. It measured 7.163m (23ft 6in) and had a 280kg (617lb) warhead made of torpex. They entered service in 1934. This torpedo came in two models. The first was the steam-driven, type G7a that had a maximum speed of 44 knots and a maximum range of 6,000m (6,600yds). It could also be set to a slow mode of 30 knots, which extended its range to 12,500m (13,700yds). However, the design was plagued by poor depth-keeping stability and tended to run under targets. These weapons' defects were not rectified until 1940. The other torpedo was the G7e. This was both more reliable and cheaper to produce. However, it had a maximum speed of 30 knots and had a range of only 5,000m (5,500yds). The torpedo's battery also required maintenance every three days. During the Norwegian campaign of April–May 1940 the U-boats missed a number of attacks on British capital ships due to faulty torpedoes. The exasperation of the U-boat crews led to an investigation that culminated in court martials of the leaders of the torpedo department. The torpedo detonators were also found to be faulty. Ultimately, the Germans were not able to circumvent this impediment. The torpedoes were refitted with contact exploders and these became the standard exploder until 1942. By the end of 1940 the torpedo failure rate fell to 13 per cent.

The Kriegsmarine's war before Operation Drumbeat
When war came with Great Britain the Kriegsmarine was unprepared to take on the navy of the British Empire. When Admiral Raeder was informed of the declaration of war he famously remarked that the German navy could 'do no more than show that they know how to die gallantly.' Dönitz was not quite so despondent. On 4 September he told his staff: 'Have no illusions about this war, it will last a long time, perhaps seven years, and we can be satisfied if we manage to end it with a draw.' At the opening of hostilities there was a total of twenty-four U-boats available for operations against Britain's shipping lanes. A formidable submarine construction programme was authorised in October 1939, but the first of these submarines were not in commission until the beginning of 1941. This construction programme was codified in 1938 as the 'Z Plan', which envisioned an unbalanced fleet. The navy's goal was to destroy England's commerce, not her navy, and so U-boats and battleships were the priorities. In February 1939 Hitler approved the plan. Over a period of nine years nine battleships, two battlecruisers, eight heavy cruisers, seventeen light cruisers, four aircraft carriers and 221 submarines of varying displacements were authorised. Hitler had further assured Raeder that war with Great Britain could be postponed until 1944, when the surface fleet would be substantially ready. U-boat construction was sporadic. There

were shortages of shipyard workers and torpedo-recovery vessels. This insufficient workforce resulted in poor work at the shipyards and it was not uncommon to have newly launched U-boats return to the yards for further work. For effective training, there was a need for considerably more torpedo-recovery vessels and due to their shortage the working-up period to get the crews and U-boats combat-ready was extended from ninety to 120 days.[25]

When war broke out the Kriegsmarine had two battlecruisers (*Scharnhorst* and *Gneisenau*), three pocket battleships, the heavy cruiser *Hipper*, about a score of destroyers and approximately twenty submarines, and with this fleet the Germans caused substantial damage to the English merchant marine, sinking over five hundred merchant ships in the first year of the war. The relationship between Raeder and Hitler was buoyed by these successes. There was never any serious attempt to link the U-boats and the surface fleet in an effort to diminish British naval hegemony as had been attempted in the First World War. Instead, for both Raeder and Dönitz, the aim of the Kriegsmarine regarding Britain was to prosecute a war against their sea lanes of communication. Between January and March 1942 a total of 533 Allied merchant ships were sent to the bottom, 242 of these by U-boats and another 203 to 'unknown causes', which were probably the result of submarine depredations. By June 1942 another 546 merchant ships had been sunk, 343 by U-boats, many of these off the American coast. Prior to Pearl Harbor, American insurance companies aided the U-boats immeasurably by openly transmitting information on convoy compositions and sailings with Swiss and British counterparts, to co-ordinate ship arrivals in Europe.[26]

The German government quickly retreated from prize rules for submarines. Newspapers rationalised the necessity to assume unrestricted submarine warfare. On 6 October 1939 a radio broadcast reported 'that the British Admiralty had ordered cargo steamers to ram German submarines on sight.' Later another broadcast stated that although the arming of merchants by the British was legal, if they used their guns they could be treated as warships. Here was a German restatement of the argument that Rickover had used before the war. The *Völkischer Beobachter*, an official publication of the Nazi Party, made a pithy assertion of the justification for unrestricted submarine warfare. It stated:

... that the crews of British passenger steamers are trained to fight submarines by gunfire and aggressive manoeuvres ... German submarines have sunk several British warships camouflaged as merchant ships ... If Great Britain scraps all rules of international warfare the responsibility for an intensification of commercial warfare at sea must be attributed to Britain.[27]

The German government declared a blockade zone around Great Britain from 17 August 1940. By 1 April 1941 it had been extended westward, past Iceland, which was now occupied by the Allies, to the territorial waters of Greenland. For the Kriegsmarine, the timorous attitude towards the United States inhibited operations. A minelaying mission was planned off Newfoundland. The mission conceived a U-boat and an auxiliary cruiser sowing a minefield off Halifax, but the high command prohibited the plan for fear of antagonising the Americans. In June, as U-boats swept across the Atlantic, they were inhibited from approaching the coast closer than the Grand Banks. Dönitz was able to get permission to send a U-boat, *U-111*, to patrol off the Newfoundland coast, between Cape Race and the Belle Isle Strait. Their orders prohibited any attacks unless upon extraordinary, valuable targets (such as the *Queen Mary* or warships of cruiser size or larger) and to maintain absolute radio silence. There was a suspicion that convoys were being routed north of the normal routes as the submarines deployed in the mid-Atlantic were finding a dearth of targets. Kapitän Wilhelm Kleinschmidt was ordered to take *U-11* to the Canadian coast and ascertain if the traffic was being diverted northward after leaving Canadian waters. He spent a week off the coast and encountered thick pack ice, but no convoys. When the U-boat returned to France he reported his findings to Dönitz and advised that it was his opinion that the convoys could not be sailing further north due to the heavy ice.[28]

The sortie by the battleship *Bismarck* and her consort, *Prinz Eugen*, in May 1941 from the Baltic was to be half of a grand commerce-raiding mission. Simultaneously, *Scharnhorst* and *Gneisenau* were to break out from Brest, France. However, the latter were unable to attack British trade routes: both *Gneisenau* and *Scharnhorst* sortied from Brest, but *Gneisenau* suffered damage due to heavy seas in the North Sea, and both ships put into Kiel as a consequence, scrubbing their portion of the operation. The four capital ships had been tasked with breaking out into the Atlantic to ravage the Allied Atlantic merchant shipping. *Bismarck* was sunk on 27 May 1941; *Prinz Eugen* retreated to France.[29]

The brunt of the war against English merchant shipping was conducted overwhelmingly by U-boats, but wolf-pack tactics could not be implemented until 1940 due to a dearth of boats. In October, Dönitz sent the first pack, comprising eight U-boats, to hunt in the waters between Iceland and the Faeroe Islands. It struck two convoys, SC7 and HX79. The next month, the pocket battleship *Admiral Scheer* sailed on a 161-day commerce-raiding cruise. January 1941 was not a happy start to the New Year for the English. Imports were less than half of what they had been a year before. The efforts of convoy escorts were not yet co-ordinated and their attacks on U-boats found to be menacing convoys were unco-ordinated. As the year progressed, the escort groups became more cohesive and competent.[30]

A more serious fetter on the U-boat's effectiveness came not from the Allies, but from Hitler. In September 1941 he ordered six U-boats to the Mediterranean Sea to interdict supplies going to the British army in Egypt. When these six were found to be inadequate in stemming the tide against the Afrika Korps, Hitler ordered another six to the Mediterranean. By the end of the year, all operational boats were either in the Mediterranean or in the western approaches to Gibraltar. Hitler then ordered nearly the entire German navy to Norway to protect the Scandinavian nation from an imagined Allied invasion. Eventually he relented and only ordered an additional eight submarines to the Arctic to buttress the seven that were on patrol there. Due to this diversion from what Dönitz felt was a sensible deployment of U-boats, he was only able to send five submarines to the East Coast of the United States when the Japanese unexpectedly bombed Pearl Harbor.[31]

The constriction of submarine operations due to the delicacy of placating American sensibilities hampered the U-boat's war against British shipping. On 17 September 1940 both Raeder and Dönitz appeared before the Führer to plead for the commencement of unrestricted warfare after the *Greer* 'incident' (see below). Although Hitler condoned the actions of Leutnant Fraatz in shooting at the American destroyer, he still adhered to a policy of restraint against American ships, regardless of the provocation. Dönitz asked that he be given a few weeks before a declaration of war against the United States, so he could plan for offensive action against the

East Coast.[32] Hitler consented, but the Japanese attack at Pearl Harbor was moving events at a faster pace.

On 17 October 1939 the pocket battleship *Deutschland* encountered the American steamer SS *City of Flint* in mid–Atlantic as she was steaming into the war zone approaching Great Britain. The Germans seized the ship, placed a prize crew aboard and sailed her to Norway, hoping to sail back circuitously to Germany, evading the British blockaders. At Tromsø the ship was permitted to take on water as allowed under international law, before sailing for Murmansk, where she arrived on 23 October. When she docked, the US Secretary of State, Cordell Hull, cabled a protest to Moscow arguing that a prize ship could only enter a neutral port to ameliorate an emergency condition. Once a ship was made seaworthy she was required to depart. If the ship remained, it was incumbent upon the host country to intern the captors and return the ship to her American captain and crew. The Soviets thence ordered the ship to sail. The ship departed and next anchored in Haugesund where the Norwegians honoured their obligations and restored the Americans to command of the ship and interned the Germans. The ship ultimately arrived at the Chesapeake Bay in January 1940 to the great embarrassment of the government in Berlin.[33]

German attacks against American and neutral shipping brought protests against Berlin. In reply, the Nazi government issued a statement justifying these attacks on neutrals before unrestricted submarine warfare was declared on 18 February 1940. The Nazis issued a list of justifications to attack neutral shipping. They issued a warning, explaining that following conditions that would warrant an attack on a neutral merchant ship:

1. Sailing in a convoy.
2. Sailing without ordinary lights or national markings.
3. Transmitting information of military value by wireless/radio.
4. Refusing to stop when ordered to do so by a German warship.[34]

The year 1940 constituted the first 'Happy Time' for the U-boat force. During the year 486 Allied merchant ships were sunk, amounting to more than 2.5 million tons. Two group attacks were mounted against the Atlantic shipping lanes. Group Prien, named for the group commander Günther Prien, commander of *U-47*, which had penetrated Scapa Flow and sunk HMS *Royal Oak*, was ordered to intercept convoy HX48 – it missed the convoy but did sink three stragglers. The second group, comprising five submarines, was named Rösing. The latter group missed its assigned convoy, and failed to make any sinkings. In August another group, including *U-47*, intercepted convoy SC2. Five ships were sunk, four of them falling to the submarine ace, Prien. On 21 September convoy HX72 was intercepted by a group of nine U-boats west of Ireland: eleven merchants were sunk under the escort of seven ASW vessels. In October a group of six submarines attacked SC7 over four days, sinking sixteen ships for 150,000 tons. The last convoy battle of the year took place in the North Atlantic. Convoy HX90 was ambushed by a small group of three boats in which six ships were sunk.

The next year began well for the Germans. In February convoy OB288 was attacked by four subs – eight ships representing 44,000 tons were sunk and another ship of 9,000 tons was damaged. However, March 1941 proved a bad month for the Ubootwaffe. Three leading aces were sunk, among them *U-47*. The cause of the sinking is unknown but the last radio message was received on 7 March. The Royal Navy corvettes *Arbutus* and *Camellia* sank *U-99*, captained by Otto Kretschmer, on 7 March, while *U-100*, Kapitäleutnant Joachim Schepke, was sunk on 17 March. She was rammed by HMS *Vanoc* after HMS *Walker* had initially attacked her. The month witnessed a precipitous decline in the number of sinkings by U-boats. In 1940 each U-boat was able to sink, on average, six Allied ships per month. One year later U-boats sank an average of less than two ships per month. During the same period U-boat losses escalated. By October the losses had mounted to six. Dönitz's concern was that the adherence to prize rules was hampering their operations and was impinging upon their safety. Dönitz had also in 1939 issued the following standing order for U-boat operations: 'Do not worry about lifeboats ... Concern yourself only with your own boat and the effort to achieve the next success as quickly as possible. We must be hard in this war.'[35]

In June 1941 an incident occurred that could have had catastrophic consequences for any attempt to keep the US out of the war in the Atlantic. On 20 June *U-203* sighted and manoeuvred to attack USS *Texas* but was unable to position herself to fire her torpedoes. The sinking of an American battleship, with a crew of over one thousand men could only hasten American entry into the war. The next day naval headquarters issued the following order to all forces at sea: 'The Führer has ordered that during the next few weeks all incidents with the USA are to be avoided ... Until further notice, only clearly identifiable enemy cruisers, battleships and aircraft carriers may be attacked.' In July, after the United States relieved the British in occupying Iceland, Raeder sought Hitler's acquiescence in rescinding the prohibition on attacking US ships. Hitler, instead, expanded it to include merchant shipping under the US flag within the blockade zone. The onus of determining a ship's nationality was, in effect, an order to cease attacking all shipping as it was often extremely difficult to determine a ship's nationality through the lens of a periscope. Hitler was convinced to moderate the prohibition and in August the order was reduced to permit attacks on destroyers and smaller warships in the blockade zone, which had been declared on 17 August 1940. Outside this zone, any clearly identified enemy ship could be attacked. The following month USS *Greer* was attacked off Iceland. Although Hitler accepted the rationale for firing torpedoes at the attacking US destroyer, he ordered that any attack was not to be responded to in kind unless it was clear it was by an enemy warship and not a US warship. Despite further incidents, these restrictions remained in force until the two countries were officially at war with one another.[36]

Despite the increasing tension between Germany and the United States, Hitler strove to maintain diplomatic relations with America. On 25 July 1941, at a conference between Hitler and Raeder, the admiral presented a situation report. Hitler decided that he would avoid war until there was a resolution to the campaign against the Soviet Union. This attitude was strained during the *Greer* incident. The response to the incident by the government in Berlin was subdued. Instead of lodging an official protest through the Foreign Ministry, a telegram was transmitted through the chargé d'affaires in Washington, DC, Hans Thomsen, on 6 September 1941, marked as 'most urgent'. Thomsen was instructed to seek the leaders of the isolationist camp in the Congress and 'in a suitably confidential manner, expose Roosevelt's war-mongering policy and thus deal it a decisive blow to the advantage of the isolationists.'[37] Three days later, Thomsen reported to Ribbentrop in Berlin that he had made clandestine contact with congressional leaders, sympathetic journalists and appropriate organisations and had started to propagate the isolationist viewpoint.

After the fall of France in June 1940 Lorient became available as a base for U-boats. This port was immediately southeast of Brest, the main naval base for the Atlantic French forces, and became a U-boat base from July 1940. This dramatically changed the conditions of the U-boat war. Now, instead of being required to enter the Atlantic by circumnavigating Great Britain, the German submarines had an egress directly into the Atlantic. The first U-boat to refuel from Lorient was *U-30*, which entered that port on 7 July 1940.[38]

On 24 August 1940 Dönitz reported on the progress of the war for the year, noting, however, that after twelve months of war the number of U-boats had not increased. In October 1939 Hitler approved a building programme to commission 352 U-boats per annum. By July 1940 this projected construction programme was reduced slightly to twenty-five submarines per month. In fact, the shipyards would launch on average half of this projection in a year. In sixteen months of war, sixty-two U-boats were commissioned. Approximately half of the submarines launched were only placed into commission after dealing with the flaws uncovered during trials.[39] He reported that as of 24 August, twenty-eight out of sixty-one operational submarines were lost. Of the 3,000 men of the Ubootwaffe, 1,200 had been lost.

The desire not to escalate any conflict with the United States remained the policy of the Nazi government up to the declaration of war on 11 December 1941. Once news of the Japanese bombing at Pearl Harbor was received in Germany, the timidity of the regime towards the United States evaporated. On 11 December 1941 Hitler protested in the Reichstag against the United States and its warmongering president. As evidence of the outrages against Germany, he cited the seven merchant ships that had been shadowed by American naval forces and 'forced' to scuttle to avoid capture. Hitler further alluded to the aggressive naval and military pressure by the United States in the Atlantic against German forces as proof of American perfidy. He denounced the 'taking over' of Iceland and Greenland and said that the attacks by *Greer* and *Kearny* were affronts to international law (he omitted to mention the sinking of *Reuben James*). He asserted that the German people were 'deeply satisfied' with the attack on Hawaii and noted the revelation in the *Chicago Tribune* newspaper of the US government's contingency plans for war as evidence of American bellicosity. He then declared war on behalf of the 'outraged' German people. Once the declaration of war was made manifest, all of the

153

restrictions on German forces regarding American ships were removed.[40] Drumbeat was about to be unleashed.

The Kriegsmarine had waged a war against British merchant shipping: this was its primary focus throughout the war. Certainly, the morale of the Ubootwaffe remained intact through Operation Drumbeat, although later in the war it did falter. Allied improvements in technology, the production of merchant ships and ASW craft, application of scientific methodology and other factors ultimately defeated the U-boats. By the time of the attack on the US East Coast the U-boats had experienced an initial 'Happy Time', and when Dönitz sent his six submarines against America for Operation Drumbeat, they were really on the defensive throughout the broader Atlantic. The opening-up of an attack on the US initially was met with great success, but once the American defences were organised and convoys instituted the German submarines were forced to retreat from the coast. Ultimately, the Ubootwaffe was thoroughly defeated.

9

Operation Drumbeat

After the declaration of war against the United States, Hitler and Raeder met to plan how they could damage their new adversary. Raeder felt that the Japanese attack would relieve pressure in the Atlantic, since the United States would transfer assets from the Atlantic to the Pacific. Due to the strictures that had been placed on U-boat operations in the western Atlantic and assignments elsewhere, there were no submarines ready to immediately assault America. However, planning was ordered for a U-boat assault on America, code name *Paukenschlag*. This translates loosely as a roll of the kettledrums as in a Wagnerian opera, hence 'Drumbeat'. Dönitz reported that he would need about a month to plan and implement the attack and he chose to deploy his six leading aces. During the intervening month, the US took rudimentary defensive measures. A minefield was laid off the Chesapeake Capes (the peninsula containing Delaware and a portion of Virginia), the approach to the naval base at Norfolk, Virginia, and boom nets for New York and other Atlantic ports were set.

Dönitz was not unfamiliar with the notion of an attack on the United States. In the 1920s he had studied a staff plan, which had been prepared in 1899 for a potential war with the United States. An invasion was theorised which presupposed naval superiority and surprise. Three battalions of infantry would invade New York harbour and a battalion of engineers would establish a beachhead on Long Island. From these bases, the navy and army would spread north to Boston and south to Norfolk. An alternative plan, the following year, envisioned the landing of an army of 100,000 men at Cape Cod after the initial seizures as in the 1899 plan. Neither the Kaiser nor the Führer gave these plans any consideration. A less grandiose plan that Hitler considered as late as May 1941 was to seize the Azores to use as an advanced bomber base. Once this was occupied, bombers could then bomb Manhattan across the Atlantic. Fortunately, no bomber was deployed that could reach America.

In February 1941 Hitler ordered the naval staff to conduct a feasibility study of a submarine assault on the major ports of the US Atlantic seaboard – Boston, New London, Newport, Hampton Roads and New York. The staff report concluded that given a state of alertness of the US Navy, an approach would have to be made submerged. This would have caused an insuperable strain on the U-boats' batteries and the staff concluded that a submarine assault was untenable. Dönitz thought this judgement timorous, for he held the United States' ASW capabilities in rather slighter regard.[1] As events unfolded, Dönitz was proven prescient.

The defence of the American seaboard from maritime threat was the responsibility of the navy. In order to organise a defence of the coast, the US Atlantic seaboard was organised as the Eastern Sea Frontier. The frontier was charged with defence of the coastal shipping traffic and enforcement of the nation's control of its territorial waters off the continental shore and the waters of the West Indies. The Eastern Sea Frontier was established on 1 July 1941 and composed of naval districts, numbered one to seven and encompassing the East Coast from Quoddy Head, Maine, to Key West, Florida. Its headquarters, and those of the Third Naval District, as well as the coastal liaison for the Army Air Force were all based at a building in Lower Manhattan, 90 Church Street. Merchant shipping, enemy contacts and location reports of air and surface units were all plotted there. Today this is a post office.

The commandant of the Eastern Sea Frontier was Vice Admiral Adolphus 'Dolly' Andrews. He retained command of the frontier through to the end of 1943. Morrison describes him as:

A sixty-two-year-old Texan, senatorial in port and speech, 'Dolly' Andrews had been on the active list for 41 years and was one of the best-known flag officers in the Navy. Presidents were one of his specialties; his friendship for President Roosevelt probably saved him from being the scapegoat for the burning of the *Normandie*, and certainly helped him to get things for his vital frontier ... His staff was exceptionally large but highly efficient, including Captain Thomas R Kurz (chief of staff),

Captain S B Bunting (assistant chief of staff), Captain John T G Stapler
(operations), Captains Harry E Shoemaker and Stephan B Robinson
(convoy and routing), Captain Ralph Hungerford (anti-submarine
warfare), Captain Henry M Mullinnix (air), and Lieutenant Commander
Harry H Hess (submarine tracking).[2]

Andrews had been assigned as commander of the Third Naval District
(New York City and environs) on 14 January 1941. He was installed as the
first commandant of the Eastern Sea Frontier on 10 March 1941, with
primary responsibility to organise and prepare the defence of the East
Coast. On 16 March 1941 Andrews circulated his first standing orders for
the defence of the coast, NA–NCF–44. This order established patrol areas,
sea-lane boundaries, tasks for available surface forces, means of harbour
defence, and the mechanisms whereby surface forces and aircraft were co-
ordinated. A final version of these orders was promulgated throughout the
frontier on 5 December 1941 as Plan 0–4. Two days later it was made
active.[3]

Between 14 and 31 December Admiral King had informed the CNO,
Admiral Stark, that there had been an observed decline in U-boat attacks
on transatlantic convoys. For King, this signalled preparations for an attack
elsewhere, and he suspected the attack to be along the US East Coast. He
also added: 'the weakness of our coastal defense force makes it essential
that the maximum practicable number of our destroyers be based at home
bases.'[4] Once King was ensconced as CNO, he did not act on his own
advice and the coast languished.

Under Rainbow War Plan 5 WPL–46, the general mandate for the
frontier was to execute the following tasks:

1. Defend the North Atlantic Naval Coastal Frontier.
2. Protect and Route Shipping.
3. Support the United States Fleet [An older name for the Atlantic
    Fleet].
4. Support the Army and associated forces within the Frontier.

In order to execute these mandates, Andrews announced these
clarifications:

A. Small enemy surface raiding forces may penetrate the coastal zone, either as disguised merchantmen or men of war.

B. Minor raids by air may be conducted by shipborne aircraft using bombs, torpedoes, mines.

C. Submarine activity may be expected with submarines operating against shipping with either torpedoes, mines or gunfire.

D. Effort may be made to penetrate harbors with small motor torpedo boats.

E. Large scale attacks will probably not occur unless the enemy manages to obtain a base within operating distance of the Frontier.[5]

Adolphus Andrews had a mixed reputation after forty years' service. Secretary of War Henry Stimson was dismissive of the admiral: he was a 'terrible old fusspocket'. NBC radio presenters Drew Pearson and Robert Allen described the admiral as a 'handsome, rather theatrical-looking officer somewhat nastily as "famous in Washington for his beautifully tailored clothes and for having been aide to Presidents of the United States."' But he had also served as chief of the Bureau of Navigation and had enjoyed various sea commands, including that of the Hawaiian Detachment. In 1942/43 he commanded the Eastern Sea Frontier, as such being in charge of the navy's anti-submarine operations therein. In that capacity he struck Stimson as 'perfectly useless'.[6]

The Eastern Sea Frontier had some aircraft assets. Once the war officially began, there were seven patrol wings organised for naval defence. These wings were each composed of four, twelve-plane squadrons. There were also two more wings in the process of forming. These patrol groups were composed almost entirely of Catalina (PBY-5A) seaplanes. However, these wings were intended to accompany the fleet and act as long-range scouts; they were equipped with their own tenders and maintenance crews. The Army Air Force had control of all long-range land-based bombers. Between 6 July 1942 and 9 October 1943 Andrews had six air groups operating at sixteen airfields throughout the command. He also had control over a lighter than air airship group at Lakehurst, New Jersey, and an air convoy escort group.[7]

Andrews had a foreboding of the imminent assault and he was disconcerted that the forces in his frontier were not adequate for the coming battle. On 22 December he wrote to the outgoing Chief of Naval

Operations, Admiral Stark: 'There is not a vessel available that an enemy submarine could not outdistance when operating on the surface. In most cases the guns of these vessels would be outranged by those of the submarine.' On 12 January 1942, the day of initiation of the U-boat assault on the East Coast, the Atlantic Fleet had destroyers spread from Brazil to Iceland. Thirty-nine destroyers and six *Treasury*-class Coast Guard cutters were assigned to five escort groups based at Argentia, Newfoundland, and Hvalfjörður, Iceland (although six destroyers were undergoing maintenance or repair in US East-Coast shipyards). Twelve destroyers were patrolling in the Gulf of Mexico and the Caribbean, with a further five operating near Bermuda. Five destroyers were assigned to patrol in the South Atlantic. A remaining nineteen destroyers were at dockside between Maine and Virginia.

However, Andrews did have one substantial asset. Every day he was forwarded an intelligence estimate, originating from the British Operational Intelligence Centre, in London, as filtered through Washington, DC. This estimate was the Royal Navy's best guess as to where the U-boats were stationed. On 7 January Admiral King's office telegraphed Admiral Andrews's headquarters, stating: There are strong indications that 16 German submarines are proceeding to the area off the southeast coast of Newfoundland. ——The object of this operation is not understood.' The next day the tanker SS *Cyclops* was torpedoed. The intentions of the German submarines were made plain by the merchant's sinking.[8] Throughout the assault the aforementioned nineteen destroyers remained docked, since they were designated to escort a troop convoy to Ireland. On 12 January a conference was held at headquarters that lasted until 02:00 the following day. A memorandum to the First Bomber Command informed them that at least four submarines were known to be operating three hundred miles east of New York's Long Island and were expected to be sailing westward. Despite this conference, US defences proved to be woefully inadequate.

First attacks

After the Japanese attack at Pearl Harbor, the country steeled itself for war. On the West Coast, newspapers were reporting that man-on-the-street interviews revealed a population that was confident of victory. On the East Coast there was little sense of crisis. There was a business-as-usual attitude

159

that pervaded the general population on the eastern seaboard, despite the drives to support Britain and the outbursts of conflict, for and against the Nazis. The navy made an effort to conceal the dire circumstances into which Operation Paukenschlag plunged the Allied war effort. Andrews's office both suppressed information about the extent of the damage wrought off the coast and magnified the efforts of ASW forces. On 23 January an announcement was made that a naval patrol plane had sunk a U-boat, but a public relations agent had made this claim without any corroboration. Between 1 January and 30 April 1942 only one U-boat was sunk in American waters, *U-85*. Through the first half of 1942, three U-boats were sunk within the Eastern Sea Frontier, one in April, another in May and a third in July. On 1 April the navy, in an attempt to obscure the extent of the devastation, issued a statement to the effect that there had been a total of twenty-eight submarines sunk by US forces, four by army planes and the rest by naval forces. In contrast to these public announcements, further releases downplayed the losses that had been inflicted on merchant shipping. On 11 March the public affairs office announced that henceforth announcements of sinkings would be 'limited'. According to the press office, as of that date twenty-eight ships had been sunk by U-boats in American waters, while the actual number was ninety-one.[9]

The first attack by a U-boat deployed for Operation Drumbeat was made by *U-123*, commanded by Kapitänleutnant Reinhard Hardegen, on 12 January 1941. The British steamer *Cyclops* was torpedoed and sunk approximately three hundred miles off the Chesapeake Capes.[10] The East Coast of the United States was under attack. The port of New York, the busiest port in the world, was now the target of Germany's submarine assault.

U-123 struck again two days later, off Cape Cod. The 9,577-ton, Panamanian-flagged tanker *Norness* was carrying a cargo of 12,200 tons of oil to Liverpool. Three torpedoes sent her to the bottom, although a total of five were fired. Two men were killed and the remaining thirty-nine crewmen made it safely into the two lifeboats or a raft. The ship sank in twenty-seven minutes, but not before relaying an emergency radio signal. However, no warship or aircraft scrambled to meet the attacking submarine. The next day the troop transport convoy, Task Force 15, sailed. This was composed of a battleship, an aircraft carrier, three cruisers and eighteen destroyers. It was these destroyers' commitment to the task force

160

that stripped the coast of its ASW vessels. However, the task force delivered 4,508 soldiers to Iceland and Ireland without mishap.[11]

The following day U-123 was in the approaches to New York City where her captain had been before. When Hardegen was a cadet (class of 1933), he had visited New York and was much taken with the city. While he was watching from his submarine's conning tower, he was hit by a feeling of nostalgia. He wrote: 'it was unbelievably beautiful and great ... We were the first to be here, and for the first time in this war a German soldier looked out upon the coast of the USA.' As U-123 crept shoreward, a tanker was sighted approaching from astern. The British tanker, Coimbra, of 6,768 tons was returning to England, unescorted, with a cargo of 9,000 tons of lubricating oil. A torpedo was fired into the ship and she erupted into fire, gun crews racing to their weapons. Another torpedo struck amidships and she broke in half.[14.] She sank approximately twenty-seven miles from the Long Island town of Southampton. Dozens witnessed the glow from the fiery destruction of the tanker. When U-123 returned to France, Dönitz, as was his custom, met the boat as it docked and awarded Hardegen the Knight's Cross. Dönitz entered the following comment on the U-boat's patrol log: 'Very well thought-out and executed patrol – a brilliant success. The commander has taken full advantage of the first appearance off the coast of North America by his dash and tenacity.'[12]

Between January and May 1942, thirty U-boats operated in US waters and sank 360 ships, amounting to 2,250,000 tons. Of these thirty submarines, five were allocated to Operation Drumbeat, the initial surge to the East Coast of America. The cost on the German side for this destruction was the loss of eight submarines. To maintain this 'Second Happy Time' as it was known, the U-tanker U-459, or 'milch-cow', sailed to American waters. She arrived on station in mid-April. From 19 April to 5 May she revictualled twelve U-boats. A second milch-cow took station in the western Atlantic and resupplied an additional six submarines.

U-boats deployed to the East Coast carried sufficient supplies to operate for two weeks. The typical tactic was to approach the offshore shipping lanes at night and wait on the surface for the passing traffic. As a target passed before the U-boat, the lights from coastal cities silhouetted it. The navy had considered a plan to reduce coastal illumination before the U-boat assault – the Third Naval District promulgated an Illumination Control Plan, calling for a blackout of shore lights in New York City and the nearby communities. All lighthouses, beacons and aids to navigation lights should be extinguished. However, the plan called for this to be implemented in the case of air raids. A 'request' was made for illumination to be curtailed at shore-side communities on 18 December. A few towns in New Jersey 'considered' complying with this request. Shore-side communities were loath to turn off these lights, arguing that this would impinge on tourism and thus damage local communities' economies. Coastal communities' illumination was within the province of the army, but did not seem significant to jeopardise army–community relations – the lights were not ordered off until April, when sufficient devastation had been wrought. On 18 April 1942 the army's Eastern Defense Command ordered all lights to be extinguished at night.[13]

The five U-boats assigned for Operation Drumbeat each had designated patrol areas. It took three weeks to cross the Atlantic from Lorient, and the U-boats sailed between 23 and 27 December. *U-123* was to patrol off Long Island and the approaches to New York City. *U-66* was assigned the southernmost area, off Cape Hatteras. *U-125* was assigned the area off New York and New Jersey. *U-130* was to operate off Nova Scotia and Newfoundland. *U-109* was ordered to hunt in the waters of the Gulf of St Lawrence.[14]

As the campaign progressed, the Germans became emboldened by the porousness of the American defences, the submarines even remaining on the surface during daylight to make their attacks. In the two weeks of the initial attack, thirteen ships, nearly three-quarters of which were tankers, were sunk between New York City and Cape Hatteras, North Carolina, amounting to 95,000 tons of shipping.

Admiral Andrews, as Commandant of the Eastern Sea Frontier and responsible for the entire eastern seaboard of the United States, had negligible forces at his command at the start of the German campaign. Due to the pre-war accord with the Army Air Force, army planes conducted anti-submarine patrols and a total of nine planes were available when the U-boats struck: three at Westover, Massachusetts, three at Langley Field near Hampton Roads, Virginia, and three at Mitchell Field on Long Island. By 1 April 1942 this force had been buttressed to nineteen bases with eighty-four army and eighty-six navy planes, a result of allocations from new construction. For surface forces Andrews had at his disposal the following craft: four patrol yachts (PY), four submarine chasers (SC), one 165ft Coast Guard cutter, six 125ft Coast Guard cutters, two patrol gunboats (PG) and three Eagle boats (anti-submarine vessels).[15] An early measure taken within the Eastern Sea Frontier – and a failure – was the Ship Lane Patrol, which Andrews ordered at the end of January. This was reminiscent of the patrolling conducted during the First World War, whereby escort vessels would patrol the shipping lanes of the convoys along the coast. Among the craft used were 83ft Coast Guard cutters. However, as tanker sinkings prompted gasoline rationing, it was ordered that these cutters operate a 'drifting patrol' once they arrived on station. These patrols contributed nothing to beat back the U-boats.

However, by April 1942 there were the following forces available for ASW patrol: twenty-three 90ft and forty-two 75- or 83ft Coast Guard patrol vessels, three 173ft patrol craft, twelve Eagle boats (from the First World War) and fourteen Royal Navy ASW trawlers lent by the British, but crewed by US naval personnel. The Royal Navy also operated twenty-three ASW trawlers, off the Gulf of Mexico and the eastern seaboard. Although these trawlers were crewed by former British merchant sailors enlisted into the Royal Navy, they operated as part of the Eastern Sea Frontier and were subject to American orders.[16] The Atlantic Fleet, based at Norfolk, Virginia, reassigned six destroyers to the Eastern Sea Frontier in the first week of April 1942. Of these, USS *Hambleton* and USS *Emmons* were assigned a patrol area off Cape Hatteras, where British intelligence reported five U-boats were operating, and they arrived on station on 2 April. This area contained the largest concentration of U-boats.

On 4 April *U-160* was cruising in the vicinity of Cape Hatteras and dived underneath the two destroyers, which sailed by oblivious of the predator's presence.[17] The next day the American–flagged tanker *Bidwell* was targeted by the submarine as she sailed unescorted northwards. The two destroyers spotted the plume of fire and smoke rising from the single torpedo that exploded against the tanker and raced back to help the stricken ship. Although they did not locate the U-boat, their presence thwarted any further attack. The crew surveyed the damage and found the ship to be salvageable. Steam was raised and she was able to proceed to New York under her own power. By 9 April the destroyers concluded their patrol and returned to Norfolk. During the course of the two destroyers' patrol, they had neither spotted nor engaged any submarines.

The months of February and March 1942 were difficult ones for shipping off the coast. By February sinkings had accumulated to 100,000 tons since the assault in January. There was such a surfeit of available targets in the form of unprotected shipping that the submarines were able to husband their torpedoes for the most attractive ones. Up to 7 March there seemed to be a respite in the sinkings off the coast, but through the next two weeks a further twenty-one ships were destroyed. On the 16th four ships were sunk in one day and the average for the whole month of March was three ships sunk per day. In response, on 12 March Admiral Andrews recommended the 'scarecrow patrols'. He would send civilian aeroplane patrols over the coast as a way to curtail some of the U-boats' freedom. Admiral King did not approve the idea for logistical reasons but the destruction continued without abatement. In the Eastern Sea Frontier War Diary Andrews wrote: 'Should this warfare continue as it has begun, it is possible to anticipate not only profound dislocations of our domestic economy but the retarding of the entire war effort of the Allies as well.'[18]

During the course of the first week of April, eight U-boats off the Atlantic frontier sank ten merchant ships, totalling 66,026 tons, and damaged another two, amounting to a further 13,894 tons, which made it to port for repairs. The senior officer aboard the two destroyers, Commander Charles Wellborn, Jr, the division commanding officer, wrote in his action report: 'It will be extremely rare for patrolling destroyers to make actual contact with a submarine in which an alert submarine commander attempts to avoid contact ... The submarine menace on our Atlantic coast can be defeated only through the operation of a coastal convoy system.'[19] After four months, the existing tactics were proving fruitless.

First Bomber Command

The principal Army Air Force formation on the East Coast at the time of the US entry to the war and throughout the U-boat attack on the United States was the First Bomber Command, under Brigadier General Arnold Krogstad. This unit had a force of fifty bombers, nine of which were the long-range B-17s. The remainder of the aircraft were medium-range B-25s and 26s. On the day after the bombing at Pearl Harbor, two plane patrols flew from each of the East Coast bases. These bases were at Bangor, Maine; Westover Field, Massachusetts; Mitchel Field, New York; and Langley

Field, Virginia. The aircraft were not well suited for ASW patrols, having no effective bombsights or radar, no aerial depth charges and crews with no training in hunting submarines. Another considerable handicap was that the ASW role of the command was not codified. Prior to the war, there had been a tug-of-war between the navy and army over responsibility for ASW patrols by aircraft over the coast. The planes operated ASW patrols as an emergency measure and at any time they could be ordered to revert to their primary mission and training, attacking potential land targets. The ambiguity of the authority for ASW patrolling can be dated to 1920. In that year Congress legislated 'that Army aviation should control all aerial operations from land bases and that naval aviation should control all such activity attached to the Fleet, including the maintenance of such shore installations as were necessary for operation, experimentation, and training connected with the Fleet.' There was some clarification in 1935. Regulation FTp-155 affirmed that naval aviation could be used to support the Fleet as above and had authority for all inshore and offshore patrolling to protect shipping and to defend the coast. Also, army aircraft could be used to temporarily perform naval aviation functions.[20]

However, the navy did nothing to prepare for its role in ASW patrolling along the Eastern Sea Frontier. During pre-war training off the Atlantic coast, the only contingency exercised against was an enemy task force of surface ships supported by carrier-borne aircraft raiding the coast. When the U-boats began to prowl the sea off the coast, there was no doctrine to combat them with naval aviation. The joint chiefs of staff ultimately decided the matter on 26 March 1942. They issued an order to all commanding generals of defence commands. It read, in part:

> Joint Action of the Army and Navy, 1935, is hereby vested in Sea Frontier Commands over all Navy forces duly allocated thereto and over all Army air units allocated by defense commanders over the sea for the protection of shipping and for antisubmarine and other operations ... Defense commanders will allocate Army air units on full time basis but may rotate them in not less than two week periods as requisite for essential training.[21]

On 8 December First Bomber began ASW patrols. Planes patrolled approximately forty miles off the coast from Portland, Maine, to Wilmington, North Carolina. These planes had an endurance to support

165

patrols of two to three hours. In January 1942 this force was reduced further. There were four bombing groups on the East Coast at the start of the war. Three heavy (B–17s and 18s) groups and one medium (B–25s and 26s). Within three months after Pearl Harbor's bombing, three of these groups were detached and transferred to the Pacific, two to Australia and one to the West Coast, due to the apprehension that the West Coast was in immediate peril.

Slaughter off the coast

By February 1942 the cumulative sinkings of merchant shipping in the Eastern Sea Frontier passed 100,000 tons. Total number of sinkings for the month was fourteen and occurred everywhere along the East Coast. In response, shipping was ordered to anchor at night and harbours along the coast were mined. A ship could steam from Jacksonville, Florida, to New York in four daylight runs. However, submarines would now lay in wait off these protected anchorages, stalking the ships as they got underway at dawn. Three U–boats maintained a patrol off of Cape Hatteras in February which became the most fertile killing field.

Admiral Andrews began to introduce substantial defensive measures in February in response to the destruction emerging off the coast. He instituted anti-submarine patrols by destroyers between the 6th and 8th of the month, despite this tactic having been found ineffective in the First World War. He asked to use fifteen destroyers from those already in the Western Atlantic, assigned for coastal defence and was afforded seven, temporarily: *H P Jones*, *Roe*, *Ludlow*, *Wainwright*, *Mayrant*, *Trippe* and *Rowan.* These were deployed along the coast, three concentrated in the Norfolk area. These ships were temporarily assigned to Andrews while they were waiting to be used as escorts or other assignments. When Andrews asked King for a more durable assignment of forces, King denied him. King wrote to Andrews: 'A review of the situation indicates that it would be inadvisable to detach any vessels from their present duty with the fleets, at least until additional new construction destroyers have been commissioned and have joined'.[22]

On 4 February the tanker ss *India Arrow* was torpedoed and sent a distress call that was received at 18:58, thirteen minutes after having been hit. The ship's owners estimated that the ship was off the coast of New Jersey and a patrol vessel was immediately dispatched while a request was made for a plane from Langley Field, Virginia, to patrol for the U-boat. The controllers at the Army Air Force field replied that they could not even say if they had a plane on patrol in the area without the permission of the commander of the North Atlantic Naval Coastal Frontier. The reporting structure was convoluted. A sighting would be relayed from an airbase (ie Langley Field) to a district headquarters (ie the Fifth Naval District, Virginia) by direct telephone line. Any report by ASW patrol bombers would go directly to the Eastern Sea Frontier headquarters. The Sea Frontier would then have to call appropriate districts for the dispatch of airborne ASW forces. However, by the time the information was relayed for the dispatch of these forces, the information was too out of date to be pertinent.[23] A submarine sighting would be called to district headquarters. This headquarters would then contact the Eastern Sea Frontier in New York. Then the frontier command would call the district headquarters back with orders to pursue the contact.

Sequence of Airborne ASW sighting and attack procedures:
I.   Aircraft sighting of submarine – reports to airfield.
II. Airfield reports to Naval District headquarters.
III. District headquarters reports contact Eastern Sea Frontier.
IV. The Sea Frontier then authorises an attack to the district headquarters.
V.   The Naval District Headquarters then orders an attack from the airfield in closest proximity to the sighting.

On 23 January Andrews had requested one destroyer be assigned to the frontier, at Hampton Roads, and USS *Roe* was deployed for ten days' duty. By 5 February an additional six escorts were assigned to Andrews. Within two weeks, however, they were reassigned and sent to Iceland. As in the First World War, the priority for ASW and escort vessels was the protection of troopships and convoys. Destroyers were assigned to the frontier as a stopgap. Once the escorts were assigned to troopship sailings, these had priority over the defence of the Atlantic seaboard. As compensation, four destroyers were assigned to the frontier temporarily by the end of February between tasks. The usefulness of these dispositions was marginal, because the continual assignment to the frontier and then removal never afforded sufficient stability for the ships

167

to attain any ASW proficiency. A policy was instituted on 8 March that whenever a destroyer was on the coast for repair or refit, they would be placed under Andrews's command for the purpose of patrolling the threatened coast. Fourteen destroyers were assigned to the frontier over the course of the month. These assignments facilitated sixty-three days of patrolling through March. This varied from one day to eighteen per destroyer. Overall, this was trying to get the work of two destroyers from one. The average time a destroyer spent in the frontier on patrol during March was two days. There was a concomitant loss in the efficiency of these ships.[24] Instead of using the time allocated on the coast for relaxation by the crew, or repairing and refurbishing these vessels, the navy tried to use these vessels on operations without a let-up. Over time, this ceaseless employment ground down the ships' material well-being and exhausted the crews.

Though the initial operations of U-boats off the East Coast in January were devastating, there was a foreboding that worse was to come. The Situation Room at the British Operational Intelligence Centre sent its assessment for the week ending 9 February. It was bleak. They had lost the ability to read the naval Enigma messages, which meant that deployments could not be accurately scrutinised. However, the Royal Navy's HF/DF tracking indicated, through picking up U-boat radio signals, that at least ten submarines were making their way across the Atlantic. The navy had no ASW vessels that it could assign for a dedicated defence for the coming assault.

As the devastation mounted, Admiral King wrote a memorandum proposing that the navy take control of all ASW forces, both navy and army air assets in June 1942. Secretary of War Stimson rejected this, as he supported the autonomy of the Army Air Force. The ASW assets being an organic part of the AAF establishment, he would not countenance their detachment. General Marshall, the chairman of the joint chiefs of staff, then proposed that the joint chiefs of staff create an overall anti-submarine command, answerable to the joint chiefs. This command would incorporate both air and surface forces, but this time Admiral King rejected the proposal as an infringement against the navy's autonomy. Admiral King's notions of ASW were spelled out in his memorandum of June as follows:

1. All-out attack mounted from Britain on German building yards and submarine bases.
2. Operational: Bring all shipping under escort and air cover.
3. Tactical: Introduction of hunter-killer system.
4. Institutional: Training of personnel in the specific techniques of anti-submarine warfare.
5. Organisational: Unification of all antisubmarine warfare activities under control exercised by himself.

The problem for King, as it was for Andrews, was the dearth of escorts, both ships and aircraft, but he urged, 'Do the best you can with what you have.'[25]

In late February the destroyer USS *Jacob Jones* was assigned to Andrews. She had been escorting ships across the Atlantic and underwent an overhaul in New York. On 27 February 1942 her captain, Lieutenant Commander Hugh Black, reported to Andrews that his ship was ready for duty. She was assigned to anti-submarine patrol between New Jersey and Virginia and by 28 February at 05:00 she was conducting a patrol in her assigned area off the Delaware Capes. She was not zigzagging and the crew was in 'condition 2' (with one-third of the crew on stand-by). *U-578* spotted the destroyer and launched torpedoes. Two torpedoes hit and the resulting explosions blew off everything forward of her bridge, as well as her transom. As the after-part of the ship sank, the depth charges exploded, killing some of the men by then in the water. Twelve men survived, though one died as the rescuing ship USS *Eagle* brought the survivors to Cape May, New Jersey. This was the first warship sunk by the enemy in the Eastern Sea Frontier.[26]

During March twenty-eight merchant ships were sunk in the Eastern Sea Frontier for a loss of 159,340 tons. Merchant marine crews' morale was deteriorating and schedules were disrupted. On 16 March Admiral King ordered a conference be convened to discuss convoying. For the first time during this assault, the US Navy was taking the situation off the East Coast as an urgent problem. Representatives from the Eastern, Gulf and Caribbean Sea Frontiers and the Atlantic Fleet were ordered to meet in Washington, DC. On 27 March a report was sent to the commander-in-chief, Admiral King, which emphasised the fact that an average of thirty-five ships left the Gulf and Caribbean for northern ports daily; it concluded that a convoy of forty to fifty ships should be organised every three days.

The recommendations proposed the establishment of a Gulf terminal at Key West, Florida, and another at Guantanamo, Cuba. Ships that could sail at more than 15 knots and those that could do no more than 10 knots were to sail independently. After sailing during the day and anchoring at protected roads during the night, the convoys would arrive off the Virginia Capes where they would split up. Some would proceed to Norfolk and the Chesapeake Bay, while those continuing north would split and turn for Philadelphia once they arrived off the Delaware Capes later the same day. The next day (the fifth since departing Key West) the remaining ships would either sail for New York, or continue northward and eventually arrive at Boston, where they would form up with ships bound for Halifax and thence across the Atlantic for Britain. Southbound shipping would follow the same plan in reverse. Six escort groups would be required, with two replenishing in port while four escorted shipping along the coast. It was estimated this would entail thirty-one destroyers, and forty-seven corvettes/patrol craft. Admiral King's office returned the report to the conference on 27 March, with the suggested timetable that the Key West–New York convoys should be ready by 15 May and the Caribbean convoys by July. These plans were all well and good. However, Admiral King told the conference that escorts in sufficient numbers to make their plans viable would not be available until mid-May. Andrews would be the commander of all escort forces assigned between Boston and the Caribbean. On the day that King's office responded to the report, the available forces amounted to three destroyers on temporary duty, three patrol craft and five sub-chasers.[27]

The forerunner of what would eventually defeat the assault was the formation of an interim rudimentary convoy system. Admiral Andrews insisted that there were inadequate numbers of escorts. His position was that a poorly protected convoy was worse than none at all. In a reply to Admiral King asking his opinion about establishing coastal convoys, Andrews advised 'that no attempt be made to protect coastwise shipping by a convoy system until an adequate number of suitable escort vessels is available.' Andrews was not just a 'naysayer' – he did have recommendations. He recommended the following steps be taken in lieu of a 'premature' convoy system:

A. Every possible use be made of inland waters and canals.

B. Ships be routed as close inshore as safe navigation permitted with schedules so arranged that particular danger points would be passed during daylight.

C. Coastwise lanes be given every possible protection with every type of available plane and craft.

D. If the enemy abandoned his present method of offshore sinkings to operate against inshore lanes, daylight runs between such points as New York and Delaware Capes, and Hampton Roads be instituted with concentration of patrol around Hatteras.

E. All shipping, including overseas shipping to and from the West Indies, South America and Cape Town be routed along the coastal B. lanes since escort vessels were not available for ships routed offshore.

F. Coastal convoy from Cape Cod to Halifax be instituted.

He went on to emphasise that convoys should only be introduced if these measures failed and that convoys should not be established unless there was a sufficient number of escorts available, which he figured at sixty-four, which was more than twice the number then available.[28] Andrews therefore argued that convoying was a last resort.

However, on 1 April he relented and a partial convoy system was inaugurated. Ships moved from one protected anchorage to another, escorted by whatever local escort crafts were available. They steamed during the day, as close to the shore as possible, and then anchored in a protected anchorage for the night. Conveniently, good anchorages along the East Coast were spaced approximately 120 miles apart north of Cape Hatteras. Andrews aptly termed this effort the 'bucket brigade'. However, as Andrews asserted, there was a dangerous dearth of escorts. Approximately 120–130 merchant ships steamed along the coast daily. To escort them Andrews had a total of twenty-eight surface vessels available within the frontier. Every escort vessel on escort duty stripped an escort from defending harbours. During the first four months of 1942, eighty-two merchant ships were sunk, equalling a half million tons, within the Eastern Sea Frontier.[29]

The establishment of the 'bucket brigade' was merely a stopgap, so Admiral King appointed a board to lay plans for a formal convoy system. This board was composed of representatives from Cominch, Cinclant, and

171

the commanders of the Eastern, Gulf and Caribbean Sea Frontiers. On 27 March 1942 the board presented their recommendations to Admiral King. On 2 April Admiral King made a few minor changes and then passed these recommendations to Admiral Andrews for implementation. This implementation included oceanic convoys from Halifax to Guantanamo and coastal convoys from Key West to New York. The board calculated that a convoy of forty-five ships would require three days to complete a transit from Key West to New York. To escort this agglomeration of merchant shipping would require thirty-one destroyers and forty-seven corvettes or patrol boats. These escorts were more than the navy had available. The report stated that each convoy should have at least five escorts, two of which should be destroyers. The ASW vessels should be able to make 18 knots. The escorts should have sound detection gear (18 knots is the maximum at which the gear would function) and depth charges.[30] Once Andrews accepted these recommendations, Admiral Ingersoll transferred ships to the Eastern Sea Frontier from the Atlantic Fleet. The escort ships were organised into six groups of seven ships each. Each escort group consisted of two destroyers, two ASW trawlers and three miscellaneous escort ships. By the end of May, a complete convoy system was established, extending from Key West to Halifax and back. Once the interlocking convoy system was functioning, sinkings in the Eastern Sea fell from twenty-three in April to three in July. In the following months the sinkings ceased completely.

The Atlantic Fleet's destroyers were deployed on either troop convoy escort or capital ship escorting operations. These operations devoured more than fifty destroyers. The ASW assets of the Atlantic Fleet were already stretched so thin that there were few resources available to protect the Atlantic seaboard, in addition to escorts assigned for transatlantic merchant convoys.[31]

The beginning of April saw eight destroyers on duty. However, by 9 April only *Herbert* and *Noa* remained, as the other ships were temporarily assigned and sent to other duties. On 16 April King ordered the Atlantic Fleet to assign three destroyers and to make others available, as it was practicable, to bring the total to nine. Throughout the month there was an average of six destroyers on ASW duty in the frontier. Their orders were to patrol for enemy submarines and no mention was made of convoying or escorting merchant shipping. Despite responding to merchant ships' reports of U-boats, none of the destroyers actually made contact with any. Typical of these patrols were the experiences of USS *Hambleton* and USS *Emmons*. The commanding officer of Destroyer Division 19, of which *Hambleton* and *Emmons* were assigned, made the observation that, 'While patrolling operations of this type are of some value in combatting enemy submarine activities, the submarine menace on our Atlantic Coast can only be defeated through the operation of a coastal convoy system.'[32]

On 8 April Andrews wrote to King that the Eastern Sea Frontier, as it was then established, was not tenable. He wrote: 'this frontier, as established, does not meet present war conditions for the following reasons':

1. Commandants of Naval Districts are so preoccupied with other district activities that they can give but little attention to military and Frontier matters. The U-boat activities along the coast show clearly that the handling of forces to combat the menace requires the full time and immediate attention of local operating commanders.
2. As a result of conflicting duties, the authority of District Commandants is delegated to subordinates – either retired or reserve officers – not fully experienced or competent to handle situations that arise and not fully prepared to make decisions without reference to Commandants.
3. The inclusion of Army Air Forces within the Frontier structure makes it highly desirable that officers actually exercising command should be active officers of high rank.[33]

Admiral King approved these observations by Andrews that sea frontier commandants could delegate to task force/group commanders authority for both air and surface forces conducting ASW operations on 2 May. These officers were drawn from the ranks of the regular line officers.

In May a new surge of nine U-boats arrived off the East Coast, extending from Newfoundland southward through the American East Coast to the Caribbean. The U-boats were *U-504*, *U-158*, *U-172*, *U-68*, *U-159*, *U-157*, *U-373*, *U-87* and *U-701*, and had sailed from France between 2 and 19 May. Eleven minefields were sown off the major ports by U-boats throughout the entire campaign. The only significant damages occurred when, on 12 June 1942, *U-701* laid fifteen mines off the Chesapeake Capes. One tanker, one coal barge and an ASW trawler were sunk, and the destroyer USS *Bainbridge* and another tanker were damaged subsequently. Another minefield at the Chesapeake Capes claimed a tugboat. Five fields were swept before there was any damage done, and the remaining fields were so badly laid that they were not discovered until German records indicated their location.[34] It was from a minefield that the port of New York suffered the only closure experienced during the war, between 12 and 14 November 1942, while the minefield was cleared.

It was not until March that US forces in the western Atlantic destroyed any U-boat, and this occurred on 1 March at the hands of a Lockheed-Hudson from Squadron VP-82 based in Argentia, Nova Scotia. While flying off Cape Race, Newfoundland, Ensign William Tepuni sighted *U-656*, under the command of Kapitänleutnant Ernst Kröning, on the surface. The U-boat's lookouts spotted the approaching aeroplane, but it was too late. As the submarine was crash-diving, the plane's depth charges found their mark and destroyed the U-boat. The destroyer USS *Roper* sank another on the night of 13 April. She was steaming southwards from Norfolk at 18 knots when her radar signalled a contact at 2,700yds. She increased speed to 20 knots and closed with the target. A torpedo passed the ship about 700yds distant. When the destroyer had closed to a range of 300yds, the searchlight was turned on and the contact was discovered to be a U-boat. *Roper* opened fire with every weapon that would bear (3in cannons and machine guns) and the U-boat crew found themselves unable to man their guns under the destroyer's fusillade. As *U-85* started to dive, shells were seen to penetrate the hull and then once it was under water, depth charges were dropped; in the morning, twenty-nine bodies were recovered. The U-boat was on its second deployment to United States waters, and had been in commission since June 1941.

The US Coast Guard also had some success: USCG *Icarus* successfully engaged a U-boat on the afternoon of 9 May after their sound gear discovered *U-352* lurking in shallow waters off Cape Lookout. The submarine fired a torpedo at the cutter, which missed. The cutter dropped depth charges and damaged the submarine, which then surfaced. The crew surrendered to the Coast Guard cutter before scuttling their boat.[35]

Another German casualty was *U-701*, under the command of Horst Degen, which had left Lorient on 20 May to take up an assigned patrol area between Chesapeake Light and a point fifteen miles south of Cape Lookout. The first sign that the U-boat was present was when two torpedoes were fired, both of which missed, at a southbound freighter on 16 June. On 19 June the submarine was engaged by the patrol craft *YP-389* off Cape Hatteras, but the latter's 3in cannon jammed and a depth charge failed to explode, and she was quickly sunk.

Subsequently, a tanker was damaged and another was sunk on 28 June off Cape Hatteras, North Carolina. However, *U-701*'s luck had run out. On 7 July an Army Air Force Hudson Lockheed out of Cherry Point, North Carolina, caught her surfaced thirty miles from the Diamond Shoals lightship. The plane dropped three depth charges while the U-boat was still diving and she was sunk in approximately 50ft of water. Eighteen men were rescued, eleven drowned, and the remaining crew drifted until a blimp sighted them fifty hours later. A rubber raft and provisions were dropped, and seven of the crew were then rescued by a Coast Guard seaplane. Through the course of the war, the Coast Guard rescued 1,658 shipwrecked mariners off the US Atlantic coast. From the start of the German assault in January through to July, eight U-boats were sunk in waters under the command of the US Navy off the coast.[36]

On 15 June Dönitz reported to Hitler that profitable work could still be done off the American East Coast. He cited poor American defences, the destruction of tankers and the inadequacy of Allied new merchant ship construction to replace losses as making conditions off the coast very favourable. Any widening of a gap between merchant sinkings and construction damaged the Allies' war-making capacity. From January to July 1942 a total of forty-three tankers were destroyed, representing a loss of 331,012 tons. Of these, twenty-eight ships were American tankers amounting to 220,909 tons.[37] During an interview with a reporter in the summer of 1942 Dönitz said: 'Our submarines are operating close offshore along the coast of the United States of America, so that bathers and sometimes entire coastal cities are witness to that drama of war, whose visual climaxes are constituted by the red glorioles of blazing tankers.'[38]

On 19 June General George Marshall wrote to Admiral King, admonishing the admiral. He wrote: 'The losses by submarines off our Atlantic seaboard, and in the Caribbean now threaten our entire war effort … I am now fearful that another month or two of this will so cripple our means of transport that we will be unable to bring sufficient men and planes to bear against the enemy in critical theaters to exercise a determining influence on the war.'[39]

Losses to U-boats in the Eastern Sea Frontier

Month	Numbers sunk	Tonnage lost per month
January	14	95,670
February	17	102,846
March	28	159,340
April	23	133,184
May	5	23,326
June	13	73,585

Note: From January through April, the Eastern Sea Frontier had the greatest losses to U-boats of any theatre of operations.[40]

The losses of merchant sailors (5,000 sailors from all the Allied nations) during the first six months of 1942 surpassed the total losses for the US throughout the First World War, which amounted to less than seven hundred.[41]

The repercussions of the losses

The eighty-two ships sunk during the first four months of 1942, amounting to the loss of nearly half a million tons, were made up mostly of coastal traffic and vessels trading with Latin America. Sugar and coffee rationing were introduced, but worse still, each month 3.5 per cent of the total operating American tanker tonnage was lost. Churchill cabled Harry Hopkins on 12 March lamenting these tanker losses. Shortages of oil were beginning to be felt in the United States' vital industrial northeast, where rationing, especially of gasoline, was imposed by June. Military operations in North Africa and other theatres were imperilled. Frustration was expressed by the American army. A general in the war plans division lamented to Dwight Eisenhower in a letter dated 12 March: 'One thing that might help win this war is to get someone to shoot King.'[42]

Frustration was also felt by the British. The Royal Navy had tried to advise the US Navy. Commander Rodger Winn was sent to Washington,

DC, in the summer of 1942 to recreate his submarine tracking room and to press King to institute convoying. King agreed to create a submarine tracking room but not to convoys.[43] On 19 March Admiral of the Fleet Sir Dudley Pound wrote to King that he 'regarded the introduction of convoys as a matter of urgency, and that convoys with weak escorts were preferable to no convoys.' King was unmoved. In March also, when Admiral Stark was appointed to the command of US naval forces in Europe, Pound recounted the Royal Navy's experience fighting U-boats to date. There were four points:

1. The comparative failure of hunting forces.
2. The great value of aircraft in convoy protection.
3. The supreme importance of adequate training and practices.
4. The value of efficient radar.

Admiral Pound summarised the British navy's frustration with their ally: 'The Americans, however, certainly seem to have been slow in putting much of our experience into practice. They first tried every conceivable measure – except convoy and escort.'[44]

The great cities of the industrial core of the country in the northeast – Boston, Philadelphia, Baltimore, Chicago and paramount among all, New York – received oil from Curaçao, Aruba in the Caribbean, Venezuela and the American ports in the Gulf of Mexico, especially Corpus Christi, Houston, and Port Arthur in Texas. An additional and considerable strain on western hemisphere oil was for Great Britain. The British imported 1,500 tanker loads per annum (four tankers per day). Each tanker, if sailing in convoy could only make four to six voyages to Great Britain each year. Oil importation and consumption was a considerable source of anxiety to Allied planners. Losses of tankers became so grievous that on 16 April a dispatch was sent from Operations in Washington, DC. The dispatch ordered: 'Commercial oil tankers for Gulf and Caribbean and US Atlantic ports shall be held in port pending further orders ... Thus no oil moved in tanker bottoms along the coast for the last two weeks of the month.' The U-boat attacks on the East Coast exacerbated a bottleneck in Allied production and the distribution of oil. Churchill, when he reminisced about this period of the war, wrote: 'Had we been forced to suspend, or even seriously to restrict for a time, the movement of shipping in the Atlantic, all our joint plans would have been arrested.'[45]

Amateurs to the rescue

Another layer of coastal defence along the Atlantic and Gulf coasts was provided by the Civilian Picket Patrol. This was composed of private sailors and their craft operating as volunteers under the authority of the Coast Guard Auxiliary, an organisation which at the war's start had a membership nationally of between 7,000 and 8,000 members with 2,000 boats, who were trained to help the Coast Guard for police and rescue activity.

Integral to this civilian defence on the East Coast was an offer from the Cruising Club of America. The club had been founded in 1921 as a means to develop the sport of yacht cruising. In 1920 the future founders of the Cruising Club, William Nutting, F W Casey Baldwin and Jim Dorsett sailed the yacht *Typhoon* to England. The officers of the Royal Cruising Club greeted them warmly. When they returned to the United States they founded the club, modelled upon the British one. On 5 March 1942, as Dönitz's submarines were devastating shipping off the East Coast, Commodore Alfred Stanford of the Cruising Club of America approached Andrews and suggested that members with ocean-going yachts could be employed for anti-submarine work. Stanford offered Andrews thirty yachts and crews to patrol off the East Coast, acting as pickets against patrolling U-boats.[46] Initially, Andrews scoffed at the proffered help. He fobbed off Stanford with a line about an accelerated small craft construction programme which would mean that the navy would have all the small craft they would need. Unfortunately for Andrews, the club's amateur yachtsmen petitioned Congress and the media with the result that Andrews found himself pressured to ask Stanford to draw up a detailed proposal and plan of action.[47] An outline of a plan was presented to the board of directors of the Cruising Club on 5 March. The board gave their approval and the general membership annual meeting on 24 March approved the plan. Thirty-six vessels were volunteered and they were chartered by the navy so they could have access to supplies and repairs at government expense. Admiral Andrews assigned his chief of staff, Captain J T G Stapler, and his intelligence officer, Lieutenant C C Vickery, to work with the club. The overall supervisor assigned was Commander Vincent

Astor, Naval Reserve, and an amateur yachtsman himself.[48] On 4 May King ordered the Coast Guard to form the Auxiliary, so as to accept civilian volunteers and vessels. The core of the Auxiliary was the Civilian Picket Patrol. This group was now transformed from having a primary duty to police and rescue work to observing and patrolling against enemy submarines. King, like Andrews, was sceptical, but also felt pressured into accepting the offer.[49] The Coast Guard appellation for these vessels was the 'Corsair Fleet', though it was more commonly known as the 'Hooligan Navy'.

Vessels in the Coast Guard Auxiliary were assigned to local patrol work. However, on 23 May Admiral King ordered the Auxiliary to be transferred from local defences within naval districts to the Eastern Sea Frontier. Once brought into the Coastal Picket Patrol each vessel was to be fitted with four 300lb depth charges, one 50mm calibre machine gun and a radio set, and they were to be organised into patrol stations along the 50-fathom contour. Admiral Andrews issued orders to formalise the status of the patrol as an element in the coast's defences on 14 July 1942, by which the vessels were organised into the Northern, Narragansett, New York, Delaware, Chesapeake and Southern patrol areas. They were to 'supplement existing anti-submarine, rescue and information duties', and would be equipped with such armament as was practicable. Each vessel was provided with an Army Interceptor Command grid chart and was instructed to 'observe and report the actions and activities of all hostile, submarine, surface and air forces, and to attack and destroy enemy submarines when armament permits.'[50] The boat's owner was permitted to remain aboard, with a rank of chief boatswain's mate and they were recruited for the duration of the conflict. The crews were composed of Coast Guard recruits. Hundreds of these 'Hooligan Navy' personnel were ultimately transferred to the regular cutters, having had the basics of seamanship and some discipline inculcated in them. Ultimately, though, as an anti-submarine force the Coastal Picket Patrol proved ineffective as a deterrent. There were inadequate training facilities to make the crewmen competent anti-submarine warriors and the boats were uniformly too slow and fragile to attack a U-boat. By 30 June 1943 the 'Hooligan Navy', was composed of 35,484 personnel and 17,474 vessels in 584 flotillas, but on 1 October 1943 it was disbanded once the 83ft Coast Guard cutters were being commissioned in sufficient numbers.[51] Those who had crewed the

'Hooligan Navy', and were found to be sufficiently fit, went on to serve throughout the Coast Guard, so some went from the coastal pickets of the United States to the landing crafts of D-Day.

A more successful amateur organisation was formed in the weeks before the attack on Pearl Harbor: the Civilian Air Patrol (CAP). At that time there were around a hundred thousand private pilots in the US. Most were found unfit for combat, mostly for reasons of age and physical limitations. The patrol operated initially under the auspices of the Office of Civilian Defense and was later transferred to the control of the Army Air Force. Initially these planes were unarmed. However, later on, the larger planes were fitted with one 325lb depth charge, or two 100lb bombs, but their principal utility was spotting shipwrecked survivors. The first patrol base for the CAP was established at Rehoboth, near the Delaware Capes, on 5 March 1942. There were further patrol bases established at Lantana, Florida; Parksley, Virginia; Flagler Beach, Florida; St Simons Island, Georgia; Miami, Florida; Charleston, South Carolina; Portland and Bar Harbor, Maine; two in North Carolina at Manteo and Beaufort; Riverhead, New York (Long Island); Falmouth and Cape Cod in Massachusetts. As the organisation was entirely civilian, they bought materials and supplies on their own. Unfortunately, it was not until 1943 that the Civilian Air Patrol was flying regular escort missions over Boston–Halifax convoys. From 5 March 1942 to September 1943, CAP flew 86,685 missions. They reported 173 U-boat sightings, ninety-one vessels in distress and located 363 shipwrecked survivors. On 1 September 1943 CAP was relieved of coastal patrols when the navy took responsibility for all anti-submarine warfare duties along the coast.[52]

Q-ships

A defensive measure championed by the president was the use of Q-ships. The naval establishment was sceptical, though, but when the president 'strongly requested' that this measure be taken, they had no choice but to comply. Q-ships were disguised warships – they carried weapons with which to attack U-boats, but these were camouflaged and hidden from sight and in outward appearance they looked like a small merchant vessel. The intention was that a U-boat would approach the Q-ship either to order its surrender or engage using its deck gun to sink it, but once close, the Q-ship would drop its disguise and attack. These decoy ships were not a success when tried during the First World War and when the British introduced them again in the Second, two were sunk, but no submarines damaged. On 20 January 1942 King contacted Andrews with a request for his opinion of Q-ships. Andrews took nine days to draft a four-page response, in which he argued that the tactic should be a success, but adding the caveat that it would best be implemented employing tankers, since these seemed to be the primary target of the U-boats. Tankers were also very well suited to this work, with their deep holds filled, not with oil, but balsa wood. King did not wait for Andrews's response. Two steamers were bought in New York City and another wooden sailing schooner was bought in Boston and were fitted with secret weapons. The two steamers were commissioned as USS *Atik* and USS *Asterion*, and set sail on 23 March. Three days later *Atik* was three hundred miles from Virginia Beach when *U-123* happened upon her. A torpedo was fired as the submarine approached and then *Atik* sprang her trap. The false sides fell away and guns blazed at the U-boat, but no shell struck any vital part before she dived. That was *Atik*'s doom. After resurfacing, Hardegen, commander of *U-123*, fired a second torpedo into the machine spaces of the vessel and a massive explosion followed this. *Atik* sank and all her crew were lost. In January 1943 *Asterion* was brought into dock for refitting and it was decided, after inspection, that she was simply to poorly constructed to go on station; neither she nor *Atik* were ever fit for combat. The final Q-ship was a twenty-three-year-old-wooden sailing schooner, *Irene Myrtle*. She went to sea in September 1943 but encountered no U-boats. After being damaged in a storm she put in for repairs and the naval inspector at that point condemned her as unfit.[53] Thus was the ignominious end of the short-lived Q-ship experiment.

End of the campaign

In April 1942 twenty-four ships, 138,121 tons, were sunk within the Eastern Sea Frontier and these losses accounted for 33 per cent of all Allied shipping lost for the month worldwide. It was the most dangerous theatre in the world and within the frontier, the area off Cape Hatteras was the most deadly place. Andrews assumed that the U-boats were refuelling from tankers flying a neutral flag, or that they were resupplying from a small island off the coast of Nicaragua or Honduras. He felt that there was no means at hand to combat these elusive submarines and wrote in the War Diary of the Eastern Sea Frontier that:

it is impossible to combat the menace with forces of inadequate strength. The outlook for May is still almost as disturbing as it was at the beginning of April, though pessimism should be tempered somewhat by the recognition that ships and planes are gradually accumulating along this coast and a protective system of considerable strength has been devised for the merchant vessels in our coastal waters.[54]

By mid-April the 'bucket brigade' convoy system, the CAP and the 'Hooligan Navy' resulted in a downturn in the U-boats' depredations. They sank only fifteen merchant ships for 76,896 tons during the second two weeks of the month. The former two weeks had losses of twenty-four ships for 145,735 tons of shipping. However, it was in May that the first turns of the coastal convoys system began. By the middle of the month the losses in the Eastern Sea Frontier dropped nearly to zero. Once the defences in this frontier had been stiffened, the focus of the U-boats' attentions shifted to the Gulf and Caribbean Sea Frontiers. Ironically, the transatlantic convoys during this period were relatively unscathed. Also, new construction of merchant shipping was ameliorating some of the gloom. By July new construction was out-pacing sinkings.[55]

From 13 January to mid-July, U-boats sank 397 Allied ships and 5,000 merchant seamen lost their lives. Once the convoy system was operating, Dönitz withdrew the U-boats to other, safer waters. In summing up the campaign, on 21 June Admiral King said: 'Escort is not just one way of handling the submarine menace, it is the only way that gives any promise of success.'[56] This may be hyperbole – defeating the U-boats took the concerted efforts of civilians, scientists and, most importantly a change in how the navy did its business and thought about ASW doctrine, in addition to the accumulation of appropriate and effective escorts.

Conclusion

The U-boat assault on America was a threat of potentially war-losing magnitude, creating difficulties and shortages in supplies, and damaging morale among merchant sailors. The US Navy was under-prepared for the attack, but there was little excuse for not anticipating the U-boat assault on the East Coast. British intelligence sent daily estimates of German submarines' locations. These transmissions were sent to Admiral Ingersoll and Andrews.[57] Samuel Morrison tersely summarised the culpability of US leadership:

> This writer cannot avoid the conclusion that the United States Navy was woefully unprepared, materially and mentally, for the U-boat blitz on the Atlantic Coast that began in January 1942. He further believes that, apart from the want of air power, which was largely, the Navy's own fault ... In the end the Navy met the challenge, applied its energy and intelligence, came through magnificently and won; but this does not alter the fact that it had no plans ready for a reasonable protection to shipping when the submarines struck, and were unable to improvise them for several months.[58]

The leaders, Admirals King and Andrews, were initially resistant to the tactics that would ultimately defeat the attacking U-boats: convoys. In Michael Gannon's assessment it was Admiral King who was ultimately culpable for the navy's failure to defend the coast. Gannon cites a number of failures by King. He failed to deploy the destroyers available for defence of the coast. He then refused to apply the lessons from the British ASW experience. He did not prioritise the construction of small ASW craft. He failed to impose a coastal blackout. Lastly, he at first declined the offer by amateurs to take on submarine patrols.[59] Although Gannon's assessment is cogent, it is not complete. Admiral Adolphus Andrews must share some of the blame. Andrews shared King's disdain for amateur yachtsmen, so he would not have made the 'Hooligans' more active than when he was ordered to do so. However, Andrews's most significant blind spot was his resistance to an earlier adoption of coastal convoying. His contention that a poorly escorted convoy was worse than none was wrong. There was the British experience of both wars and his own navy's experience in the First World War, which was conclusive about the positive value of convoys. Andrews was a conservative thinker. His ideas about patrolling for submarines as opposed to escorting merchants had already been exploded by past experience. Certainly, Andrews was right when he wrote that there was precious little to defend the coast with; he was right in continuing to request ASW ships for his command. Ultimately a decision was made, as it was in the First World War, that the escort of troopships, capital ships and convoy escort were the paramount role for destroyers in the Atlantic. A consequence of that decision was that there was a dearth of these

183

precious ships for the defence of the coast. The pre-war notion that submarines were primarily to operate with the fleet and the post-First World War acceptance that ASDIC/sonar had solved the submarine problem led to a vacuum when it came to ASW/merchant shipping protection doctrine. Destroyers trained only to protect the capital ships of the fleet, not tankers or freighters.

The struggle against the U-boat, and American strategic notions about how to participate in the war, developed during the period immediately preceding America's open belligerency. Franklin Roosevelt's acrobatic-like political manoeuvring to isolate the anti-interventionists and build support for mobilisation required an agility and deftness of great delicacy. Through means arguably both disingenuous and crafty, FDR brought public support to aid the Allies.

The Germans also failed to send more submarines in adequate numbers to the East Coast once the defences there proved to be porous, even though Dönitz lobbied Hitler for more boats. On 22 January Hitler had met with Raeder's chief of staff, Vice Admiral Kurt Fricke. Hitler anticipated that Norway was to be the 'zone of destiny' for the war and demanded twenty U-boats be stationed between Iceland and Norway, so as to forestall any Allied attempt to invade Scandinavia. Eight of the U-boats that had been earmarked to attack North America were detailed instead to this Arctic region.[60] These eight U-boats, instead of fruitless patrolling for a phantom invasion, could have been much more effectively used in the waters of the eastern seaboard.

The repulse of the U-boat attacks on the East Coast involved a tough fight and changes to tactics and to a whole way of thinking. Ultimately, the U-boats were not defeated. Once Dönitz perceived that ASW measures were beginning to work and that his U-boats were encountering strong resistance, he simply moved them to new theatres. Winston Churchill summarised Dönitz's decision to abandon efforts in the Eastern Sea Frontier when he wrote: 'Admiral Dönitz forthwith changed his point of attack to the Caribbean and the Gulf of Mexico, where convoys were not yet working ... whenever Allied counter-measures began to take effect Admiral Dönitz shifted his U-boats.'[61]

Appendix: Adolphus Andrews

Before, during and after the U-boat assault the Commandant of the Eastern Sea Frontier was Vice Admiral Adolphus Andrews.

Adolphus Andrews was born on 7 October 1879 in Galveston, Texas. He had originally wanted to go to Yale. However, his father told him that upon his graduation from high school, at the age of fifteen, he was too young to leave. Instead, he went to the University of Texas, Austin. While taking classes there he received a telegram from his father instructing him to take the examination for the Naval Academy.[1] He returned, took the examination, and was instated 7 September 1897. At admission he was ranked twenty-fifth in a class of seventy-five cadets. He graduated from the Naval Academy in June 1901, with a cumulative class standing of thirteenth in a class that had been whittled down to fifty-two. Among his classmates was Ernest J King, who placed second in the same graduating class.[2]

After Annapolis, Andrews served in a series of assignments. He was the commanding officer of the presidential yacht. He served as the commanding officer of USS *Villalobos* (gunboat in China), USS *Prometheus* (repair ship), USS *Mayflower* (presidential yacht), USS *Chewink* (mine-sweeper) and USS *Texas* (BB-35). Ashore, he served as a recruiter in New York City and Dallas, Texas. He also commanded the submarine base at New London, Connecticut. Andrews was part of the naval representation to the 1927 Geneva arms control talks. He also was the head of the Bureau of Navigation (in charge of all navy personnel matters) 1935–38 and acted temporarily as Secretary of the Navy in 1936. He was Commander-in-Chief of the Scouting Force. He was an aide to

Presidents Theodore Roosevelt (junior aide), Warren Harding and Calvin
Coolidge. Andrews remained in command of the Eastern Sea Frontier
until November 1943.

In February 1939 Vice Admiral Andrews participated in Fleet Problem
XX. The fleet problems were exercises involving almost all the navy's
warships between 1923 and 1940. These explored potential operations and
tactics given a specified scenario. One group of ships was designated as the
defence, Black Force, and another as the attackers, White Force.[3]

Adolphus was given command of the Black Force. His assignment was
to prevent the White Force from approaching Puerto Rico and simulating
an amphibious assault. He was given six battleships, an aircraft carrier
(*Ranger*), eight heavy and six light cruisers, thirty-two destroyers, fifteen
auxiliaries and five aircraft tenders. The White Force, commanded by
Admiral Edward C Kalbfus, was composed of six battleships, three aircraft
carriers (*Lexington*, *Yorktown* and *Enterprise*), six heavy and six light
cruisers, twenty-nine destroyers, and twelve submarines. The target ship
Utah acted as a surrogate for three large troop transports. (Throughout
these exercises there were often ersatz ships).

Andrews made the destruction of the White Force's battle force the first
priority. This conception was good 'Mahanite' strategy, which exemplifies
his conservative way of thinking. The destruction of Kalbfus's 'transports'
would have guaranteed Andrews's success. The White submarines sank a
destroyer and damaged *Ranger*. During the initial manoeuvring there was
no official winner declared, but Kalbfus was felt to have acquitted himself
well. The second part of the exercise was a battleship duel observed by
President Roosevelt. He spent part of the observation aboard the heavy
cruiser *Houston*, part of Andrews's command. This 'engagement' lasted
six hours. Although the submarines attempted to torpedo the Black battle
line, they proved to be unable to engage the battleships due the latter's
high speed. The final part of the exercise was a simulated invasion of
Puerto Rico. At the conclusion of the exercise, Andrews recommended
that the US acquire bases at Port of Spain, Trinidad, and other Caribbean
islands.[4] This would happen in the destroyers-for-bases deal.

Andrews served as the commander of another fleet exercise force. He
was commanding officer of the Maroon force during Fleet Problem XXI
in late April and early May 1940. Maroon had nineteen submarines
assigned. His assignment was to defend Hawaii from a simulated invasion.

He used his submarines defensively, to ward off attacks, generally near the 'enemy's' objectives.[5]

He served as the commandant of the Eastern Sea Frontier and retired while in that posting, but continued to serve as a member of the Navy Manpower Survey Board (to determine the Navy's personnel needs) and as a member of the Navy Court of Inquiry on the Pearl Harbor attack.[6] Andrews's posting as the commandant of the Third Naval District/ Eastern Sea Frontier was an indication that he was ending his career, as a shore-side command at his rank was an indication that he was not considered a 'stellar' officer.[7] He died in the naval hospital in Houston, Texas, on 19 June 1948.

He was awarded the following citations: the Spanish Campaign Medal (20 April to 19 December 1898), the Mexican Campaign medal (29 April 1914 to 29 May 1914) and the Victory medal with the Atlantic Fleet clasp (28 June 1918 to 1 September 1918), the Haitian Campaign Medal (11 February 1920 to 15 February 1920), the American Defense Service Medal with Fleet Clasp (8 September 1939 to 1 February 1941), and the World War II Campaign medal, the Distinguished Service Medal. From the government of Brazil he had a commemoration conferred upon him on the occasion of his visit there commemorating the centenary of the country's independence, and the Order of Vasco Núñez de Balboa, grade of commander, on the occasion of the visit of the US fleet to Panama, 28 April to 2 May 1939.[8]

Notes

Chapter 1

1 Rear Admiral Julius Augustus
Furer, *Administration of the Navy
Department in World War II*
(Washington: Department of the
Navy, 1959), 1.
2 Robert Greenhalgh Albion, *Makers
of Naval Policy: 1798–1947*
(Annapolis: Naval Institute Press,
1980), 43–4.
3 Furer, 21.
4 Furer, 22.
5 William M McBride, *Technical
Change and the United States Navy,
1865–1945* (Baltimore: John Hopkins
University Press, 2000), 14–16.
6 Ibid, 17.
7 Ibid, 19.
8 Ibid, 24.
9 Ibid, 31.
10 Ibid, 42.
11 Potts, J R, 'HMS *Dreadnought*.
Dreadnought Battleship (1906)',
http://www.militaryfactory.com/shi
ps/detail.asp?ship_id=HMS-
Dreadnought.
12 McBride, 47; John T Kuehn,
*Agents of Innovation: The General
Board and the Design of the Fleet that
Defeated the Japanese Navy*
(Annapolis: Naval Institute Press,
2008), 8.
13 McBride, 51.
14 Ibid, 60.

15 Furer, 201.
16 Robert L O'Connell, *Sacred
Vessels: The Cult of the Battleships and
the Rise of the US Navy* (Boulder:
Westview Press, 1991), 124.
17 Ibid, 126, 135.
18 McBride, 126.
19 Naval War College, 'History',
www.usnwc.edu/About/History.asp
x?viewmode=printerfriendly.
20 Captain W M Sims, 'The
Practical Character of the Naval War
College: A lecture Delivered before
the Officers of the US Naval
Academy November 11, 1912',
www.usnwc.edu/getattachment/Abo
ut/History/SimsDoc.pdf.aspx, 1,
4, 5.
21 Ibid, 10, 12.
22 Ibid, 14.
23 Peter P Perla, *The Art of
Wargaming* (Annapolis: United
States Naval Institute, 1990), 36–7.
24 Ibid, 65.
25 McHugh, 58–61.
26 Perla, 69.
27 Dave McComb, *US Destroyers
1934–45: Pre-war classes* (Oxford:
Osprey, 2010), 6–7.
28 Theodore Roscoe, *United States
Destroyer Operations in World War II*
(Annapolis: Naval Institute Press,
1982), 14.
29 Richard Hill, *War at Sea in the*

Ironclad Age (London: Cassell, 2002), 105.
30 Roscoe, 64.
31 Assistant Chief of Air Staff, Intelligence, 'The Antisubmarine Command', April 1945, http://www.uboatarchive.net/AAFHistory.htm, 11.
32 Ibid, 13.
33 Timothy A Warnock, *The Battle Against the U-Boat in the American Theater* (Montgomery: Air Force Historical Agency), 24.
34 Assistant Chief of Air Staff, 15.
35 Samuel Eliot Morrison, *History of the United States Naval Operations in World War II, vol I: The Battle of the Atlantic, 1939–1945* (Annapolis: Naval Institute Press, 2010), li-lii.
36 Montgomery C Miegs, *Slide Rules and Submarines: American Scientists and Subsurface Warfare in World War II* (Washington, DC: National Defense University Press, 1990), 211, 214.

Chapter 2
1 James I Marino, 'The Undeclared War 1939–1941', *World War II History* (Late Fall 2012), 42.
2 Waldo Heinrichs, *Threshold of War* (New York: Oxford University Press, 1988), 4.
3 Ibid, 6.
4 Transcript of National Industrial Recovery Act (1933), 5–6, www.ourdocuments.gov.
5 Patrick Abbazia, *Mr Roosevelt's Navy: The Private War of the Atlantic Fleet, 1939–1942* (Annapolis: Naval Institute Press, 1975), 9.
6 Heinrichs, 10.
7 Thomas Bailey and Paul Ryan, *Hitler vs Roosevelt: The Undeclared Naval War* (New York: The Free Press, 1979), 103–4.
8 'Fireside Chat 16: On the

"Arsenal of Democracy"' (29 December 1940), Miller Center at the University of Virginia, http://millercenter.org/president/fdroosevelt/speeches/speech-3319.
9 Transcript of Lend-Lease Act (1941), www.ourdocuments.gov.
10 Morrison, 37.
11 Robert Greenhalgh Albion and Jennie Barnes Payne, *Sea Lanes in Wartime. The American Experience 1775–1942* (New York: W W Norton, 1942), 308.
12 Heinrichs, 11; Bailey & Ryan, 116.
13 Heinrichs, 28; Blair, Clay, *Hitler's U-boat War, vol I: The Hunters, 1939–1942* (New York: Modern Library, 2000), 419.
14 Heinrichs, 30.
15 Heinrichs, 31.
16 Robert William Love, *The Chiefs of Naval Operations* (Annapolis: Naval Institute Press, 1980), 115.
17 Heinrichs, 38.
18 Ibid, 40.
19 Ibid, 41.
20 Abbazia, 75.
21 Heinrichs, 47.
22 Ibid.
23 Lisle Rose, *Power at Sea, vol II: The Breaking Storm, 1919–1945* (Columbia: University of Missouri Press, 2007), 191; Corbin Williamson, 'Repair Work and Naval Musical Chairs: Conflict and Co-operation in Anglo-American Naval Relations in 1941', *International Journal of Naval History* (21 July 2015), 8.
24 Bailey & Ryan, 48, 122.
25 Heinrichs, 83.
26 Bailey & Ryan, 138–9.
27 Heinrichs, 84–5.
28 Kent Roberts Greenfield, 'Command Decisions' (Center of Military History, Department of the Army, Washington, DC), 84, http://www.history.army.mil/book

s/70-7_0.htm.
29 Bailey & Ryan, 129–32.
30 Heinrichs, 102.
31 Ibid, 108.
32 Ibid, 110–11.
33 Ibid, 115.
34 Ibid, 152.
35 Ibid, 156.
36 Love, 119–21.
37 Greenfield, op cit, 36–7.
38 Heinrichs, 164.
39 Ibid, 165.
40 Marc Wortman, *1941: Fighting the Shadow War. A Divided America in a World at War* (New York: Atlantic Monthly, 2016), 286–7.
41 Heinrichs, 167.
42 Ibid, 168.
43 Ibid, 173.
44 Bailey & Ryan, 196–7; USS *Kearny* Official After Action Report, October 20 1941, http://mysite.verizon.net/sepulcher/kearnyreport.html.
45 President Roosevelt speech about attack on USS *Kearny*, http://www.usmm.org/fdr/kearny.html, 2, 5.
46 Bailey & Ryan, 205.
47 Heinrichs, 210–13.
48 Ibid, 206.
49 Blair, 418, 426; Wortman, 314.

Chapter 3
1 Robert Levine, *The Politics of American Naval Rearmament, 1930–1938* (New York: Garland, 1988), 32.
2 Transcript of National Recovery Act (1933), 1, 5, www.ourdocuments.gov.
3 Love, 76, 80–1.
4 Stephen Roskill, *Naval Policy Between the Wars*, vol II (New York: Walker, 1968), 160.
5 Levine, 39–41.
6 Ibid, 53–4.
7 Roskill, *Naval Policy*, vol II, 162.
8 James F Cook, *Carl Vinson:*

Patriarch of the Armed Forces (Macon, GA: Mercer University Press, 2004), 28.
9 Ibid, 66–9.
10 Ibid, 81.
11 Levine, 99–100.
12 Furer, 816.
13 Levine, 115–18, 127.
14 http://www.globalsecurity.org/military/facility/camden.htm; Levine, 142.
15 Levine, 164.
16 McComb, 6, 9–10.
17 Levine, 182.
18 Cook, 87–9, 94–5, 98–102.
19 McComb, 11–12.
20 Cook, 117.
21 Levine, 288–9.
22 Ibid, 404, 408.
23 Ibid, 464, 468.
24 Roskill, *Naval Policy*, vol II, 325–6.
25 Vincent P O'Hara, David W Dickson and Richard Worth, *On Seas Contested: The Seven Great Navies of the Second World War* (Annapolis: Naval Institute Press, 2010), 7 (France), 54 (Germany), 113 (Great Britain); Cook, 142.
26 Cook, 144–8.
27 Ibid, 149.
28 Ibid, 153; David Kaiser, *No End Save Victory: How FDR led the Nation into War* (New York: Basic Books, 2014), 73.
29 Kaiser, 213.
30 Kaiser, 217, 222–3.
31 Cook, 171–2.

Chapter 4
1 Lisle Rose, *Power at Sea, vol I: The Age of Navalism, 1880–1918* (Columbia: University of Missouri Press, 2007), 202.
2 Ibid, 203.
3 Blair, 11–12.
4 Rose, op cit, 251.
5 Arthur J Marder, *From Dreadnought to Scapa Flow*, vol IV

(London: Oxford University Press, 1969), 50.

6 Paul G Halpern, *A Naval History of World War I* (Annapolis: Naval Institute Press, 1997), 338.

7 Marder, Arthur J, *From Dreadnought to Scapa Flow*, vol III (London: Oxford University Press, 1966), 271.

8 Marder, vol IV, 65.

9 Halpern, 341.

10 Marder, vol IV, 69–70.

11 Marder, op cit, 75–6.

12 Norman Polmar and Edward Whitman, *Hunters and Killers, vol I: Anti-Submarine Warfare from 1776 to 1943* (Annapolis: Naval Institute Press, 2015), 37.

13 Ibid, 38–40.

14 Ibid, 28–9.

15 Marder, vol IV, 116.

16 Ibid, 117.

17 Ibid, 121–6.

18 Ibid, 273.

19 Ibid, 130.

20 Arthur J Marder, *From Dreadnought to Scapa Flow*, vol V (London: Oxford University Press, 1970), 83.

21 Ibid, 85.

22 Ibid, 97.

23 Rear Admiral William Snowden Sims, *The Victory at Sea* (Annapolis: Naval Institute Press, 1984), 163.

24 Marder, op cit, 79.

25 Ibid, 123.

26 Rose, 269; James Tertius De Kay, *Roosevelt's Navy: The Education of a Wartime President, 1882–1920* (New York: Pegasus Books, 2012), 227.

27 De Kay, 185; Halpern, 430–1.

28 Halpern, 362–5.

29 W S Sims, 206–7.

30 James W Hammond, Jr, *The Treaty Navy: The Story of the US Naval Service Between the World Wars* (Victoria, Canada: Trafford Publishing, 2001), 11.

31 W S Sims, 122–3.

32 Ibid, 124–6.

33 Polmar & Whitman, 45.

34 Halpern, 430–2.

35 Rose, 268.

36 Halpern, 359.

37 Halpern, 435.

38 Rose, vol I, 265; De Kay, 73–4.

39 Marder, op cit, 170.

40 De Kay, 85, 88, 91.

41 Rose, op cit, 277.

42 Marder, op cit, 177.

43 Ibid, 183, 190.

44 W S Sims, 246.

Chapter 5

1 Ruth Henig, *Versailles and After, 1919–1933* (Annapolis: Naval Institute Press, 1995), 11.

2 Ibid, 12.

3 Jerry W Jones, 'The Naval Battle of Paris', *Naval War College Review* (Spring, 2009), 82–3.

4 Ibid, 84.

5 O'Connell, 239–40.

6 Henig, 19.

7 Ibid, 20–2.

8 Ibid, 38–9.

9 Ibid, 68.

10 Stephen Roskill, *Naval Policy Between the Wars*, vol I (New York: Walker, 1968), 21, 24.

11 Christopher M Bell, *Churchill and Sea Power* (Oxford: Oxford University Press, 2013), 94, 96.

12 Hammond, 9.

13 O'Connell, 244.

14 Ibid, 246.

15 Rose, 66.

16 O'Connell, 255–6.

17 Ibid, 259.

18 Roskill, op cit, 307; O'Connell, 262.

19 O'Connell, 264–5.

20 Ibid, 265.

21 Ibid, 266–7.

22 'Treaty relating to the use of Submarines and Noxious Gases in

Warfare, Washington, 6 February 1922', University of Minnesota, http://www1.umn.edu/humanrts/instree/1922a.htm.
23 O'Connell, 272–3; Roskill, op cit, 330; Raymond Westphal, Jr, 'Postwar Planning: Parliamentary Politics and the Royal Navy, 1919–22', *The Journal of Military History*, 74:1 (2010), 170.
24 Roskill, op cit, 498–9.
25 Ibid, 501–2.
26 O'Connell, 291–2.
27 Ibid, 298.
28 Joel Ira Holwitt, '"Execute Against Japan": Freedom-of-the-Seas, the US Navy, Fleet Submarines, and the US Decision to Conduct Unrestricted Warfare, 1919–1941', PhD diss (Ohio State University, 2005), 30.
29 Lieutenant H G Rickover, 'International Law and the Submarine', *United States Naval Proceedings* (September 1935), 1214, 1217, 1218.
30 Ibid, 1219.
31 Ibid, 1223, 1227.
32 Roskill, op cit, 345.
33 Rose, 84.
34 Ibid, 88, 91, 117.
35 Roskill, op cit, 441; Rose, 129.
36 Roskill, op cit, 534–7.
37 Ibid, 347.
38 O'Connell, 309.

Chapter 6
1 Workers of the Writers' Program of the Work Projects Administration for the City of New York, *A Maritime History of New York* (Brooklyn, NY: Going Coastal, 2004), hereafter referred to as *Maritime History*, 184, 193, 195, 200–1, 205.
2 New Jersey Department of Environmental Protection, 'Black Tom Explosion (1916)', (Division of Parks and Forests, 26 January 2005) http://www.state.nj.us/dep/parksandforests/parks/liberty_state_park/liberty_blacktomexplosion.html.
3 *Maritime History*, 238.
4 Ibid, 248, 265; Thomas F Berner, *The Brooklyn Navy Yard* (Charleston, SC: Arcadia, 1999), 7, 8.
5 *Maritime History*, 253, 255–6, 263.
6 *Maritime History*, 262; Karl Drew Hartzell, *The Empire State At War World War II* (State of New York, 1949), 326; Richard Goldstein, *Helluva Town: The Story of New York City During World War II* (New York: Free Press), 55.
7 Goldstein, 19.
8 Charles Sterling Popple, *Standard Oil Company (New Jersey) in World War II* (New York: Standard Oil Company, 1952), 131–2.
9 Ibid, 134.
10 Blair, 66; Popple, 135–6, 155–6.
11 Tim Newark, *Mafia Allies* (St Paul, Minnesota: Zenith Press, 2007), 78–9.
12 Ibid, 81.
13 Paul H Jeffers, *The Napoleon of New York: Mayor Fiorello La Guardia* (New York: John Wiley, 2012), 87–8.
14 Newark, 87–9.
15 Lorraine B Diehl, *Over Here! New York City During World War II* (New York: Harper Collins, 2010), 52.
16 Goldstein, 105, 107, 114.
17 Ibid, 117–18.
18 Diehl, 47, 51–2.
19 Jeffers, passim.
20 Goldstein, 24.
21 Ralph Da Costa Nunez, *The Poor Among Us* (New York: White Tiger Press, 2013), 294–5.
22 Ken Brown, 'The SS *Normandie* Fire', *World at War* (January 2015), 70, 72.

23 Ibid, 75.
24 Ibid, 74, 75; Steven H Jaffe, *New York at War: Four Centuries of Combat, Fear, and Intrigue in Gotham* (New York: Basic Books, 2012), 238.
25 Newark, 51–6.
26 Newark, passim.
27 Ibid, 92–4.
28 Ibid, 95–7; Sid Feder and Joachim Joesten, *The Luciano Story* (New York: Da Capo Press, 1994), 187–8.
29 Newark, 100–1.
30 Ibid, 103–4.
31 Feder & Joesten, 203.
32 Jeffers, 233.
33 Jeffers, 233, 278.
34 Jaffe, 225; Diehl, 11.
35 Jeffers, 279.
36 Traces, 'American Bund', www.traces.org/americanbund.html.
37 Newark, 72–3.
38 Traces, 'American Bund', www.traces.org/americanbund.html.
39 Ibid.
40 Goldstein, 214–15.

Chapter 7
1 Merchant Marine Act, 1936. Title VIII-Contract Provisions. Section 801 (3), (4) and Section 806 (b), www.usmm.org; Frederick C Lane, *Ships for Victory: The History of Shipbuilding under the US Maritime Commission in World War II* (Baltimore: John Hopkins Press, 1951), 12, 24.
2 L A Sawyer and W H Mitchell, *Victory Ships and Tankers* (Newton Abbot: David & Charles, 1974), 9; Justin F Gleichauf, *Unsung Sailors. The Naval Armed Guard in World War II* (Annapolis: Naval Institute Press, 1990), 85; Lane, 28, 29.
3 Emory Scott Land, *Winning the War with Ships. Land, Sea and Air – Mostly Ships* (New York: Robert McBride, 1958), 7.

4 Lane, 33–5, 39, 58.
5 Herbert Brian, *The Forgotten Heroes* (New York: Tom Doherty, 2004), 11; Lane, 3.
6 Sawyer & Mitchell, 89.
7 Brian, 205.
8 Gleichauf, 85; Lane, 28, 29.
9 Brian, 35; Lane, 3.
10 Sawyer & Mitchell, 89; Brian, 205.
11 Lane, 236.
12 Ibid, 244, 252, 255.
13 Ibid, 257; 'Rosie the Riveter', *World War II Quarterly* (Spring 2013), 37, 38.
14 Lane, passim.
15 Ibid, 288–90.
16 Lane, 299–304.
17 Lane, 451.
18 Lane, 61, 62, 65, 66.
19 Brian, 30, 43; Eric Lichtblau, 'After 40 Years, Merchant Marines Win Veterans: Finally – a "Flag and a Headstone"', *Los Angeles Times* (30 January 1988), http://articles.latimes.com/print/1988-01-30/news/mn-10163_1_u-s-merchant-marine.
20 Brian, 37.
21 Ibid, 55.
22 Ibid, 82.
23 Gleichauf, 3.
24 Ibid, 5.
25 Ibid, 6, 10.
26 Ibid, 19.
27 Ibid, 32, 33.
28 Ibid, 51, 94.
29 Ibid, 158.
30 Ibid, 256.
31 Ibid, 95.

Chapter 8
1 Jim Bloom, 'Preparing the Wolfpack: Germany's Type II U-boats', *Strategy & Tactics*, 293 (July/August 2015), 70–1.
2 Vincent P O'Hara, David W Dickson and Richard Worth, *On Seas Contested: The Seven Great*

Navies of the Second World War
(Annapolis: Naval Institute Press,
2010), 41; Admiral Karl Dönitz,
'The Conduct of the War at Sea'
(Division of Naval Intelligence,
Washington, DC, 15 January 1946),
iii; Timothy P Mulligan, *Neither
Sharks nor Wolves: the Men of Nazi
Germany's U-boat Arm, 1939–1945*
(Annapolis: Naval Institute Press,
1999), 38, 39, 50, 51.
3 Uboat.net, 'Hans-Georg von
Friedburg', Uboat.net/men/
commanders/320.html.
4 Rose, 120.
5 O'Hara et al, 42, 215; Mulligan,
174.
6 Ibid, 132; Gordon Williamson,
*Wolfpack: The Story of the U-boat
in World War II* (Oxford: Osprey,
2006), 145–7.
7 G Williamson, 151, 152.
8 Mulligan, 117.
9 Ibid, 7.
10 Ibid, 91, 94, 95.
11 Ibid, 74.
12 G Williamson, 163, 164.
13 Ibid, 168, 173.
14 Mulligan, 16, 17.
15 G Williamson, 169; Mulligan,
44, 181.
16 Mulligan, passim.
17 Ibid, 215, 216, 221.
18 Mulligan, 59, 60, 75.
19 O'Hara et al, 43.
20 Michael Gannon, *Black May*
(New York: Harper Collins, 1998),
52.
21 Mulligan, 56.
22 O'Hara et al, 49.
23 G Williamson, 26.
24 Ibid, 40, 45, 46.
25 Mulligan, 45, 46; O'Hara et al,
72; Rose, 129; Blair, 357.
26 Rose, 203, 204, 235, 286.
27 Jak P Mallmann Showell,
*Dönitz, U-boats, Convoys: The
British Version of His Memoirs from
the Admiralty's Secret Anti-*

Submarine Reports (Barnsley:
Frontline Books, 2013), 3.
28 Gunther Hessler, *German Naval
History, The U-boat War in the
Atlantic: 1939–1945* (London:
HMSO, 1989), 86; Blair, 305.
29 Rose, 237–9; Blair, 224.
30 Rose, 292, 293.
31 Ibid, 308.
32 Cajus Baker, *Hitler's Naval War*
(Garden City, NY: Doubleday,
1974), 307.
33 Bailey & Ryan, 61–4.
34 Showell, 5, 6.
35 G Williamson, 201–4;
Showell, 26, 27; Mulligan, 198.
36 Hessler, 86, 87.
37 Bailey & Ryan, 178.
38 Showell, 10.
39 Mulligan, 75.
40 Bailey & Ryan, 249, 250.

Chapter 9
1 Michael Gannon, *Operation
Drumbeat* (New York: Harper and
Row, 1991), 78–9.
2 Morrison, 207, 208.
3 U-boat Archives, War Diary,
North Atlantic Naval Coastal
Frontier, December 1941, 6, 7,
http://www.uboat.net/ESFWWar
DiaryDec41.htm. Accessed 6 April
2012.
4 Ed Offley, *The Burning Shore:
How Hitler's U-boats Brought World
War II to America* (New York: Basic
Books, 2014), 100.
5 U-boat Archives, War Diary,
North Atlantic Naval Coastal
Frontier, December 1941, 5,
http://www.uboat.net/ESFWWar
DiaryDec41.htm. Accessed 6 April
2012.
6 Offley, 98; Gordon W Prange, *At
Dawn We Slept: The Untold Story
of Pearl Harbor* (New York: Penguin
Books, 1991), 621.
7 Morrison, 248.
8 Ladislas Fargo, *The Tenth Fleet*

(New York: Ivan Obolensky, 1962), 67, 68.
9 Morrison, 126; Fargo, 70, 71.
10 U-boat Archives, War Diary, North Atlantic Naval Coastal Frontier, January 1942, 2, http://www.uboat.net/ESFWWar DiaryDec41.htm. Accessed 6 April 2012.
11 Offley, 107–9.
12 Ibid, 112, 113; U-boat Archives, *U-123* – 7th War Patrol, 53, 54, http://www.uboatarchive.net/KT B123-7.htm. Accessed 29 January 2015.
13 Gannon (1991), 186; Morrison, 130.
14 Offley, 95, 96.
15 U-boat Archives, War Diary, North Atlantic Naval Coastal Frontier, December 1942, 8, http://www.uboat.net/ESFWWar DiaryDec41.htm. Accessed 6 April 2012.
16 Morrison, 131.
17 Offley, 149, 150.
18 Eastern Sea Frontier, War Diary, March 1942, 3.
19 Offley, 151, 152.
20 Ibid, 145, 146; U-boat Archives, http://www.uboatarchive.net/AA FHistory.htm, 12, 13. Accessed 16 February 2013.
21 U-boat Archives, http://www.uboatarchive.net/AA FHistory.htm, 19. Accessed 16 February 2013.
22 Morrison, 133, 134; Offley, 99, 100.
23 U-boat Archives, War Diary, North Atlantic Naval Coastal Frontier, January 1942, 1–3, http://www.uboat.net/ESFWWar DiaryDec41.htm. Accessed 6 April 2012.
24 U-boat Archives, War Diary, North Atlantic Naval Coastal Frontier, March 1942, 3, http://www.uboat.net/ESFWWar

DiaryDec41.htm. Accessed 6 April 2012.
25 Fargo, 108.
26 U-boat Archives, War Diary, North Atlantic Naval Coastal Frontier, February 1942, 2–3, http://www.uboat.net/ESFWWar DiaryDec41.htm, accessed 6 April 2012; Gannon (1991), 309, 310.
27 U-boat Archives, War Diary, North Atlantic Naval Coastal Frontier, March 1942, 3–7, http://www.uboat.net/ESFWWar DiaryDec41.htm. Accessed 6 April 2012.
28 Offley, 153, 154.
29 Morrison, 254, 255.
30 Ibid, 255–6.
31 U-boat Archives, War Diary, North Atlantic Naval Coastal Frontier, April 1942, 2, http://www.uboat.net/ESFWWar DiaryDec41.htm. Accessed 6 April 2012.
32 U-boat Archives, War Diary, North Atlantic Naval Coastal Frontier, April 1942, 7, http://www.uboat.net/ESFWWar DiaryDec41.htm, accessed 6 April 2012; Morrison, 136, 137.
33 U-boat Archives, War Diary, North Atlantic Naval Coastal Frontier, April 1942, 1, http://www.uboat.net/ESFWWar DiaryDec41.htm. Accessed 6 April 2012.
34 Morrison, 154, 155.
35 Ibid, 156.
36 *The Coast Guard at War: Cutter, vol VIII* (Public Information Division, Coast Guard Headquarters, 1 July 1947), 1; http://uboat.net/fates/losses/194 2.htm, accessed 9 March 2017; U-boat Archives, War Diary, North Atlantic Naval Coastal Frontier, January 1942, 4, 5, http://www.uboat.net/ESFWWarDiaryD ec41.htm, accessed 6 April 2012.

37 Gannon (1991), 765.
38 Morrison, 157.
39 Fargo, 63, 64.
40 Morrison, 413.
41 Gannon (1998), 85; 'Merchant Marine in World War I', www.usmm.org/ww1merchant.html.
42 Gannon (1991), 391.
43 Offley, 128, 129.
44 Roskill, *War at Sea*, vol II, 97–8.
45 U-boat Archives, War Diary, North Atlantic Naval Coastal Frontier, April 1942, 6, http://www.uboat.net/ESFWWar DiaryDec41.htm, accessed 6 April 2012; Fargo, 60.
46 The Cruising Club of America, https://www.cruisingclub.org/abo ut_history.htm.
47 Fargo, 119.
48 U-boat Archives, War Diary, North Atlantic Naval Coastal Frontier, March 1942, 13, 15, http://www.uboat.net/ESFWWar DiaryDec41.htm. Accessed 6 April 2012.
49 Morrison, 268, 269.
50 Ibid, 269, 270.
51 *The Coast Guard at War: Auxiliary, vol XIX* (Public Information Division, Coast Guard Headquarters, 1 July 1947), 10.
52 Morrison, 276–9, 280, 281.
53 Gannon (1991), 305, 307, 323, 327–30.
54 U-boat Archives, War Diary, North Atlantic Naval Coastal Frontier, April 1942, 4, http://www.uboat.net/ESFWWarDiaryD ec41.htm. Accessed 6 April 2012.

55 Offley, 158; Admiral Ernest J King, 'US Navy at War 1941–1945. First Report of the Secretary of the Navy', 81, www.ibilio.org/hyperwar/USN/USN, accessed 6 June 2012; Gannon (1998), 85.
56 Morrison, 199–200.
57 Gannon (1991), 412.
58 Morrison, 201.
59 Gannon (1991), 414.
60 Offley, 139, 140.
61 Churchill, 107.

Appendix
1 Carol Moore, 'Adolphus Andrews, Sr', Find A Grave Memorial, http://www.findagrave.com/cgi-bin/fg.cgi?page=gr&GRid=588694 70.
2 United States Department of the Navy, Merit Roll of the Naval Cadets of the First Class-Annual Examination, June 1901, 74.
3 Albert A Nofi, *To Train the Fleet for War; The US Navy Fleet Problems, 1923–1940* (Newport: Naval War College Press, 2010), 241.
4 Ibid, 243–7.
5 Ibid, 257–9.
6 National Personnel Records Center, Record of Officers, Andrews, Adolphus, 1–3.
7 Telephone conversation between author and Michael Gannon on 19 September 2016.
8 National Personnel Records Center, Record of Officers, Andrews, Adolphus, 3.

Bibliography

Abbazia, Patrick, *Mr Roosevelt's Navy: The Private War of the Atlantic Fleet, 1939–1942* (Annapolis: Naval Institute Press, 1975)

Albion, Robert Greenhalgh, *Makers of Naval Policy: 1798–1947* (Annapolis: Naval Institute Press, 1980)

Albion, Robert Greenhalgh, and Jennie Barnes Payne, *Sea Lanes in Wartime. The American Experience 1775–1942* (New York: W W Norton, 1942)

American Merchant Marine at War, 'Merchant Marine in World War I', www.usmm.org/ww1merchant.html

Assistant Chief of Air Staff, Intelligence, 'The Antisubmarine Command', April 1945, http://www.uboatarchive.net/AAFHistory.htm

Bailey, Thomas, and Paul Ryan, *Hitler vs Roosevelt: The Undeclared Naval War* (New York: The Free Press, 1979)

Baker, Cajus, *Hitler's Naval War* (Garden City, NY: Doubleday, 1974)

Bell, Christopher M, *Churchill and Sea Power* (Oxford: Oxford University Press, 2013)

Berner, Thomas F, *The Brooklyn Navy Yard* (Charleston, SC: Arcadia, 1999)

Blair, Clay, *Hitler's U-boat War, vol I: The Hunters, 1939–1942* (New York: Modern Library, 2000)

Bloom, Jim, 'Preparing the Wolfpack: Germany's Type II U-boats', *Strategy & Tactics*, 293 (July/August 2015)

Brian, Herbert, *The Forgotten Heroes* (New York: Tom Doherty, 2004)

Brown, Ken, 'The SS *Normandie* Fire', *World at War* (January 2015)

Churchill, Winston S, *The Second World War, vol IV* (Boston, MA: Mariner Books, 1950)

Cook, James F, *Carl Vinson: Patriarch of the Armed Forces* (Macon, GA: Mercer University Press, 2004)

Cooper, Henry, 'Operation Paukenschlag', *Sea Classics* (July 2016)

Cruising Club of America, 'History', https://www.cruisingclub.org/about_history.htm

Da Costa Nunez, Ralph, *The Poor Among Us* (New York: White Tiger Press, 2013)

De Kay, James Tertius, *Roosevelt's Navy: The Education of a Wartime President, 1882–1920* (New York: Pegasus Books, 2012)

Diehl, Lorraine B, *Over Here! New York City During World War II* (New York: Harper Collins, 2010)

Dönitz, Admiral Karl, 'The Conduct of the War at Sea' (Division of Naval Intelligence, Washington, DC, 15 January 1946)

Fargo, Ladislas, *The Tenth Fleet* (New York: Ivan Obolensky, 1962)

Feder, Sid, and Joachim Joesten, *The Luciano Story* (New York: Da Capo Press, 1994)

Furer, Rear Admiral Julius Augustus, *Administration of the Navy Department in World War II* (Washington: Department of the Navy, 1959)

Gannon, Michael, *Operation Drumbeat* (New York: Harper and Row, 1991)

———, *Black May* (New York: Harper Collins, 1998)

Gleichauf, Justin F, *Unsung Sailors. The Naval Armed Guard in World War II* (Annapolis: Naval Institute Press, 1990)

Goldstein, Richard, *Helluva Town: The Story of New York City During World War II* (New York: Free Press)

Greenfield, Kent Roberts, 'Command Decisions' (Washington, DC: Center of Military History, Department of the Army)

Halpern, Paul G, *A Naval History of World War I* (Annapolis: Naval Institute Press, 1997)

Hammond, James W, Jr, *The Treaty Navy: The Story of the US Naval Service Between the World Wars* (Victoria, Canada: Trafford Publishing, 2001)

Hartzell, Karl Drew, *The Empire State At War World War II* (State of New York, 1949)

Hattendorf, John B, ed, *Doing Naval History: Essays Toward Improvement* (Newport, RI: Naval War College, 1995)

Heinrichs, Waldo, *Threshold of War* (New York: Oxford University Press, 1988)

Henig, Ruth, *Versailles and After, 1919–1933* (Annapolis: Naval Institute Press, 1995)

Hessler, Gunther, *German Naval History, The U-boat War in the Atlantic: 1939–1945* (London: HMSO, 1989)

Hill, Richard, *War at Sea in the Ironclad Age* (London: Cassell, 2002)

Holwitt, Joel Ira, '"Execute Against Japan": Freedom-of-the-Seas, the US Navy, Fleet Submarines, and the US Decision to Conduct Unrestricted Warfare, 1919–1941', PhD diss (Ohio State University, 2005)

Jaffe, Steven H, *New York at War: Four Centuries of Combat, Fear, and Intrigue in Gotham* (New York: Basic Books, 2012)

Jeffers, Paul H, *The Napoleon of New York: Mayor Fiorello La Guardia* (New York: John Wiley, 2012)

Jones, Jerry W, 'The Naval Battle of Paris', *Naval War College Review* (Spring, 2009)

Kaiser, David, *No End Save Victory: How FDR led the Nation into War* (New York: Basic Books, 2014)

King, Admiral Ernest J, 'US Navy at War 1941–1945. First Report of the Secretary of the Navy', www.ibilio.org/hyperwar/USN/USN

Kuehn, John T, *Agents of Innovation: The General Board and the Design of the Fleet that Defeated the Japanese Navy* (Annapolis: Naval Institute Press, 2008)

Land, Emory Scott, *Winning the War with Ships. Land, Sea and Air – Mostly Ships* (New York: Robert McBride, 1958)

Lane, Frederick C, *Ships for Victory: The History of Shipbuilding under the US Maritime Commission in World War II* (Baltimore: John Hopkins Press, 1951)

Lend-Lease Act (1941), www.ourdocuments.gov

Levine, Robert, *The Politics of American Naval Rearmament, 1930–1938* (New York: Garland, 1988)

Lichtblau, Eric, 'After 40 Years, Merchant Marines Win Veterans: Finally – a "Flag and a Headstone"', *Los Angeles Times* (30 January 1988)

Love, Robert William, *The Chiefs of Naval Operations* (Annapolis: Naval Institute Press, 1980)

McBride, William M, *Technical Change and the United States Navy, 1865–1945* (Baltimore: John Hopkins University Press, 2000)

McComb, Dave, *US Destroyers 1934–45: Pre-war classes* (Oxford: Osprey, 2010)

McHugh, Francis J, *US Navy Fundamentals of War Gaming* (New York: Skyhorse, 2013)

Mahan, Alfred Thayer, *Mahan on Naval Warfare* (Mineola, NY: Dover, 1999)

Marder, Arthur J, *From Dreadnought to Scapa Flow*, vols III, IV, V (London: Oxford University Press, 1966, 1969, 1970)

Marino, James I, 'The Undeclared War 1939–1941', *World War II History* (Late Fall 2012)

Merchant Marine Act, 1936. Title VIII-Contract Provisions. Section 801 (3), (4) and Section 806 (b), www.usmm.org

Miegs, Montgomery C, *Slide Rules and Submarines: American Scientists and Subsurface Warfare in World War II* (Washington, DC: National Defense University Press, 1990)

Morrison, Samuel Eliot, *History of the United States Naval Operations in World War II, vol I: The Battle of the Atlantic, 1939–1945* (Annapolis: Naval Institute Press, 2010)

Mulligan, Timothy P, *Neither Sharks nor Wolves: the Men of Nazi Germany's U-boat Arm, 1939–1945* (Annapolis: Naval Institute Press, 1999)

National Industrial Recovery Act (1933), www.ourdocuments.gov

New Jersey Department of Environmental Protection, 'Black Tom Explosion (1916)' (Division of Parks and Forests, 26 January 2005) http://www.state.nj.us/dep/parksandforests/parks/liberty_state_p ark/liberty_blacktomexplosion.html

Newark, Tim, *Mafia Allies* (St Paul, Minnesota: Zenith Press, 2007)

Nofi, Albert A, *To Train the Fleet for War; The US Navy Fleet Problems, 1923–1940* (Newport: Naval War College Press, 2010)

O'Connell, Robert L, *Sacred Vessels: The Cult of the Battleships and the Rise of the US Navy* (Boulder: Westview Press, 1991)

O'Hara, Vincent P, David W Dickson, and Richard Worth, *On Seas Contested: The Seven Great Navies of the Second World War* (Annapolis: Naval Institute Press, 2010)

Offley, Ed, *The Burning Shore: How Hitler's U-boats Brought World War II to America* (New York: Basic Books, 2014)

Perla, Peter P, *The Art of Wargaming* (Annapolis: United States Naval Institute, 1990)

Polmar, Norman, and Edward Whitman, *Hunters and Killers, vol I: Anti-Submarine Warfare from 1776 to 1943* (Annapolis: Naval Institute Press, 2015)

Popple, Charles Sterling, *Standard Oil Company (New Jersey) in World War II* (New York: Standard Oil Company, 1952)

Potts, J R, 'HMS Dreadnought. Dreadnought Battleship (1906)', http://www.militaryfactory.com/ships/detail.asp?ship_id=HMS-Dreadnought

Prange, Gordon W, *At Dawn We Slept: The Untold Story of Pearl Harbor* (New York: Penguin Books, 1991)

Rickover, Lieutenant H G, ' International Law and the Submarine', *United States Naval Proceedings* (September 1935)

Roosevelt, Franklin D, 'Fireside Chat 16: On the "Arsenal of Democracy"' (December 29, 1940), Miller Center at the University of Virginia, http://millercenter.org/president/fdroosevelt/speeches/speech-3319

———, 'Address over the radio on Navy Day concerning the attack upon the destroyer U. S. S. Kearny, October 27, 1941', http://www.usmm.org/fdr/kearny.html

Roscoe, Theodore, *United States Destroyer Operations in World War II* (Annapolis: Naval Institute Press, 1982)

Rose, Lisle, *Power at Sea, vol I: The Age of Navalism, 1880–1918*, and *vol II: The Breaking Storm, 1919–1945* (Columbia: University of Missouri Press, 2007)

Roskill, Stephen, *Naval Policy Between the Wars*, vols I and II (New York: Walker, 1968)

———, *The War at Sea*, vol II (London: HMSO, 1958)

Sawyer, L A, and W H Mitchell, *Victory Ships and Tankers* (Newton Abbot: David & Charles, 1974)

Showell, Jak P Mallmann, *Dönitz, U-boats, Convoys: The British Version of His Memoirs from the Admiralty's Secret Anti-Submarine Reports* (Barnsley: Frontline Books, 2013)

Sims, Captain W M, 'The Practical Character of the Naval War College:

A lecture Delivered before the Officers of the US Naval Academy November 11, 1912', www.usnwc.edu/getattachment/About/History/SimsDoc.pdf.aspx

Sims, Rear Admiral William Snowden, *The Victory at Sea* (Annapolis: Naval Institute Press, 1984)

U-boat Archives, 'U-123 – 7th War Patrol', http://www.uboatarchive.net/KTB123-7.htm

———, 'War Diary, North Atlantic Naval Coastal Frontier', http://www.uboat.net/ESFWWarDiaryDec41.htm

———, 'U-boat losses during 1942', http://uboat.net/fates/losses/1942.htm

US Coast Guard Public Information Division, *The Coast Guard at War, vol XIX: Auxiliary* (Washington, DC: US Coast Guard, 1 July 1947)

———, *The Coast Guard at War, vol VIII: Cutter* (Washington, DC: US Coast Guard, 1 July 1947)

United States Department of the Navy, *Merit Roll of the Naval Cadets of the First Class-Annual Examination, June 1901*

University of Minnesota, 'Treaty relating to the use of Submarines and Noxious Gases in Warfare, Washington, 6 February 1922', http://www1.umn.edu/humanrts/ instree/1922a.htm

Warnock, Timothy A, *The Battle Against the U-Boat in the American Theater* (Montgomery: Air Force Historical Agency)

Westphal, Raymond, Jr, 'Postwar Planning: Parliamentary Politics and the Royal Navy, 1919–22', *The Journal of Military History*, 74:1 (2010)

Williamson, Corbin, 'Repair Work and Naval Musical Chairs: Conflict and Co-operation in Anglo-American Naval Relations in 1941', *International Journal of Naval History* (21 July 2015)

Williamson, Gordon, *Wolfpack: The Story of the U-boat in World War II* (Oxford: Osprey, 2006)

Workers of the Writers' Program of the Work Projects Administration for the City of New York, *A Maritime History of New York* (Brooklyn, NY: Going Coastal, 2004)

Wortman, Marc, *1941: Fighting the Shadow War. A Divided America in a World at War* (New York: Atlantic Monthly, 2016)

Index